Christian Commitment

Christian Commitment

An Apologetic

Edward John Carnell

BAKER BOOK HOUSE
Grand Rapids, Michigan 49506

Copyright 1957 by Edward John Carnell
Paperback edition issued 1982 by
Baker Book House
with permission of copyright owner

ISBN: 0-8010-2473-0

PHOTOLITHOPRINTED BY CUSHING - MALLOY, INC.
ANN ARBOR, MICHIGAN, UNITED STATES OF AMERICA

Affectionately dedicated to the distinguished dean of American radio evangelists, Charles E. Fuller. For over a third of a century he has brought a compassionate gospel to those who labor in hard and remote places. He was not disobedient to the heavenly vision.

PREFACE

Many have heralded the warning that some day, beyond the gloom of the grave, men will meet God. It seems to me, true though this is, that the emphasis is in the wrong place. It is my firm moral persuasion that such a rendezvous ought to take place here and now. "Behold, now is the acceptable time; behold, now is the day of salvation" (II Corinthians 6:2). I contend that man, in a very special sense of the term, already *knows* God, and that the moment he has the spiritual mettle to humble himself he will also *meet* God. "God has two dwellings; one in Heaven; and the other in a meek and thankful heart."* We cannot comprehend why God has privileged us to have fellowship with him. We bow before the mystery. But this we do know: that if such fellowship *is* available, no energies should be spared in gaining it.

This is a study in Christian apologetics. Apologetics is that branch of systematic theology which shows why Christianity is true. The duty to defend the faith is included in faith itself. "Always be prepared to make a defense to any one who calls you to account for the hope that is in you, yet do it with gentleness and reverence" (I Peter 3:15). Many Christians have hope, but few can give a reason for their hope.

Since apologetics is an art and not a science, there is no "official" way to go about defending the Christian faith. The defense must answer to the spirit of the times. For example, Joseph Butler's *The Analogy of Religion* was designed to answer deists who affirmed a God of transcendence but not a God of immanence. Judged with

---

* Izaak Walton, *The Compleat Angler* (Oxford), p. 223.

this goal in view, the work is a masterpiece. But judged by the spirit of our modern world, it is curiously devoid of force. William Paley's *Natural Theology* addressed an age that was greatly impressed with the teleological order of nature. But the evolving presuppositions of science have evacuated the apologetical force of final causes. The climate of our modern world is dynamic and existential. People speak of Kierkegaard's "individual," of "confrontation" and "crisis." This is why we have sought to impress the contemporary mind with evidences drawn from man's marvelous power of moral and rational self-transcendence.* "Who has plumbed its depths? Yet it is a power of mine, and appertains unto my nature; nor do I myself grasp all that I am. Therefore is the mind too narrow to contain itself. And where should that be which it does not contain of itself? Is it outside and not in itself? How is it, then, that it does not grasp itself? A great admiration rises upon me; astonishment seizes me."†

Some apologists try to safeguard the finality of Christianity by repudiating the possibility of truth outside of Christianity. But their effort, as one might suspect, is a failure. Christ himself defended degrees of truth in the natural man. "You know how to interpret the appearance of the sky, but you cannot interpret the signs of the times" (Matthew 16:3). Astute secular thinkers are like a ship that has ten good days at sea, only to sink on the eleventh. The voyage was ill-fated from the beginning. Non-Christians can develop relative truths about nature and life, but they cannot answer the profound question, "How can a sinner be just before God?"

Other apologists go to the opposite extreme of defending Christianity by an appeal to evidences that are accessible to human self-sufficiency. The effort is equally futile. Although it does justice to the clear Biblical teaching that God's eternal power and deity are perceived in the things that have been made (Romans 1:20), it neglects the equally clear teaching that "The unspiritual man

* Man also enjoys power of *aesthetic* self-transcendence. A valid perception of beauty is, in some sense, a valid perception of God. But in the interests of economy we shall have to by-pass this part of man's complex endowment.
† Augustine, *The Confessions*, X, 8.

does not receive the gifts of the Spirit of God, for they are folly to him, and he is not able to understand them because they are spiritually discerned" (I Corinthians 2:14). God is not rightly known until one is spiritually moved by a sense of his own moral distance from God.

Let me illustrate this. Aquinas claimed that the existence of God can be demonstrated from the being and attributes of a flower. The "five proofs" support this assertion. But such proofs are spiritually vapid, for they assume that God can be apprehended by rational dialectic. The conclusion "God exists" evokes no more spiritual interest than the conclusion "Europe exists." After an exercise in Thomistic dialectic, one can casually remark, "How jolly glad I am that I happened on this, for now I can prove God's existence to my friends in the camera club!" It is possible that such an individual *does* believe in God. "Even the demons believe —and shudder" (James 2:19). But he certainly does not believe very profoundly, for a profound knowledge of God presupposes a profound knowledge of sin.

Hence, I am careful to speak of a "spiritual approach to God" rather than a "rational proof of God's existence." Although both approach and proof presuppose critically assessed evidences, they differ in the moral attitude of the investigator himself. An approach to God calls for an exercise of spiritual as well as rational facilities, while a proof of God's existence calls for an exercise of only the rational. A wretched man can intellectually assent to God's existence, but only a man of character can spiritually approach God's person.

Therefore, it seems much more in accord with Biblical revelation to argue that human beings dwell in the person of God from the first moment of moral self-consciousness, but that they remain unaware of this enclosure until worldly pride yields to spiritual humility. God himself is the moral and spiritual environment of an upright man. "For 'In him we live and move and have our being' " (Acts 17:28). "God is love, and he who abides in love abides in God, and God abides in him" (I John 4:16).

Some may try to void this by denying the *reality* of the moral and spiritual environment, but they merely show their want of education. Whoever is sensitive to the manner of his own life will recognize that he is held in such an environment by existence itself. The simplest experiment will establish this. Suppose we notice that another person is looking at us. Unless he gives evidence of a moral contract, he has no right to look. He must smile, nod, or show some other mutually accepted sign of friendship. If he continues to look, but reveals no evidence of accepting us as a friend, he arouses a sense of moral indignation and we judge him an annoyingly prying person. No one may invade the sanctity of our life without participating in the moral and spiritual environment.

But this leads to an interesting question. If the scientific method clarifies our physical environment, while philosophical method clarifies our rational environment, what method clarifies our moral and spiritual environment? To the best of my present knowledge, none has been developed. The purpose of this book is to devise and apply a method by which an alert individual can acquaint himself with the claims of this environment.

But before one can accomplish this, and thus discover his place in God, he must venture complex judgments about the nature of man, types of truth, methods and conditions of knowing, and the primary moral and rational convictions that already hold one as he stands in line at the bank or listens to a band concert. The task is mainly one of displacement, for truth takes on dignity only as error is discredited. Refuting error is a difficult and involved task, to be sure, but the effort cannot be avoided. As Mill observes, "Misrepresentation is always beautifully brief; refutation always tediously long." If we want to find God, we must make a deliberate effort. Let us remember Spinoza's observation, that all things worth while are equally difficult.

* * *

I acknowledge thanks to the following: to *The Great Books of the Western World*, published by Encyclopædia Britannica, for

Preface

the use of Darwin's *The Descent of Man* and Boswell's *Life of Samuel Johnson LL.D.*; to Oxford University Press for the use of the following works in The World's Classics series: Izaak Walton, *The Compleat Angler and Lives*; Thomas de Quincey, *Confessions of an English Opium-Eater*; Thucydides, *The Peloponnesian War*; Oliver Goldsmith, *The Vicar of Wakefield*; Jonathan Swift, *Gulliver's Travels*; John Stuart Mill, *Autobiography*; Anthony Trollope, *An Autobiography*; and Thomas Carlyle, *On Heroes, Hero-Worship, and the Heroic in History*; to Pocket Books, Inc., for the use of Benjamin Franklin's *Autobiography*; and to the American-Scandinavian Foundation for the use of Sören Kierkegaard's *Concluding Unscientific Postscript*.

The Scripture quotations are from the Revised Standard Version of the Bible, copyrighted 1946 and 1952, and are used by permission of the copyright owners, the National Council of the Churches of Christ in the U.S.A.

I also owe a special word of thanks to Mrs. Anne Kimber for her painstaking care in the preparation of the typescript.

E. J. C.

Fuller Theological Seminary
Pasadena, California

CONTENTS

PREFACE   vii

INTRODUCTION
- I. Spiritual Responsibility and the Rise of a World View   2
  1. The deficiency of classical thought   2
  2. Developing a starting point   3
  3. A word about procedure   7

Part One:
DEVELOPING THE THIRD METHOD OF KNOWING

- II. Types of Truth and Methods of Knowing   10
  1. The rise of the third method of knowing   10
  2. The naming of an absolute truth   12
  3. Philosophy and personal responsibility   14
  4. The two kinds of truth   14
  5. The third kind of truth   15
  6. The two conventional methods of knowing   17
  7. The limitations of knowledge by acquaintance   19
  8. The limitations of knowledge by inference   20
  9. The third method of knowing   21
  10. The relation between the three methods of knowing   23
  11. The three conditions of knowing   24
  12. A final review   29

Part Two:
APPLYING THE THIRD METHOD OF KNOWING

- III. A Preliminary Probe   32
  1. Transition through aesthetics   32
  2. A plain and simple experiment in the city park   34

	3. The discovery of a universal starting point	35
	4. Descartes' starting point	37
	5. Aristotle and the law of contradiction	38
	6. The law of contradiction and moral self-acceptance	41
	7. The law of uniformity and moral self-acceptance	42
	8. The realism of the third method of knowing	44
IV.	Moral Self-Acceptance and Social Relations	47
	1. A refinement of procedure	47
	2. Finding an index to human actions	49
	3. Challenging the theory that all morals are relative	52
	4. Moral self-acceptance and values	54
	5. Moral self-acceptance and social relations	55
	6. Our moral demands on strangers	57
	7. Moral responsibility when entering friendship	58
	8. Moral demands within friendship	60
	9. The second criterion	61
	10. The problem of animals	63
	11. Conscience and moral relativity	64
	12. The paradox of morals	66
	13. The balance of moral self-acceptance as a method	71
	14. Kierkegaard	73
V.	Moral Self-Acceptance and the Judicial Sentiment	80
	1. A transition through Kant's practical imperative	80
	2. An empirical trial of the practical imperative	82
	3. A further clarification of procedure	84
	4. Human rights and moral self-acceptance	87
	5. The judicial sentiment	91
	6. The judicial predicament	94
	7. Harmonizing duty and desire	96
	8. The reality of the administrator of justice	101
	9. The elimination of false alternatives	104
	10. The person of God as the administrator of justice	107
	11. Kant's appeal to conscience	110
	12. A final word about Kant	114

Part Three:
BECOMING ACQUAINTED WITH THE PERSON OF GOD

VI.	Preparations for Meeting God	118
	1. Going beyond Spinoza	118
	2. Going beyond Aristotle	120
	3. Extending the cycle of fellowship	121
	4. Spiritual preparation and the perception of truth	125

5. The moral predicament	128
6. The character of God	130
7. The univocal point of identity between time and eternity	135
8. The problem of God's finitude	142
9. The problem of evil	144
10. Moral self-acceptance and the terms of fellowship	149
11. The anatomy of humility	153
VII. The Admission of Guilt	156
1. A revision of procedure	156
2. The paradox of humility	157
3. Direct and indirect fulfillment	158
4. The two qualities of moral response	160
5. A clarification of direction	162
6. The anatomy of an apology	164
7. Why we cannot apologize to God	166
8. The anatomy of repentance	167
9. The problem of repenting before God	169
VIII. Defining the Law of Life	171
1. The pith and marrow of the imperative essence	171
2. The law by which we judge others	172
3. The law of justice	172
4. Difficulties with justice	174
5. Justice and repentance	176
6. Exceptions to justice	177
7. The problem of evidences	179
8. A further word about the counsel of Christ	185
9. Why we must humbly ask a favor	186
10. The law of consideration	188
11. Implications and inferences	192
12. A new dimension to the moral predicament	195
13. The dialectic of striving	200
14. Consideration and repentance	203
15. Justice and consideration	204
16. Beyond consideration	205
17. The law of love	207
IX. The Logic of Repentance	212
1. The paradox of moral striving	212
2. Venturing a radical hypothesis	214
3. Selfishness and the judicial sentiment	215
4. A check against haste	216
5. A faulty application of method	217
6. A correction of procedure	219

Contents

    7. The buttressing force of cumulative evidences   220
    8. Tragic moral choices   223
    9. The claims of love on the heart   230
   10. The conditioned element in conscience   233
   11. The problem of the heathen   237
   12. A final review of the moral predicament   240
   13. Why it is necessary to repent   241

Part Four:
CONCLUDING INFERENCES AND PROBLEMS

X. Christ the Power and the Wisdom of God   246
    1. The possibilities and limits of human wisdom   246
    2. The judicial sentiment in God   248
    3. The cross of Christ   249
    4. The cross and personal repentance   254
    5. The filial bond   255
    6. Objections to positional righteousness   257
    7. The principle of federal headship   262
    8. Objections to federal headship   263
    9. Objections to total depravity   264
   10. Saving faith   267
   11. God's sovereignty and the problem of evil   269
   12. The filial bond and the problem of evil   273
   13. The dialogue of Habakkuk   273
   14. The faith of Abraham   277
   15. Man's search for ultimate meaning   278
   16. The problem of evil and the cross of Christ   281

XI. The finality of Jesus Christ   284
    1. The verification of the Christian world view   284
    2. A terminal difficulty   286
    3. The Protestant Reformation   290
    4. Christianity and other world religions   293
    5. The height and depth of the religious perspective   295
    6. The righteousness of correct thinking   297
    7. The righteousness of self-denial   299
    8. The righteousness of keeping the law   300
    9. Conclusion   302

INDEXES

  Index of Scripture Passages   305
  Index of Names and Subjects   306

INTRODUCTION

Chapter One

SPIRITUAL RESPONSIBILITY AND THE RISE OF A WORLD VIEW

1. THE DEFICIENCY OF CLASSICAL THOUGHT

When formulating a philosophy of life, I contend that the least accessible fact, and thus the most baffling to isolate and classify, is the complex moral and spiritual environment of the philosopher himself. Most efforts in abstraction fail to impress the common man because sages seldom take time to interpret life from within the center of their own perspective as individuals. The more carefully I have meditated on this, the more convinced I have become that a world view remains truncated to the degree that a thinker fails to deal with data gained by a humble participation in the moral and spiritual environment.

Philosophers err when they confine their attention to "universal man." There is only one real man: the suffering, fearing individual on the street; he who is here today and gone tomorrow; he whose heart is the scene of a relentless conflict between the self as it is and the self as it ought to be. Whenever a philosopher speaks of mankind in the abstract, rather than concrete individuals at home and in the market, he deceives both himself and all who have faith in his teaching.

What it means to be held in a moral and spiritual environment can only be learned as one acquaints himself with the realities that already hold him from existence itself. This pilgrimage into inwardness is a painfully personal responsibility, for only the individual himself has access to the secrets of his moral and spiritual life. The task cannot be wrought by proxy. It is sheer affectation to try to be another person. "We are not to judge of the feelings of others by what we might feel if in their place."* The particularities of selfhood are not open for public inspection; they lie too deep for discovery.

If this be the case, however, some will justly wonder why I am developing a method by which the moral and spiritual environment can be known. The answer is, I am lifting the veil from *my* experiences in order that others might be guided into a more accurate understanding of their own. Although each person must drink the cup of inwardness for himself, it is helpful to know where the fountain is and how one goes about drinking.

This noble desire to guide others is my first motive in writing. The second is less noble. I shall not conceal the fact that I am developing this method in order that I might reassess a number of presuppositions which I scorned in my youth as undignified, but which in later years I have found increasingly attractive. What these presuppositions are will appear as we proceed.

It is not easy for one to use his own life as a paradigm in the development of apologetical method. Yet, I am quick to confess that a sense of pleasure preponderates my fear. Although it is painful to unbosom the self, such uneasiness is more than balanced by the feeling of cleanness that comes when the self is honest with the self.

2. DEVELOPING A STARTING POINT

When meditating on how to clarify the moral and spiritual environment, I decided to tease out the causal connection between the major moral convictions in my heart and the totality of reality over against me. This partly explains why I have cast my method in semiautobiographical form. In pursuing this method, however, I have tried to be careful neither to prejudice my selec-

---

* Oliver Goldsmith, *The Vicar of Wakefield* (Oxford), p. 32.

tion by personal preference nor to assign a more certain causal connection at any point than could be justified by the conclusions of patient inquiry.

I have never been happy with the fact that philosophers tend to dismiss starting point as a trifle to be decided on either aesthetic or prudential grounds. Classical philosophy seems to think that *where* one begins his investigation, and what spiritual dispositions he brings to the evidences, are not important. I am firmly convinced that this is irresponsible counsel. What one thinks of a particular realm of evidences will depend on what he thinks of the moral and spiritual environment of which he is dynamically a part. "The fear of the Lord is the beginning of knowledge" (Proverbs 1:7). Pride unconsciously angles the investigator's approach. One is apt to believe what he wants to believe.

No sooner has a self-sufficient student in philosophy pledged his obedience to the whole of experience than he unconsciously corrupts the purity of his pledge by betraying a preference for aspects of experience that leave the moral life unexamined. Since data come in two different qualities of cloth—the first, sense perception, by which we learn the facts of the external world; the second, spiritual perception, by which we learn the facts of the internal world—it usually happens that self-sufficiency places a greater value on the scientific and rational aspects of life than on the moral and spiritual. By diverting attention from the moral ambiguity of the heart, one can make bold personal pretenses of rectitude and virtue.

The history of philosophy abundantly illustrates the ease with which thinkers abandon their devotion to the whole of experience: as in the fierce contest between empiricism and rationalism in ancient Greece (empiricism arguing from sense perception that *everything* is in motion, and rationalism arguing from logic that *nothing* is in motion);—as in the inflexible assertions of idealism, romanticism, and naturalism that all reality can be explained from the point of view of mind, feelings, or the material world, respectively;—as in the warm debate between absolutists and relativists (the absolutists solemnly averring that the true, the good, and the beautiful have unconditional being; the relativists countering that such values are contingent to the finite observer). If science were to betray such erratic tendencies, it long ago would have fallen into public disrepute.

Little wonder that college sophomores become so soured with the "strife of systems" that they altogether despair of philosophy's possibilities. If professionally trained thinkers fail to agree on such basic matters as truth and method, where will the tyro stand?

Were I to say how I escaped becoming embittered, it would be my awareness of the fact that it is *impossible* to avoid philosophizing. Whether I cared to own it or not, I was already committed to certain presuppositions by the very way I conducted myself toward reality; for actions prove what one really believes. To asperse philosophy, therefore, is simply to asperse oneself. Just as one may control the purity of the air he breathes, but not the necessity of breathing, so one may control a particular philosophic effort, but not the necessity of systematic reflection. Whoever negates philosophy is already tightly held in the grip of bad philosophy.

Though I was spared the folly of abusing philosophy, I was not spared the error of following a faulty method. Without ado I pledged myself an acolyte in the service of classical empiricism. I felt that since rocks and projectiles are open for public inspection, they are the real stuff of being; while feelings and compunctions, having the substance of a dream, are a welter of unclassification that can only lead to bad subjectivism.

Once I had taken my vows to defend mathematically measurable being, I became impatient—nay, disgusted—with those who defended the inner tensions of the moral life as the true wellspring of wisdom. And chief among the savants I assailed was the roving Athenian Socrates.

When first I meditated on the exhortation *Know thyself!* the counsel seemed so banal, and so utterly void of rational counsel, that I was quite at a loss to explain why it was so highly esteemed in the Socratic method. Since nothing can enter consciousness until we are first aware of it, I did not see how it was possible to *escape* knowing the self. An intuitive, presentational awareness of our own person is the surest piece of information we have. To urge what cannot be avoided, therefore, is pointless exhortation. Charmides, Chaerephon, and Critias may have perceived rich, mystical significance in the Delphic epigram, but I could see nothing but a flat platitude.

It is easy to perceive where I erred. I could not appreciate the place of inwardness in philosophical method because I was unconscious of my own enclosure in the moral and spiritual environment. I was viewing life through a lens so perfectly ground and so splendidly adjusted to my eyes that I was unaware of my dependence on it for daily vision. As long as the reality of this dependence was concealed from consciousness, it was natural to make the error of thinking that I enjoyed perfect vision, and that the advice of Socrates simply did not apply to me. Had I taken time to tell what I *meant* by the self, I would have replied, with haste and confidence: "It is but the flow of consciousness." Socrates would have pitied my pathetic pretense to knowledge, but I would have gone my merry way, a smug little Euthyphro who quite overlooked the fact that one rightly knows neither the self nor the universe until he spiritually comprehends himself in relation to the universe. As a very unripe child in philosophy, I did not appreciate the reciprocal relation between rectitude and the perception of objective reality. In due time, of course, I realized that the self is neither as simple in essence as I imagined, nor nearly as rationally subject to my control as I presumed; and that the Delphic inscription, far from banality, was rich with spiritual admonition.

Now that I look back on the philosophical disorganization of my earlier life, I find it easy to chide myself. But is this fair? Correction I needed, yes, but not reproach; for I did only what I sincerely thought was right. It would be imprudent to judge an adolescent by the standards of an adult, there being an appropriate time and place for everything under the sun. Conduct is meet

Spiritual Responsibility and the Rise of a World View

for rebuke only when it is unfit, as when a man delights in adolescent ways or when an adolescent fancies himself a man.

3. A WORD ABOUT PROCEDURE

A clear intuition counseled me to emulate the determination of a mechanic who rebuilds an intricate piece of machinery. Each aspect of the moral and spiritual environment must be examined, the small and large together; the irrelevant findings to be discarded and the relevant to be refurbished and labeled. This task of removal, classification, and replacement must continue until the place of the self in the moral and spiritual environment is bared for critical investigation. Thus, with the simplicity of fiat, after the manner of a fairy tale, I presumed myself qualified to overhaul the intricacies of the moral life.

It was not until I was deeply committed to graduate studies in the university that I began to appreciate the complexity of things. Although formal instruction in the classroom did not give me a direct answer to my dilemma, it nevertheless stimulated me to seek out the answer for myself. Let me briefly review how this happened.

At the start of my studies I dutifully complied with the academic presupposition that all knowledge can be communicated through class lectures, books, or seminar discussions. I failed to see that moral facts are never rationally known until they are spiritually felt.

I did not remain ignorant long, however, for the more painstakingly I pondered the significance of university studies, the more I realized that formal instruction about man referred to the thin abstraction *Homo sapiens*, and not to any particular person, living or dead, on or off the campus. The "man" so eloquently reviewed by the professor was nothing but an attractive composite of the essential attributes of the race. This meant that instead of being taught the uniqueness of the self and its relation to reality in general, I was simply being stocked with a quantity of interesting data about the species. And what distressed me was not the secondary value of such information, but the capital error of assuming that a knowledge of the self is analytically included in a knowledge of the species. Since personal uniqueness interpermeates every phase of one's being, one's life can be materially identified with the race at no point.

Checked with a momentary fear that I was acting in haste, I determined to test the validity of this charge by using my own body in an experiment. If any part of an individual is materially equivalent with the race, it is his body; for all normal human beings have the same skeleton, blood vessels, nerves, muscles, and fluids.

I spent many days pondering the problem, fully determined to hold the question before me until I was critically satisfied. At the end of this period of reflection my conviction was corroborated. There is only one body we call our own: that through which our desires are actuated; a frame that must be patiently dealt with; one that is the vehicle of pleasure, temptation, and pain—this and no other. Not a single lecture in anatomy, physiology, or anthropology can accurately describe what it means to be housed in our particular frame. Lips and legs are more than flesh and bones. Flabby or stiff, each somewhat mirrors the rich individuality of our person: lips that betray the inner man, legs that sometimes bear us, sometimes fail. No element can be materially absorbed into the species without destroying its particularity. Each gnawing pain, each distracting yawn, each repulsive pimple is of unique concern to the self.

When students of anatomy pore over a cadaver, or when students of sociology correlate men in group relations, they are acquainting themselves with data that are accurate as far as, but no further than, the species. And the feature that inflamed me, let me repeat, was the noxious error of encouraging students to believe that in knowing the race they likewise knew themselves. Only a perverted standard of values would induce others to neglect their individuality in favor of a scientific description of the race. To comprehend the species, but not the self, is sham scholarship.

Part One

DEVELOPING THE THIRD METHOD OF KNOWING

Chapter Two

TYPES OF TRUTH AND METHODS OF KNOWING

1. THE RISE OF THE THIRD METHOD OF KNOWING

Now that many profitable years have come and gone since receiving the dubious honor of a doctor's degree, I feel strangely distant from the self that used to be. As I ponder the past in calm retrospect, it is even difficult to recall the agony of language examinations and thesis writing. I do not mean to imply that I have been delivered from the habit of fretting. On the contrary, the passage of time has simply changed the names of the things that distress me.

It is very easy to accent the disappointing features of graduate work—and there were many. But I confidently believe that without such disappointments I might never have been goaded to develop a substitute, and more fruitful, approach to life for myself. The more I recoiled from conventional techniques in the university, the wider my eyes opened to the significance of what I now call the "third method of knowing." But before reviewing the meaning of this method, and especially the way in which it comprehends realities that are overlooked by conventional techniques, let me briefly paint in the background of the discovery itself. I found the truth through an odd train of circumstances.

Although I have always been reasonably healthy, insomnia has plagued me from adolescence until now. Only those who are unable to sleep at night can appreciate the distressing toll this ailment takes on one's life: the omnipresent sense of fatigue, the susceptibility to irritation, and the grossness of an unrefreshed mind. All through the university I struggled against a never ending torpor, mental and animal. Each night the disquiets of mind prevailed over weariness. And the more the tensions of graduate work mounted, the more I fought off the effects of insufficient sleep. One Friday afternoon, as I prepared for the spring language examinations, I emotionally exploded. Having lost sleep with such regularity, I lacked courage to face the future. My mind was like a mass of live rubber: continually expanding, it threatened to divide down the center. This would leave me powerless to cope with responsibilities in the university. Out of all patience with myself, therefore, I seized a stack of German idiom cards and angrily hurled them against the wall. Vengeance was mine.

Within a few minutes I was walking down the spur tracks leading away from town. Never before had the difference between my own roily soul and the serenity of nature stood out in sharper contrast. Although I longed to be identified with the natural harmony of the grass and the trees, I knew that this could only be enjoyed by denuding the self of all that comprises the essence of freedom. This left me with an overpowering sense of my own finitude. I could *consider* an ant, but I could not be one; and the more I tried to be one, the more I used moral freedom as an escape from the perils and responsibilities of moral freedom. Everything I conceived became a burden; every anticipated obligation threatened to impale me. Even so ordinary a responsibility as conversing with others overwhelmed me with consternation. Nor dare I conceal the fact that even suicide took on a certain attractiveness.

As I stood on the railroad track, rubbing my forehead and watching the flaming sunset, I intuitively grasped the following truth: *One's ability to see reality is somewhat conditioned to the tone of one's affections.* An extended loss of sleep radically alters my outlook. My will-to-live decays; I become mordacious toward others; I experience *Weltschmerz*. But after a powerful sedative, I see things in a different light. The harmony of nature is restored; I am patient with others; the zest for creative living revives. This was an important discovery, one that is rarely appreciated in the university. Observe the power of passion to corrupt one's conception of the right. When King Saul became jealous of the young David, the distortion of his moral faculty was so complete that even murder took on the form of a good. "And on the morrow an evil spirit from God rushed upon Saul, and he raved within his house, while David was playing the lyre, as he did day by day. Saul had his spear in his hand; and Saul cast the spear, for he thought, 'I will pin David to the wall.' But David evaded him twice" (I Samuel 18:10-11). This suggests that there is a real causal connection between the tone of one's affections and his ability to perceive reality. An imbalance in the neurophysical life will be reflected in the moral-spiritual life. An angry person can appreciate neither the lily nor the God behind the lily.

Random though my conduct appeared, it was sufficient to acquaint me with the clue that led to the third method of knowing. When one is threatened with a nervous breakdown, he has no difficulty acknowledging his own limitations. He spiritually reckons with the fact that forces other than his own are in control of his destiny. No further proof is needed.

2. THE NAMING OF AN ABSOLUTE TRUTH

Once I had the mettle to accept the realities to which I was already committed by existence itself, it did not take me long to see that, despite the stress on relativity in the university, I was already in possession of an absolute truth. In defending this absolute, however, I know I cannot convince pedants who construct their world view in isolation from the realities that hold them as they go through the cafeteria line or take part in a faculty discussion. Unless one looks in the right place, important aspects of reality remain hidden.

Here is the truth which is as absolute as either the laws of logic or the axioms of geometry: *Man is not the author of his own existence*. The fact that this assertion cannot be formally demonstrated is quite beside the point, for only an individual so utterly pompous as to overlook his own finitude would deny its truth. This absolute needs only to be impressed, not demonstrated.

One can call this truth to his attention without having to face a nervous breakdown, of course, for the reality of human dependence can be perceived in many separate ways. Reflect, for example, on the mystery of our beating heart. What sustains this complex muscle? And what is the relation between moral freedom and the flow of blood? No really profound answers to these questions can be given. And even more mysterious than the circulation of the blood, and thus more shattering to self-sufficiency, is the baffling fact of rational and moral self-transcendence. What is thought? And how can an immaterial idea affect a material body? Whoever meditates on these questions with an eye to the mystery of life will immediately acknowledge that he is not the author of his own existence. If one does not even know the meaning of life, how can he pretend to be its creator?

Here, then, is the first clue to the third method of knowing: *Ultimate reality cannot be grasped unless rational knowledge is savored by spiritual conviction*. We do not know the significance of "dependence" until a mental awareness of this relation fructifies in a whole-souled adjustment to its claims. Dependence must be felt; it cannot be a mere object of thought. Even as guilt implies the feeling of culpability, and even as indebtedness implies the feeling of obligation, so dependence implies the feeling of subordination. Hence, a person does not rightly apprehend dependence until he conforms himself to the relation. The necessity of this conformity is included in the relation itself. If an individual *professes* to be dependent, while he lives as if he were self-sufficient, he deceives himself and the truth is not in him. His proud life shows that his admission is academic and formal, not moral and spiritual. He is a hypocrite.

3. PHILOSOPHY AND PERSONAL RESPONSIBILITY

If a philosopher will not limit his speculation by the realities that already hold him, how can he possibly develop a consistent approach to ultimate reality? Ultimates cannot be comprehended until one reflects on them with a spiritual eye to his own finitude. A known attribute of ultimate reality is this: we are dependent on it for existence. If a philosopher fails to build his approach on this one known attribute, his final metaphysic, though he have a millennium in which to develop it, will remain truncated.

Since this is a very serious charge, a goodly space must be devoted to its defense. The third method of knowing will never enjoy prestige until the limitations of conventional philosophical methods are acknowledged.

Because kinds of truth and methods of knowing are supporting phases of one question, however, it is bootless to evaluate methods of knowing until one acquaints himself with the particular kind of truth to which each method answers. Methods illuminate our search for truth; but without a clarification of the nature of truth we should not know what to look for.

4. THE TWO KINDS OF TRUTH

Since "being" is the subject of any investigation, philosophers never quibble over the fact that the real is the true. One may say, for example, "This is truly a pleasant afternoon," or, "This is truly part of the American way of life." Whatever is, is true. To the extent that something participates in being, it is true. This is called *ontological truth*.

Were there no more to the problem than mere academic agreement on the proposition "The real is the true," philosophers would never wrangle about truth. No matter what the stuff of reality is, it has being, and to this degree it is true.

But how can reality be known? How can we critically distinguish reality from appearance? If ontological truth is to be of any service, therefore, a procedure must be devised that will put man's mind in touch with reality. This procedure is rational inference. Whenever a person enters a new environment, he is compelled to make inferences, for man is curious by nature. Symbols or terms represent concepts, and the valid construing of these symbols is truth. *Propositional truth*, thus, is the second kind of truth. Whenever judgments conceptually house the real, they possess the quality of truth.

It makes no difference whether ideas *are* the real, or whether they *correspond* to the real. In either instance the proposition is the receptacle of truth. Nor is it of any moment how particular philosophers verify propositional truth: whether by the power of propositions to guide our experience without frustration (systematic consistency); by the correspondence of ideas to things (correspondence); by the consistency of ideas with each other (coherence); or by operational differences in controlled experiment (pragmatism). Whatever the stripe of a philosopher may be, he still has to think, and in thinking he must make inferences. The manner of his life proves that the proposition is the cradle of truth.

With the rarest exceptions—such as Socrates, Pascal, and Kierkegaard—thinkers have rather consistently confined themselves to a defense of these two kinds of truth. Such a restriction, I assert, is a fruit of philosophy's dreadful habit of ignoring the moral and spiritual realities that already hold man as a creature made in the image of God.

5. THE THIRD KIND OF TRUTH

It is no simple task to unmask the deficiency of classical philosophy, however, for its error is more one of omission than of commission. I am fully persuaded that if one criticizes philosophy's passion to be precise in either ontological or propositional truth, he simply shows his own want of good sense. Were classical philosophy to be judged by its devotion to the conventional kinds of truth, we would have to doff our hats in praise. Reality is the "given" in truth, while experience and judgment make it possible for the whole man to contact reality.

But what if a third kind of truth exists, one that is the precise equivalent of neither ontological nor propositional truth? What if there were a kind of truth which, in Kierkegaard's words, "comes into being" only as one is transformed by ethical decision? Philosophers think that when they have developed an elaborate system of propositional truth, they can rest on their laurels, quite content that the task is finished. But if Socrates and Kierkegaard are right, such a retirement is culpably premature. The *real* business of philosophy has not even started.

By the term "third kind of truth" I mean *truth as personal rectitude*. The possibility of rectitude is implied in the very meaning of moral freedom itself, for uprightness does not come into being until man as he is coincides with man as he ought to be. For example, if one ought to be transformed by the fact that he is dependent on powers greater than himself, truth as personal rectitude has no existence until one morally and spiritually conforms the whole of his life to this relation. Essence and existence are united by right moral decision. If one chooses to scorn this responsibility, the third type of truth is shorn of reality.

Since man is part of nature, and yet enjoys moral freedom over nature, it is easy to suppose that man's affinity with nature invests him with the same harmony that is enjoyed by a flower. Let us call man's natural features the "descriptive essence." This essence takes in all that belongs to man as he is: legs, organs, reproductive desires, and so on. Viewed from the perspective of his descriptive essence, man really and truly is; existence and essence are federated harmoniously.

Unlike brutes, however, man remains spiritually free to make or undo the most important aspect of his being. Men have moral freedom; they are entrusted with the responsibility of creating or destroying rectitude by the quality **of their own** decisions.

Types of Truth and Methods of Knowing 17

Let us call the stuff of rectitude the "imperative essence." Even as the descriptive essence comprehends all that man is, so the imperative essence comprehends all that man ought to be. Moral and spiritual decision cannot be shunned without deteriorating character, for essence and existence are not in harmony until one elects to live uprightly.

6. THE TWO CONVENTIONAL METHODS OF KNOWING

If the fulfillment of duty is man's most important responsibility, however, one would think that classical philosophy would have devoted its best talents to devising a method which answers the question, "How is a knowledge of the imperative essence possible?" But this certainly has not been the case. Just as it has been assumed that there are only two types of truth,—ontological and propositional—so it has been assumed that there are only two methods of knowing: knowledge by acquaintance and knowledge by inference. Let us briefly review these two types of knowing, showing why neither is able to lead the mind into a conceptual awareness of the imperative essence. If one expects to grasp the third type of truth—truth as personal rectitude—he must develop a theory of knowledge which can make peace with the data of the moral and spiritual environment.

Knowledge by acquaintance is the passage of the mind to a conclusion without the aid of a middle premise. Acquaintance is direct experience. For example, when Thomas De Quincey tried to tell what it meant to bask in the ecstasy of opium, precise words failed him. His experience paragoned description. "Eloquent opium! that with thy potent rhetoric stealest away the purposes of wrath, pleadest effectually for relenting pity, and through one night's heavenly sleep callest back to the guilty man the visions of his infancy, and hands washed pure from blood."* Intimate emotions, such as love, joy, and grief, are effectively known only

---

* *Confessions of an English Opium-Eater* (Oxford), p. 217.

as they are felt. The same is true about the more universal aspects of nature. For example, Samuel Johnson wisely observes that though we *know* what light is, it is not easy to *tell* what light is. Augustine said the same thing about the meaning of time.

Knowledge by acquaintance answers to ontological truth. If one wants to know the sunset in all its presentational immediacy, he must face the west and open his eyes. He must experience the sunset. Since whatever is, is true, and since experience is our only way of apprehending the wholeness of what is, it follows that only knowledge by acquaintance can directly apprehend ontological truth. A child defines a cat by pointing at it. Since he experiences the cat, he knows the cat.

Knowledge by inference is the passage of the mind to a conclusion with the aid of a middle premise.* The syllogism is the foundation of valid inference: "All men are mortals; Socrates is a man; therefore, Socrates is a mortal." Valid inference can be simple or complex, but it must always follow the rules of logic. Knowledge by inference begins with simple judgment—"This is a horse"—and it ends with vast libraries of ponderous tomes. A system of thought is the consummate fruit of human reflection. But systems must be reflected on; they cannot be directly intuited.

Nothing will be gained by laboring this. It is sufficient to note that whenever a judgment is formed about the real, the thinker relies on rational inference to acquaint his mind with truth. If an expert geologist makes a series of judgments about the meaning of certain rock strata, his inferences are valid if they place the mind in contact with the real. This, quite obviously, is why knowledge by inference answers to truth as propositional correspondence to reality. A valid inference always yields a true conclusion—providing it is based on true premises.

But if knowledge by acquaintance directly introduces the mind

---

* In broadest terms, of course, *all* knowledge is inferential. Knowledge by acquaintance completes the inference without a middle premise, while knowledge by inference does not. Let us not be confused. We have simply distinguished these two species of inference in order that our efforts may enjoy greater precision.

Types of Truth and Methods of Knowing

to reality, while knowledge by inference houses the real by means of symbols and words, what method escorts the mind into the imperative essence? How can we grasp the nature of that one species of being which has no existence until free, moral decision closes the gap between what an individual is and what he ought to be? That is the problem.

7. THE LIMITATIONS OF KNOWLEDGE BY ACQUAINTANCE

Some moralists have tried to gain a knowledge of duty by an empirical review of the conflicting practices of mankind. Suggestive though this is, it fails for two very important reasons.

First, a description of the moral habits of the race cannot acquaint the mind with a sense of duty, for duty is in the imperative, not the descriptive, mood. Duty is rationally known only as it is spiritually felt. Claims to duty are in a different genus than actual duty. Second, an empirical review of moral practice is worthless unless it is proved that men are, in fact, doing their duty. Many men may, even as most do, outwardly pretend what they do not inwardly believe. Human beings are capable of infinite self-deception. "The heart is deceitful above all things, and desperately corrupt; who can understand it?" (Jeremiah 17:9). One may see and profess the right, while in act he does the wrong. Men live more by interest than principle.

Other moralists suppose that if we critically survey the feelings of duty in our own heart, a knowledge of the imperative essence can be distilled. This procedure at least faces in the right direction, for it recognizes that a sense of duty can be felt only as an individual stands in the center of the moral and spiritual environment. Whether duty is actually felt, however, will depend upon the degree to which one begins within the sense of duty itself. If one examines his moral life with an eye to gaining an empirical knowledge of duty, he repeats the error of trying to use descriptive data when developing imperative truths. In all eternity this cannot be done. *Claims* to duty are as far removed from *duty* as Christ is from Beelzebul. Duty can only be known as one stands within duty. Moral resolution and knowledge by acquaintance must combine, for duty does not appear until the heart is confronted by an acknowledged sense of obligation.

In sum: since knowledge by acquaintance authorizes an individual to suspend himself transcendentally over the various moral claims in his own soul, it must end in the very descriptive mood with which it began. Nothing is duty unless it captures the heart as a command.

8. THE LIMITATIONS OF KNOWLEDGE BY INFERENCE

Probably the most ambitious rational effort in morals was undertaken by Immanuel Kant. The key to Kant's formalistic ethics is the celebrated rule of self-consistent conduct, the categorical imperative: "Act only on that maxim whereby you can at the same time will that it should become a law universal." This is a rational statement of the supreme moral law of self-determined beings. It negates all imperatives which command less than universal duty by admitting exceptions. Any action that is a means to something else is hypothetical; but if the action is conceived as good in itself, and consequently as the principle of a will that conforms to reason, it is categorical. Because it is rational, it is compelling; and because it is categorical it is universal.

With the mere mention of Kant, memory wings me back to the tense seminars in graduate school where, about a heavy oak table, we examined the Kantian ethic. I recall how awed I was by the technical thoroughness of the Kantian system. But even more awesome was the realization that the system was quite void of moral power. I was mentally challenged by Kant, but not spiritually convicted.

Although followers of Kant may insist that I comprehensively reconstruct formalistic ethics before pressing criticisms, I am persuaded that such a work is as inconvenient at this juncture as it is irrelevant. Here is the issue, and a library of Kantian defense cannot change a tittle of it: *Kantian ethics seeks to acquaint the mind with duty by a rational statement of duty.* Such an approach is doomed before it even begins.

It happens that man is morally free to raise the question, "Why *should* one be rationally self-consistent?" Unless one is already held by an antecedent moral obligation to be rational, a statement of duty is spiritually powerless to communicate a sense of duty. The missing link is moral duty itself. One does not know duty until he is held by duty. Therefore, regardless of how effectively propositional knowledge may clarify the rational components in self-consistent conduct, it has no power, in and of itself, to convince a man that he ought to be rational. Logical validity is without appeal until an individual's conscience is gripped by a moral compulsion to be logical. The moral must precede the rational, for individuals are motivated by power as well as mind. If it is to one's interest to believe contradictions, he will assuredly find reasons to justify his preference. Hobbes well observes that when reason is against a man, a man will be against reason.

In sum: since people are free to decide whether or not they want to be rational, a formal statement of duty can confront the heart with nothing but *claims* to duty.

If it happens that a person is already held by a moral urge to be rationally self-consistent, then the categorical imperative, if valid, does no more than clarify a sense of compulsion that already exists. It does not give this sense of compulsion; and it does not because it cannot.

9. THE THIRD METHOD OF KNOWING

Since man enjoys veto rights over his own impulses, one can only know the content of the imperative essence by a total spiritual acceptance of the duties to which he is already committed by existence itself.* Rather than experientially or speculatively fingering mere claims to duty, one must allow himself to be transformed by the duties that hold him as he drives his car or shops for a new furnace.

Man is a spiritual creature; praiseworthy moral decision forms the very essence of his dignity. But if one will not spiritually acquaint himself with the components of his moral life, nothing from the outside can move him—whether it be a system of ethics, a self-transcendent survey of his own impulses, or a scientific review of how men conduct themselves in other cultures. The obligation to meet duty is part of duty. Duty can never be measured by thought; its essence eludes detection until one is morally and spiritually controlled by a sense of duty.

This is why I assert that a knowledge of the imperative essence will never be felt until one places himself in the center of those obligations which form the moral and spiritual environment of his life. If he shrinks from this, preferring to deal with either rational or empirical claims to duty, he will never move one inch toward a correct knowledge of the imperative essence.

But what name shall I give the third method of knowing, in order that it may henceforth be referred to with convenience and accuracy? Let us remember that terms are only useful; they cannot be true or false. A name is serviceable to the degree that it accurately denotes the ideas one has in mind.

I shall call the third method of knowing *knowledge by moral self-acceptance*. The content of the imperative essence cannot be apprehended until one is spiritually transformed by the sum of those duties which already hold him.

I realize that very little has been said about the precise meaning of moral self-acceptance. May the reader have patience. Since

---

* This expression, "the duties to which he is already committed by existence itself," will doubtless sound gratuitous and naïve to the reader. How does "existence itself" establish a line of argument from a person reared on Christian soil to a German conditioned by Hitler? Of what value, then, is an appeal to duties that already hold us? I have no other response than that I am conscious of these problems and that in due time I shall give my attention to them.

Types of Truth and Methods of Knowing 23

much of the book will be devoted to a dilation of this method, precision should increase as subsequent chapters unfold.

10. THE RELATION BETWEEN THE THREE METHODS OF KNOWING

Knowledge by acquaintance confronts the mind with the presentational wholeness of reality, while knowledge by inference confronts it with a conceptual grasp of reality. But if this is the case, how can knowledge by moral self-acceptance touch aspects of reality that remain inaccessible to other theories of knowledge?

As a formal fact, knowledge by moral self-acceptance can do *nothing* without the aid of knowledge by acquaintance and knowledge by inference. Even as the mind functions through the brain, but is not the same as the brain, so the third method of knowing functions through acquaintance and inference, though it is not the same as these.

An illustration may help clarify the matter. Suppose an archaeologist seeks permission to excavate a distant mound. Since the foreign government controls the site, while the archaeologist controls the techniques, only by friendly cooperation will either the government or the scientist know the meaning of the mound. The government has no direct access to knowledge; but without its authorization the archaeologist cannot begin to dig. So with moral self-acceptance: although knowledge by acquaintance and knowledge by inference are the only ways in which the content of the imperative essence can be brought before the mind, only moral self-acceptance can release the data which make up this essence. If a person will not submit to the moral sense, he will remain spiritually blind; for neither acquaintance nor inference has access to the pith and marrow of the imperative essence. Only moral self-acceptance can release a sense of duty into consciousness. Once duty has been released, of course, it then can be directly experienced or conceptually represented.

11. THE THREE CONDITIONS OF KNOWING

With this preliminary work before us, we may now review the three conditions of knowing. So we ask, "When does one possess knowledge?" Conditions of knowing answer to types of truth and methods of knowing. I define knowledge as "man's systematic contact with the real."

First, *To know is to experience*. Whenever a person consciously experiences anything, he meets the first condition of knowing. If he feels pain, he knows what pain means. His knowledge may be so clear that henceforth he dreads the very thought of pain.

Second, *To know is to enjoy a conceptual account of reality*. If a graduate student passes all his examinations, he enters the fellowship of learning. He meets the second condition of knowing because he relates his thoughts consistently. He can entertain accurate judgments about life; he can write scholarly articles.

But what condition of knowing answers to moral self-acceptance? If we enjoy either a direct experience, or a conceptual grasp, of reality, what more could be wanted? Let us see.

It is man's moral responsibility to determine whether a given action is worthy or unworthy. If a person freely does something, he announces to others, if not to himself, that he is subjectively willing to accept the implications of such a decision. For example, since fire will sear man's skin, a normal individual must bear whatever pain he feels when he deliberately touches fire. The pain could have been anticipated by a judicious use of moral freedom. Moral freedom, let us remember, is the very stuff of our dignity. Whenever the consequences of a choice can be anticipated, a decision to act implies the responsibility to live by these consequences.

Suppose a tourist is visiting England and the Continent. He has an allotted amount of money. If he squanders this money during the first week of the tour, his distress will arouse little sympathy in others. Since he was free to anticipate the conse-

Types of Truth and Methods of Knowing 25

quences of improvident living, he must live with the fruit of his choice. He should have acted more circumspectly.

It is important to notice how Wisdom answers one who acts rashly, for Wisdom's word may resolve our difficulty. Anxious to save one from the effect of his own imprudence, it says, "Why, you know better than that!" Foolish conduct is a sin against knowledge. To say that an individual "knows" better is merely another way of saying that he is responsible for acquainting himself with the outcome of his choices. And this is precisely what is meant by the third condition of knowing: *To know is to be morally responsible for knowing.* Although one does not meet the first condition of knowing until he experiences something, and although one does not meet the second condition of knowing until he reasons consistently, one already meets the third condition of knowing by virtue of his being a normal human being. Moral responsibility is the third condition of knowing. A person must spiritually anticipate the outcome of his actions.

All normal men are committed to the truth of this maxim: *Never do anything you will regret.* "Regret" is perhaps the bitterest word in the language. Even as men strive to make the best use of each opportunity, so they feel insecure when, through carelessness, they fail. No man will knowingly act to his own hurt.

Observe the dialogue we have with ourselves whenever we act precipitately. Suppose we spend money on something that is inferior in value, or which we find we do not need. Since our hard-earned money is gone, a memory of the act carries a note of condemnation. This is why foolishness has a moral basis, for whoever acts to his own hurt has done what he ought not to have done.

Again, suppose we blurt something we intended to conceal. We chide ourselves for our lack of self-control. A lost temper evokes a similar dialogue. "Alas, sir," said the wise Samuel Johnson, "on how few things can we look back with satisfaction."

The third condition of knowing is so deeply ingrained in human affairs that Jesus appealed to it when urging the eager multitudes not to enroll as his disciples until they pondered the consequences. "For which of you, desiring to build a tower, does not first sit down and count the cost, whether he has enough to complete it? Otherwise, when he has laid a foundation, and is not able to finish, all who see it begin to mock him, saying, 'This man began to build, and was not able to finish'" (Luke 14:28-30). An unfinished tower invites taunts and jeers because those who begin to build know what is required of them. They *know* because they are morally *responsible* for knowing. If one fails to count the cost, he plays the fool by sinning against the counsels of prudence.

But it may be asked, "How much does an individual know?" The answer is: He knows as much as he may be held accountable for. "If I had not come and spoken to them, they would not have sin; but now they have no excuse for their sin" (John 15:22). Age, social rank, and personal station are accidents, for the calculus of responsibility is decided by the total complex of a person's station and place. The insane know nothing because they are morally responsible for nothing; the child knows more because he is morally responsible for more; and the adult knows most because he is morally responsible for most. The extent of the third condition of knowing is measured by the power of moral and rational self-transcendence to acquaint the mind with consequences that flow from freely motivated conduct.

The tie-in between knowledge and action should be comprehended in the richest possible way. Moral self-transcendence is authorized to evaluate the reach of everything that can be anticipated by a judicious use of freedom. A distant link in the chain, no less than one that is near, must be anticipated. If a person degrades himself by spirits, for example, he is morally responsible for the effects of liquor on his health, his employment, his social standing in the community, and his dignity as head of the family. If he murders another while inebriated, the law holds him liable— even though the foul play was committed under nonmoral conditions. Having knowingly and willingly set this concatenation of events into motion, he is morally answerable to the whole.

The third condition of knowing does not prevail, of course,

Types of Truth and Methods of Knowing

unless the outcome of conduct can be anticipated by a judicious use of moral and rational self-transcendence. If one is shot by a stray bullet while walking through the park, it is meaningless to speak of moral responsibility. But if one hastily swallows poison, while thinking it is medicine, he is responsible, for he should have been more cautious in his choice.

A dog cannot be tried by jury. Neither can a child. The dog has no powers of self-transcendence, and the powers in the child are dormant. Hence, it is meaningless to speak of the third condition of knowing in either case. But when the child reaches its majority and innocence gives way to moral accountability, the third condition of knowing is born. The status of the dog remains the same, but not that of the child. Whereas the child can make both himself and his decisions an object of thought, the dog cannot.

The third condition of knowing will grow in importance as later arguments develop. In anticipation, however, let me simply say that if an individual will morally acquaint himself with the realities to which he is committed by existence itself, he may discover, to his surprise, that he is already in possession of the rough outline of a coherent view of God and the world. *It is my conviction that man's difficulty is not lack of knowledge, but lack of moral courage to act on the knowledge he already has.* If this is true, only a refusal to be spiritually honest prevents one from consciously recognizing the place of God in his life. Since moral and rational self-transcendence is able to acquaint the self with implications that flow from freely inspired decisions, an ignorance of these implications can be traced back to indolence in the individual himself. Hence, all are without excuse—all normal people, that is.

In saying this, I am saying no more than what the Apostle Paul has asserted from the beginning. "For what can be known about God is plain to them, because God has shown it to them. Ever since the creation of the world his invisible nature, namely, his eternal power and deity, has been clearly perceived in the things that have been made. So they are without excuse" (Romans 1:19-20).

When one inquires why so many remain ignorant of the

realities to which existence itself commits them, he should be careful to approach the question through the manner of his own life; otherwise he will be tempted to put all or none of the blame on personal perversity. Whoever examines his own habits will see that truth lies somewhere between these two extremes. Blindness to the third condition of knowing is neither as deliberate as religious zealots suppose, nor as innocent as moralists would like to pretend. The heart of man is both innocent and guilty, both consciously and unconsciously deceived.

Nor do we violate the law of contradiction by asserting that an individual can be ignorant and informed at the same time. It happens that there are *three* conditions of knowing. A person may be ignorant when judged by one condition, but very much in possession of knowledge when judged by another. The law of contradiction asserts that a thing cannot both be and not be in the same sense. But terms have different senses. If we mean that a man may be experientially or conceptually unaware of the implications that flow from his actions, he then may be called ignorant. He is not rationally conscious of the realities that hold him. But if we mean that an individual is morally and spiritually responsible for acquainting himself with such realities, and thus *ought* to have a conceptual grasp of their meaning, he may be said to know. When philosophers restrict conditions of knowing to either direct experience or conceptual representation, they simply announce one more of their many prejudices.

Let us remember how I have defined knowledge: Knowledge is "man's systematic contact with the real."* It is important to ob-

---

* By "systematic" I mean orderly, integrated, and dependable. Such things as knack, hunch, and opinion are not orderly; therefore they are not knowledge. Knowledge implies relatedness; it guides one systematically into the real. There are degrees of orderliness, of course, and thus degrees of knowledge. The principles of mathematics are more systematic than the guiding principles of psychology; but mathematics and psychology are both branches of knowledge. The proposition "I am a person" is no less knowledge than the proposition "Two and two make four." We must strive for increased precision in knowledge, to be sure, but we must avoid being betrayed into absurdity. Logical positivism has reached the place where even the exhortation "Logical positivists should say in word what they intend in meaning" is not knowledge. Aristotle wisely observes that the ability to judge what degree of precision may fairly be expected in any inquiry is the mark of an educated man.

Types of Truth and Methods of Knowing

serve that this definition does not include the word "conscious." I assert that man can be systematically in contact with the real without knowing it. But this want of awareness in no way alters the reality of the knowledge. Since self-transcendence is authorized to survey the sweep of one's relation to the real, an individual could know what he knows, if only he would *will* to know. The manner of his life is a revelation of what he already believes. It is his moral responsibility to acquaint himself with this belief.

If he continues to interact with reality, but refuses to acquaint himself with the implications of this interaction, he simply reinforces our contention that the basic trouble with man is moral, not rational.

12. A FINAL REVIEW

In an effort to tie the discussion together, let us give a pithy review of the kinds of truth, methods of knowing, and conditions of knowing.

The three kinds of truth: ontological truth, truth as propositional correspondence to reality, and truth as personal rectitude. *The three methods of knowing:* knowledge by acquaintance, knowledge by inference, and knowledge by moral self-acceptance. *The three conditions of knowing:* direct experience, the conceptual ordering of reality, and moral responsibility.

These three elements, in turn, form three separate concatenations. *The first chain:* ontological truth, knowledge by acquaintance, and direct experience. *The second chain:* truth as propositional correspondence to reality, knowledge by inference, and the conceptual ordering of reality. *The third chain:* truth as personal rectitude, knowledge by moral self-acceptance, and moral responsibility.

Like a body with all of its parts fitly knit together, no part can say to another, "I have no need of you." Methods of knowing are no less complex than the types of truth to which they answer. The method that measures the distance between stars is inappropriate when inquiring into the essence of beauty; and the method that inquires into beauty is inappropriate when searching for the essence of duty. Moralists are tempted to negate science in order to safeguard absolutes, while technicians are tempted to nullify absolutes in order to safeguard science. Such business is neither necessary nor wholesome. A rich and free use of the three methods of knowing will lead one through the three conditions of knowing into the three kinds of truth. A wise man should strive to comprehend the whole of reality, physical, rational, aesthetic, and moral and spiritual.

Part Two

APPLYING THE THIRD METHOD OF KNOWING

Chapter Three

A PRELIMINARY PROBE

1. TRANSITION THROUGH AESTHETICS

When I tried to apply the third method of knowing, however, I discovered, to my distress, that I had no clear notion of how to go about the matter. Moral self-acceptance is assuredly the third method of knowing, but what, precisely, does it *mean* to accept the self? Shall I say, "Here I am; I accept myself"? This clearly omened that it would be no easier applying the new method than it had been to devise and define it in the first place.

But since I had to start somewhere, I decided to try my hand at describing a unique experience. The purpose of this was to encourage the habit of looking at reality from the perspective of my own life. Until a habit of this sort developed, it would be difficult, if not impossible, to accept the realities which already held me. Such realities would remain hidden as long as I viewed things through the eyes of the race.

Memory immediately carried me back to the hot July afternoon on a friend's farm, where with great fascination I watched a group of wheat threshers going about their sweaty business. Anxious to show that I was a man, I made my way to the top of the wagon and began tossing ripe bundles of grain to the clapping belt below me. It was then that tragedy nearly struck. Careless of my footing for a moment, I began to slip down the side of the wagon and into the voracious jaws of the tremendous monster. If a farm hand

A Preliminary Probe

had not seen my plight and brought the machine to a grinding halt, I doubtless would have been torn to bits in its glistening parts.

The experience was unique, to be sure, but each time I tried to describe what it meant to face death by mangling, words failed me. I *experienced* what it meant—thus witnessing to the richness and validity of knowledge by acquaintance. But I could not communicate this meaning to others. Adjectives such as terrifying, frightful, and poignant were too universal to denote the particularity of my plight. They were inaccurate modes of expression.

This failure not only made me envious of novelists who excite empathy by the sheer use of words, but it reminded me of a truth already established, namely, that since the aesthetic experience deals with data in the descriptive mood, it can never acquaint an individual with the claims of the moral and spiritual environment. Moral data are in the imperative mood.

But is it not true that we are spiritually inspired by a great work of art? And does this not suggest that the aesthetic experience, in some sense, places one in contact with rectitude?

Further meditation gave me a satisfying answer. Although art spiritually confronts a person with universal human truths, in and of itself it is powerless to be the vehicle of duty. Whether art leaves deposits of moral conviction on the heart depends on the extent that one has already resolved to begin within duty. The aesthetic experience cannot pass beyond claims to duty unless one stands in the center of duty itself. One can weep while reading *Les Miserables*, only to turn back to his tearless, perfunctory life, quite unaltered by the experience and quite heedless of moral responsibility.

If art *does* change the heart, it is because one has been spiritually willing to accept the implications of the aesthetic experience; in which case it is the third method of knowing, not art, that acquaints the mind with duty.

This means that even if one could boast the skill of Gustave Flaubert, the most painstaking of the French stylists, he would not necessarily be nearer a knowledge of the moral and spiritual environment than a rogue. Art cannot communicate moral conviction until a sense of duty is released by moral self-acceptance. Being an artist does not give one a moral advantage. Artist or hod carrier, an upright person is transformed by duty because he has the courage and the consistency to begin with duty. The moral task is equal in all; no one can boast of superior opportunities. All are held by the third condition of knowing from existence itself.

2. A PLAIN AND SIMPLE EXPERIMENT IN THE CITY PARK

Venturing the possibility that I was making an easy thing difficult—a surmise which later proved to be true—I decided to break from philosophic tradition by humbly stooping to a very artless experiment. Since it is one's moral responsibility to acquaint himself with the realities that already hold him, I decided I had no choice other than to analyze a typical instance of conduct. And since I happened to be feeding pigeons in the city park when this decision was made, I wrote the following question at the top of my notebook: "To what am I committed as I freely choose to go to the city park?" Philosophers and scientists may be too occupied with cosmic things to worry about the place of the self in a city park, but it happens that cosmic things cannot properly be understood until one learns how to approach simple things through moral self-acceptance. It was in the course of this naïve little experiment that, to my complete delight, I discovered the elusive key to moral self-acceptance.

But rather than forthrightly telling how I managed to pass from an observation to an acceptance of the self, let me fill in each detail as it developed.

First, I had to concentrate on the guiding proposition *To know is to be morally responsible for knowing*. Since I already met the third condition of knowing, it was my spiritual responsibility to acquaint myself with the realities implied in any particular act. This is why I asked, "To what am I committed as I freely choose to go to the park?"

A Preliminary Probe

I immediately saw that in going to the park I made myself liable to all of the risks which threaten one who ventures out of doors. So, I quickly jotted down a list of the hazards incurred—everything from the threat of rain to the peril of being overpowered and robbed. Since the possibility of these evils was implied in my freely inspired conduct, should I not admit the fact?

When I grew weary of adding new risks to the list, however, I decided that nothing would be gained until I defined the exact relation between such risks and the proposition *To know is to be morally responsible for knowing*.

Resolving the problem was not easy, for it seemed that my experiment simultaneously did, and did not, illustrate the third condition of knowing. Suppose a person catches a disease while attending a symphony concert. He should have anticipated such an outcome. This is one way to view the matter. From another viewpoint, however, catching such a disease was unavoidable; and it is morally repugnant to be blamed for what cannot be helped. One is not within the third condition of knowing until consequences can be anticipated by reasonable foresight.

Despite the disappointment of this impasse, I was not unhappy with the progress of the argument. Although it yielded no *significant* information, the experiment in the park nonetheless taught me how to raise questions from the proper perspective. This certainly was gain.

3. THE DISCOVERY OF A UNIVERSAL STARTING POINT

Further reflection convinced me that the act of going to the park had nothing particularly distinctive about it. Eating a banana or writing a letter would have served just as well, for no act is wholly exempt from threats and perils. Every freely initiated action is attended by risks. If one remained at home, rather than going to the park, he would hazard the possibility of choking on a cracker or falling down the back stairs. All of life is ordered against a legion of insecurities.

This would be a very trite observation were it not for the fact that it fortifies the third method of knowing with the following universal starting point: *All men must act.* How men act is irrelevant. If they go swimming, they expose themselves to the possibility of cramps; if they take a walk, they may be hit by a car.

Some will doubtless rebut that this starting point was not established by the third method of knowing. The observation is valid, but irrelevant. The third method of knowing did not establish the reality of the park, either. Neither here nor elsewhere have I argued that moral self-acceptance is the only method of knowing. There are three methods—knowledge by acquaintance, knowledge by inference, and knowledge by moral self-acceptance—and each is appropriate to the particular data with which it deals. Since the starting point, "All men must act," is not part of the imperative essence, its validity is established by rational inference, not moral self-acceptance.

Philosophers have often striven to find a starting point that will coordinate all reality. Some have sought it in the quality of being, as in materialism and idealism; others have sought it in a universal method, as in empiricism and rationalism. But history abundantly witnesses to the failure of such efforts. The dream of finding a perfect coordinate will *never* be realized. Since reality is plural, approach must be plural; and since approach must be plural, starting point and method must be plural. The stuff of a rock is different from the stuff of morals, and a starting point which leads to a knowledge of a rock will not lead to a knowledge of morals.

My starting point—all men must act—sums up the important fact that no normal individual can avoid the third condition of knowing. Whether or not we care to admit it, all of us *must* act. And since a course of conduct is never freely chosen until we are morally satisfied that the right conditions prevail, the manner of our lives proves what we really believe. For example, if we decide to sit in a particular chair, we reveal our belief in the reality of the chair. And if we are upright individuals, we shall cordially acknowledge this belief; we shall not try to conceal it from others.

A Preliminary Probe

This is extremely crucial. The human race meets the third condition of knowing from creation itself. We *know* the realities which make freely inspired action possible because we are morally *responsible* for knowing. All normal individuals are answerable for what they do with the power of moral self-transcendence. If a person refuses to acknowledge the realities which hold him as he mingles with men in society, he culpably outrages the image of God in him. Man's glory consists in rectitude, but rectitude does not come into being until one is honest.

4. DESCARTES' STARTING POINT

Before proceeding further, however, I decided it would be profitable to compare my starting point with that of a typical classical philosopher. I chose René Descartes.

I simply cannot join the swelling ranks of those who make Descartes' *cogito* a whipping boy for all the ills in modern philosophy. I have always been warmly attracted to the Cartesian starting point, for it has close affinities with my own procedure.

Descartes began with the assertion, "I think, therefore I am." Critics tend to reduce the *cogito* either to tautology—"I, who exist, think; therefore I exist"—or to antilogy—"I, who do not exist, think; therefore I exist."

The critics' dissatisfaction with the *cogito* has always puzzled me, for I do not see how a morally inspired person can evade the force of the Cartesian argument. Determined to resolve the problem, I began to meditate on why I was so attracted to the *cogito* while Descartes' critics were so repelled.

I finally found an answer that satisfied me. Whenever I ponder the *cogito*, I sense a responsibility to include the manner of my own life among the data being considered. Here is what I defend: "I think, therefore I am morally obliged to admit the reality of my own existence." Were I to refuse to come at the problem by way of moral self-acceptance, I could easily reduce the *cogito* to either tautology or antilogy. This single element—one's moral responsibility to accept the implications of his own actions—makes the difference between sympathy and cavil.

This review was very instructive, for it clearly warned that my own starting point would fare no better than that of Descartes. Unless a person is spiritually willing to be responsible for his own conduct, the assertion, "All men must act," will be nothing but a truism. It will communicate no interesting information.

Although Descartes and I share the same limitation in approach, I make bold to assert that in the event an individual *is* morally willing to live by the implications of his own conduct, my starting point is markedly superior to that of Descartes. Descartes, I feel, did not make strategic use of the *cogito*. After brilliantly defending a truth to which all men are committed from existence itself, he then shifted to an arid survey of clear and distinct ideas. Although I feel personally responsible to admit the conclusion of the *cogito*, I am only rationally curious about the finished Cartesian system. This is why I have always wanted to walk up to Descartes and say: "Thinking involves the necessity of admitting one's existence, but what of it? Let us turn to some other matter, for nothing profound is before the house."

Here is why I believe my starting point is of unique significance. Since freely inspired action is a revelation of what one really believes, the third method of knowing places moral and rational demands on every normal member of the human race. A man has no right to call himself upright until he spiritually acknowledges the realities which hold him as he orders a new lawn mower or argues politics. Actions betray one's convictions, and moral self-acceptance is the method by which these convictions are apprehended and measured.

5. ARISTOTLE AND THE LAW OF CONTRADICTION

The relation between moral character and rational ability is perfectly illustrated by Aristotle's answer to the skeptics who denied the law of contradiction. The law says that a thing cannot both be and not be at the same time. Just as rectitude forms the

A Preliminary Probe

moral and spiritual environment of an upright heart, so the law of contradiction forms the rational environment of a consistent mind. When Aristotle tried to refute the skeptics, however, he encountered the frustrating fact that the skeptics *used* the law of contradiction to *deny* the law of contradiction. But how could this be shown? That was the difficulty.

After exhausting all his dialectical powers, Aristotle had to bow to the truth that only men of character can apprehend rational ultimates. Unless the skeptics were willing to approach the problem by way of moral self-acceptance, they necessarily would remain unconvinced. There was no straight-line way to demonstrate the law of contradiction. *The skeptics had to include the manner of their own lives among the data being considered, for one cannot attack the law of contradiction without appealing to the law of contradiction.* This is why Aristotle urged the skeptics to stand in the center of the truths to which they were committed whenever they said something significant.

Since this is one of the most interesting chapters in the history of philosophy, I shall let the Stagirite review his own difficulty. "There are some who, as we said, both themselves assert that it is possible for the same thing to be and not to be, and say that people can judge this to be the case. And among others many writers about nature use this language. But we have now posited that it is impossible for anything at the same time to be and not to be, and by this means have shown that this is the most indisputable of all principles.—Some indeed demand that even this shall be demonstrated, but this they do through want of education, for not to know of what things one should demand demonstration, and of what one should not, argues want of education. For it is impossible that there should be demonstration of absolutely everything (there would be an infinite regress, so that there would still be no demonstration); but if there are things of which one should not demand demonstration, these persons could not say what principle they maintain to be more self-evident than the present one.

"We can, however, demonstrate negatively even that this view is impossible, if our opponent will only say something; and if he says nothing, it is absurd to seek to give an account of our views to one who cannot give an account of anything, in so far as he cannot do so. For such a man, as such, is from the start no better than a vegetable. . . . The starting-point for all such arguments is not the demand that our opponent shall say that something either is or is not (for this one might perhaps take to be a begging of the question), but that he shall say something which is *significant* both for himself and for another; for this is necessary, if he really is to say anything . . . (It makes no difference even if one were to say a word has several meanings, if only they are limited in number; for to each definition there might be assigned a different word. . . . If, however, they were not limited but one were to say that the word has an infinite number of meanings, obviously reasoning would be impossible; for not to have one meaning is to have no meaning, and if words have no meaning our reasoning with one another, and indeed with ourselves, has been annihilated; for it is impossible to think of anything if we do not think of one thing; but if this *is* possible, one name might be assigned to this thing.)"*

In sum: if a person intends to speak significantly, his terms cannot simultaneously designate one thing and its opposite; for when nothing specific is meant, nothing at all is meant. Significant speech *must* obey the law of contradiction. It seems to me that this is the most perfect philosophical argument ever devised. A skeptic establishes the law of contradiction by his very effort to deny it. There is no meaningful way to escape the force of this demonstration.

But bear in mind that Aristotle could not begin his negative demonstration until a skeptic met two conditions: not only did he have to *say* something significant, but he had to be morally willing to accept the implications of his speech. Both parts belong to the Aristotelian demand. Actions betray what one believes; but one will not become conscious of such belief until he is spiritually willing to be honest.

* *Metaphysics*, IV (1005b-1006b).

A Preliminary Probe 41

Aristotle called his demonstration "self-evident." But in truth it is far from self-evident. It is hidden from the eyes of all who refuse to be responsible for the realities to which they are committed by existence itself. Aristotle, like Kant, illuminates the fact that the rational life cannot get on with it unless the moral life is firm.

This review of Aristotle inspired me with a measure of renewed confidence that the hour had now come to formulate a fresh approach to the person of God. If Aristotle had conceived man's relation to God in the same way that he conceived man's relation to logic, he would have rendered philosophy a unique service. But it apparently never occurred to him that the person of God comprises the environment of man's moral and spiritual life in the same way that the law of contradiction comprises the environment of man's rational life.* Or at least if he saw it, he never did anything about it.

6. THE LAW OF CONTRADICTION AND MORAL SELF-ACCEPTANCE

I soon recognized that the law of contradiction is the purest possible reality to which one is already committed by existence itself. I should have known this when I undertook my experiment in the park. If I had had more of the sense of Aristotle, I should have perceived that a reliance on the axioms of logic antecedes any significant contemplation of threats and risks. Before I could think about a park, I had to be in possession of a criterion of judgment. I had to be assured that the park was not other than itself. It could not both be and not be at the same time and in the same sense. A resting in the truth of the law of contradiction is the rational precondition for all other activity. This is why Aristotle's

---

* Christ is the "wisdom of God." Whenever we enjoy the possession of wisdom, we share in the mind of Christ. This is a privilege accorded no animal. "And yet the validity of logical sequences is not a thing devised by men, but is observed and noted by them that they may be able to learn and teach it; for it exists eternally in the reason of things, and has its origin with God." Augustine, *On Christian Doctrine*, II, 50.

negative demonstration constitutes the purest possible application of moral self-acceptance. No future use of the third method of knowing can surpass it in excellence.

It is my hope, nonetheless, that even as one's reliance on the law of contradiction is established whenever one *speaks* significantly, so one's reliance on the person of God is established whenever one *judges* significantly. If the third method of knowing is applied with care, man's life in God ought to be proved with a force that is somewhat analogous to Aristotle's negative demonstration of the law of contradiction. Equivalent precision is impossible, of course, for as we move from mind to spirit, not only is the surface of possible error extended, but the moral warfare in the heart increases. If skeptics had to wage a spiritual battle before they would concede the validity of the law of contradiction, how much greater will the struggle be when man is confronted with a truth that threatens to shatter his moral complacency at every point?

In any event, I decided that even as meaningful speech implies the law of contradiction, and even as the *cogito* implies a thinker's existence, so the wider actions of men imply the general outline of a complete world view; and that this world view is no less established by the fact of man's conduct than either the law of contradiction or the reality of a thinker's existence.

7. THE LAW OF UNIFORMITY AND MORAL SELF-ACCEPTANCE

In order that the meaning of moral self-acceptance might be clarified even further, I decided to show how one would go about establishing the law of uniformity in nature. A demonstration of such a law is roughly parallel to Aristotle's negative demonstration of the law of contradiction.* Even as the truth of the law of

---

* Observe that this demonstration is only *roughly* parallel. Our expectation of regularity hovers somewhere between a priori necessity and arbitrary postulation. We do not know exactly where. This leaves the door ajar for the possibility of miracles. One purpose of a miracle is to remind us that the will of

A Preliminary Probe

contradiction is established whenever one *speaks* significantly, so the truth of the law of uniformity is established whenever one *acts* significantly. All meaningfully directed conduct rests on the antecedent confidence that nature is regular. The proof is as simple as that.

I realize how specious this will sound to those who will not come at the matter with a moral and spiritual willingness to accept the realities that already hold them. Relativists assert that the law of uniformity in nature is merely an operational hypothesis which helps them get on with the business of interpreting and controlling nature. They forget that though there is no scientific proof of regularity, action carries a proof all of its own. Conduct betrays one's firm assurance that nature is regular.

I forthrightly challenge relativists to approach this question with a firm spiritual willingness to abide by the implications of their own actions. If they try to deny the antecedent truth of uniformity, they will begin within deception; for the very floor on which they stand is part of an anticipated system of regularity. Whether they care to admit it or not, their confident posture is a loud announcement of their belief that the floor will remain wood, instead of turning to poison ivy or buckets of green paint. There is no *direct* way to show this, of course. If relativists refuse to view the matter through the realities that already hold them, they will remain as blind to the law of uniformity as skeptics are to the law of contradiction. Ultimates cannot be seen unless the heart is controlled by right affections.

Relativists who boast of an open universe are either exceedingly ignorant or exceedingly mendacious. They remind me of the times at school when a bully would pin a weaker boy to the ground. The defeated lad would writhe in pain. Yet, would he admit it? Oh, no! He would rally all his courage to assure everybody that he was not hurt. Those who watched, however, knew this was a lie.

God, not immanent law, is the final ground of regularity. God promises to keep nature steady, in order that we may regulate our lives safely and predictably. "While the earth remains, seedtime and harvest, cold and heat, summer and winter, day and night, shall not cease" (Genesis 8:22).

I might mention, in conclusion, that Immanuel Kant strove valiantly to establish the unity of the world as a "limiting concept." His effort would have been much more convincing if he had followed a theory of knowledge which took in the third condition of knowing. His notion of a limiting concept was rather crudely tacked on to what could have been a very challenging effort in pure reason. We shall enlarge on this at a later point.

8. THE REALISM OF THE THIRD METHOD OF KNOWING

In whatever way conventional philosophic methods neglect realities which touch the hearth and the market, such a neglect can never be charged against the third method of knowing. Moral self-acceptance adheres very closely to the real. It proceeds on the assumption that men in action are more natural, and thus are less likely to conceal their true convictions, than men while professionally philosophizing. Speculation is partly an unconscious projection of personal interests.

If one will observe the freely inspired actions of another person long enough, sooner or later he will discover this person's true convictions; for native actions invariably betray true beliefs. Pyrrho, for example, solemnly averred that lasting happiness was a fruit of a disciplined suspension of judgment. But when wild dogs were after him, or when a rumbling chariot headed his way, with a sharp eye to physical well-being he abandoned his suspended judgment and fled to safety. His actions contradicted his philosophy, and the real Pyrrho was the Pyrrho in act.

There is nothing new about this insight. Penal authorities appeal to it whenever a suspect submits to a lie detector. Although the accused may conceal all outward evidence of guilt, there is a natural limit to his control over inner response. He can never completely throttle the witness of the nervous system. Each effort to conceal guilt sets neural reverberations in motion, and a sensitive lie detector can measure this quantity.

A Preliminary Probe

Moral self-acceptance is relieved of all kinds of difficulties. Since men *must* act, and since action reveals what men really believe, it is not necessary to approach people as skeptics, atheists, or dogmatists. Rather than probing into convictions that divide men, the third method of knowing confines itself to convictions that unite them. Men salute the same flag, march off to the same war, and weep or rejoice over the same drama. They applaud the hero and hiss the coward. They praise the good and condemn the bad.

This was crisply illustrated one autumn afternoon as I sat with nearly a hundred thousand students and alumni, watching a game of university football. The spiritual unity of the crowd impressed me. Although the spectators represented many different religious, political, and ideological points of view, their prejudices were either consciously waived during the game or forgotten altogether. A set of lovely fraternal ties knit each person with his neighbor. The crowd rose and sat in a fellowship that was most inspiring to watch—empiricist and rationalist, relativist and absolutist, Protestant, Catholic, and Jew, it made no difference. They applauded skill; they hissed unnecessary roughness; and they laughed when a small dog ran between the legs of the players. Here was the nearest expression of natural harmony to be found anywhere in society. A bond of primary values fused the vast throng into one living organism. I suppose this is why the athletic contest will always be a part of the human venture. It proves how many truths and values we all hold in common.

But when the gun sounded and the crowd began to move, ant-like, toward the tunnels, this spell of vital unity was broken and an alien spirit took over. A robust self-love converted jolly young people into grumbling drivers trying to thread their way out of the crowded parking lot. Each was once again anxious to make a point of his religion, his politics, and his philosophy.

I shall not presume to say which was the true man: the man in fellowship at the game or the irate driver in the sea of stalled cars. I only assert that if philosophers are ever going to get on with it, they must base their case on the raw, conflicting facts that make up man's fourfold environment: physical, aesthetic, rational, and moral and spiritual. And I certainly do not mean that philosophers should attend as many football games as possible—observing how often people sneeze or noting at what point fellowship converts to anger. Philosophers ought, rather, to stand in the center of their *own* commitments. The true data of inwardness cannot be comprehended until one arouses a spiritual willingness to accept the realities that already hold him. This is a painfully private task; it cannot be wrought by proxy.

Chapter Four

MORAL SELF-ACCEPTANCE AND SOCIAL RELATIONS

1. A REFINEMENT OF PROCEDURE

Hitherto I have argued that the third condition of knowing means "moral responsibility for both the fact and the outcome of freely inspired conduct." Before proceeding further, however, it may be helpful to dilate this somewhat. There are two separate elements in responsibility, each of which is important in its own right.

First, there is "responsibility of admission." This signifies one's moral obligation to own all the realities to which existence itself commits him. Second, there is "responsibility of consequence." This signifies one's moral obligation to absorb the consequences which flow from freely inspired action.

No aspect of life is ever wholly exempt from these two kinds of responsibility. For example, if a man elects to drive a car, he should admit that he is already committed to the law of uniformity. *This is responsibility of admission.* If he complains that he would never have bought a car, had he known how high the taxes were, he is forthrightly reminded that he should have thought of that before the purchase was made. *This is responsibility of consequence expressed as inconvenience.* And if he argues that he cannot justly be fined for breaking an unknown law, he is told with equal forthrightness that whenever one decides to operate a car he makes himself responsible for the laws governing right driving. These laws should be studied before one takes to the road. *This is responsibility of consequence expressed as judicial obligation.*

It is necessary that this clarification be made, lest it be thought that moral self-acceptance consists in nothing but the rather perfunctory responsibility of absorbing inconvenient or disagreeable fruits of action. There are moral and judicial responsibilities which must be met, responsibilities that affect the very structure of the soul. Personal tastes cannot even be indulged unless one is negatively assured that his act does not endanger the health and welfare of the community. If one deliberately disregards moral obligation, he outrages the essence of his own dignity, for dignity *consists* in rectitude.

I am not unaware of the legal maxim *Ignorantia facti excusat* (Ignorance of the fact excuses). A reasonable mistake of fact, honestly acted on, voids the charge of malicious intent in most cases. Even the maxim *Ignorantia juris neminem excusat* (Ignorance of the law excuses no one) has been tempered in civil-law countries. A mistaking of law, except in criminal cases, is treated as a mistaking of fact. These maxims warn against the *abuse*, but not the truth, of the third condition of knowing. The third condition of knowing prevails whenever the implications of one's conduct can be anticipated by a reasonable and untaxed use of moral and rational self-transcendence. A college freshman will be forgiven an honest mistaking of fact or law; but he will not be forgiven—and to this degree he illustrates the third condition of knowing—if he does not even bother to acquaint himself with the rules of the university. This distinction must be kept in mind, for neither here nor elsewhere is it our intention to press the third condition of knowing to the point where it embarrasses accepted juridical canons. For instance, when we assert that men *know* God because they are morally *responsible* for knowing, we intend to make full allowance for an honest mistaking of fact or law. God judges by truth and justice, not caprice. The third condition of knowing has no existence unless the consequences of freely inspired conduct can be reasonably anticipated by the one who acts.

2. FINDING AN INDEX TO HUMAN ACTIONS

In attempting to apply the third method of knowing, one immediately confronts the complex connections that make up human conduct. Life is a continuum. At what point, therefore, can a man interrupt this unity, in order that he might come to terms with the realities that already hold him? And how can he be sure that here is the place to break in, rather than another? This means that even though one may be quite *willing* to apply the third method of knowing, the very complexity of existence may discourage him before he even starts.

I concluded, after due reflection, that conduct can be classified according to the degrees of personal enthusiasm with which one acts. If ordinary action is a revelation of what one believes, it certainly follows that the more enthusiastically one undertakes a project, the stronger is one's belief. This possibility, at least, merited critical investigation.

Here is the rule of thumb I decided to apply: *Routine conduct reveals our belief in general being; excited conduct our belief in values; and morally inspired conduct our belief in rectitude.*

Hiking down a trail betrays one's confidence in the reality of both the trail and the law of natural uniformity. But if one greatly prefers hiking to swimming, so that a consistent pattern of preference protrudes, an acute observer can justly conclude that, in the mind of this other person, hiking not only has being, but it has the peculiar kind of being called "value." A value is anything prized or held with esteem. Values engage the self more intimately than sheer being, as witnessed by the power of a preference to increase or decrease our happiness. Values answer to the well-being of the soul.

If enthusiastic action is an index to what one values, then ethically inspired action is an index to one's moral convictions. Moral convictions touch the self more intimately than values, for they are excited by a concerned response to the moral and spiritual environment.

If this rule of thumb is acceptable, we now have access to the third kind of truth by way of the third method of knowing, for morally inspired conduct is an index to convictions that lurk deep in the recesses of the heart.

If a man drinks a glass of water, he shows his belief in the reality of water. But suppose his mind chances to wander to his favorite trout stream. The very thought of the mountain retreat stirs up nostalgic memories. This excitement proves his belief in the value of the stream. Now, suppose he is curtly told that he no longer has a right to fish. He clenches his fist, pounds the table, and solemnly warns that he will *never* forfeit the privilege of fishing. This increased enthusiasm proves his belief in the right to fish. He may be quite mistaken about such a right, but that is beside the point. Since he *acts* as if he has a right to fish, it is his solemn responsibility to admit it.

In sum: casual action mirrors general being; enthusiastic action mirrors the being of values; and juridical action mirrors the being of rectitude. Each aspect of being is part of the totality of the real: being as sheer existence; being as value; and being as rectitude. Each type of being is as real as any other, though each differs from the others in essential characteristics.

I fully realize how inane this will sound to positivists who insist on measuring all reality by a restricted application of the scientific method. They will tartly ask, "Does the being of a river change when different people are differently related to it?" I see no way of answering those who refuse to be spiritually responsible for the types of being which degrees of enthusiasm mirror. If one cannot perceive that rectitude has a different quality of being than a tree, blindness must remain.

But this, at least, can be said: Whoever is indifferent to types of being will never clarify his relation to the person of God. Personality cannot be an object of scientific scrutiny. It is rationally known only as it is spiritually felt. If man is dependent on God,

Moral Self-Acceptance and Social Relations

God can never be known until man proceeds through a moral and spiritual acceptance of this relation. "Blessed are the pure in heart, for they shall see God" (Matthew 5:8).*

Others may challenge my procedure on the ground that conduct is not *necessarily* a revelation of belief, for men frequently deceive one another. They inwardly acknowledge one thing, while outwardly they pretend something quite different. "Take me not off with the wicked, with those who are workers of evil, who speak peace with their neighbors, while mischief is in their hearts" (Psalm 28:3).

This new objection is so well taken that I must immediately temper an earlier assertion. I said that if one observes another person long enough, the native convictions of that person are bound to be revealed. I now realize that this may or may not be the case. It depends on whether the person deliberately tries to cloak his true feelings. If it is to his advantage to feign convictions, he can prolong his lie indefinitely. And when this happens, *no* reliable expectations can be grounded on the manner of his conduct. Action is revelatory only to the degree that one is held by a sincerity that is free from any desire to deceive.

Since this is the case, it is necessary to revise our assertions somewhat. Action is a form of revelation, to be sure, even as degrees of enthusiasm mirror the types of being that engage one; *but only the individual, in the solitude and honesty of his inner life, can detect and measure this revelation.* For example, an honest person will admit that his outward pretension of security is often an evidence of inner insecurity. He may deceive others, but he cannot deceive himself—or, better, he cannot deceive himself as long as he is spiritually willing to live by the realities that already hold him.

---

* I am conscious of the grave problem which emerges at this juncture. Is there a univocal point of identity in the propositions "Man is a person" and "God is a person"? If there is, how can we avoid pantheism? And if there is not, how can we make meaningful predications about God?

I inject these questions, so the reader may know that I am not unaware of their existence. But there is a time for everything, and this is not the time. Additional background information is needed if the problem is to be resolved with reasonable precision.

Down deep in his heart he knows the truth. And knowing it, he should accept it.

This clarification does not alter the principle in any essential way. It simply reinforces the fact that the way to the moral and spiritual environment, and thus the way to God, is painfully private. Man *knows* his place in God because he is morally *responsible* for knowing; he meets the third condition of knowing from existence itself.

3. CHALLENGING THE THEORY THAT ALL MORALS ARE RELATIVE

If we may call the self in its inner privacy the "honest self," while reserving the name "social self" for the outward manner of the self as it seeks to impress others with its worth and security, we have a vantage point from which to break a lance with the modern dogma that "all morals are relative." Faith in this dogma has arisen, in the main, from an empirical review of the various tribes and nations under the sun. Having discovered that moral convictions tend to change with the times, the conclusion is drawn that standards are relative to the culture in which they take their rise. Moral criteria have no absolute content; they have no transcultural reference. What is right in one society is often wrong in another.

I am not yet sufficiently far along in moral self-acceptance to establish the absoluteness of morals, but enough evidence has been marshaled to warn the student of comparative ethics that the problem may be vastly more complex than the scientific method suggests. Since a person will reveal no more of his true convictions than he cares to, a scientific review of moral habits can only serve, at best, as an index to what others *profess* to believe. The true moral convictions of an individual may lie beneath the veneer of social pretense, and science is powerless to penetrate this stratum. Unless it draws its data from moral self-acceptance, therefore, the scientific method is as irrelevant in morals as the third method of knowing is in matters of science. Whenever either method usurps the work of the other, wisdom converts to foolishness.

Moral Self-Acceptance and Social Relations 53

Thus, there are many reasons to deny, and none to believe, that an empirical review of moral habits gives a trustworthy insight into the true convictions of a tribe. One may outwardly pretend what he inwardly disbelieves. He may participate in the terms of rectitude, and thus know the absoluteness of morals; but he remains spiritually free to defy this insight. Defective affections betray him into hypocrisy. "Though they know God's decree that those who do such things deserve to die, they not only do them but approve those who practice them" (Romans 1:32). If a *single* individual can deceive others by pretension, so can a tribe. Whenever personal gain flows from pretense, it is easy to justify the pretense; and the stronger the gain becomes, the more deliberate is the justification.

Furthermore, empiricism can give no really decisive account of why prophets speak against the mores of their culture. It may well be that the prophets are defending truths which the tribe fears, but which it has no moral interest in following. For example, the ancients thought it was beautiful to fondle little boys. But Socrates and Marcus Aurelius could not practice this with the consent of their nobler faculties. It was a habit they did not want their loved ones to adopt. So, they prophetically witnessed against their own age. I do not say that empiricism has *no* explanation of this phenomenon; I simply say its explanation is not *decisive*. For example, it cannot profoundly account for Socrates' refusal to escape from prison. "For I am inclined to think that these muscles and bones of mine would have gone off long ago to Megara or Boeotia —by the dog, they would, if they had been moved only by their own idea of what was best, and if I had not chosen the better and nobler part, instead of playing truant and running away, of enduring any punishment which the state inflicts."* The prophet may possibly be in contact with standards which take their rise in eternity. Both Plato and the Christian would assert that this is, in fact, the case.

This, I think, is sufficient to discredit the popular dogma of moral relativity. Since an individual will unbosom no more of

* *Phaedo*, 99.

his true convictions than the whole self finds it advantageous to reveal, it is foolish of ethicists to think they can decide the relativity or absoluteness of morals by an empirical study of the race. A man will never knowingly reveal things to his own hurt—especially to his moral hurt. The surface relativities of a culture may only cloak a set of absolutes which are inwardly known and spiritually feared. "For what can be known about God is plain to them, because God has shown it to them" (Romans 1:19).

4. MORAL SELF-ACCEPTANCE AND VALUES

We have asserted that one can measure types of being by the degrees of enthusiasm with which he undertakes a project. The time has now come to test this assertion. We shall begin with values.

Many things evoke a feeling of value: eating steaks, receiving praise, and any personal attention that accents our prestige or power. And many things pique us: inclement weather, frustrated opportunities, and sundry threats and insecurities too numerous to list. The strength of the value tends to fluctuate with the changing dispositions of the self. If we are well, only large things can annoy us; but if we are physically weary the self is peeved by such insignificant trifles as a piercing noise or the discourtesy of a bumpkin.

This might seem to be striving after wind, but such is not the case. Let me show why. First, is it not significant that we are able to classify values as better and worse? Unless we already possessed a criterion, how could we meaningfully entertain such judgments? If we succeed in isolating this criterion, we may have a clue to the content of the imperative essence. Second, the experiment proves something very important about social relations. The moment we face another individual, sensitive contact is made with the moral and spiritual environment. People do what animals and nature cannot do: they force us to defend the dignity of our own life. The sheer presence of others alerts us to issues of justice and injustice.

Moral Self-Acceptance and Social Relations

This second insight was very rewarding, for it clarified the direction in which we should move. If we ever expect to plunge into the real business of moral self-acceptance, we must return with Socrates to the market place, there to examine the realities that already hold us as we mingle with others. Enthusiastic, judicial excitement is a revelation of moral convictions, and no more effective place can be found for the arousing of such convictions than the streets and shops of the thronging city.

5. MORAL SELF-ACCEPTANCE AND SOCIAL RELATIONS

Therefore, even as I formerly asked, "To what realities am I committed when I freely go to the park?" so I now ask, "To what realities am I committed when I freely stand in the society of others?" Just as I was spiritually willing to acknowledge the realities that held me when I went to the park, so I now am equally willing to acknowledge the realities that hold me when I enter the society of others. This may seem like a circuitous way to clarify the moral and spiritual environment, but the indirection cannot be avoided. Method must correspond to the type of data under scrutiny.

Once we enter society with an eye to the third condition of knowing, we find that we are powerless to trust others unless they give evidence of accepting the dignity of our person. Men of character cannot be indifferent to the moral response of a neighbor. If one seeks fellowship, he must extend fellowship. No one can force us to act.* Suppose a stranger is driving through town. He cannot get out of his car and *compel* us to give him directions. We feel no compulsion unless he shows moral signs of receiving the dignity of our person. If he disregards the terms of fellowship,

---

* Even official authority is limited by our dignity. The state can force us to buy a driver's license, but it cannot force us to be fingerprinted. The fingerprint on the license may be an excellent safeguard, yet one cannot be forced to give his fingerprint. This would be a violation of his dignity. The same is true in jurisprudence. A man cannot be forced to take a lie-detector test. Evidence gained by duress is inadmissible.

he will learn nothing from us. Friendly response is always a fruit of loving affections, never a work of legal striving.

Regardless of where we may happen to be—whether in high society among kings or in low society among rogues—the quality of our moral demand remains unaltered. An upright man is no more able to have fellowship with a cheat than a rational man is able to believe a contradiction. The moral and spiritual environment binds the soul, and the rational environment binds the mind. The sheer presence of our person places others under moral responsibility.

The force of this will escape us unless we recall our procedure. If meaningful speech commits us to the law of contradiction, and if meaningful action commits us to the law of uniformity, then meaningful judicial response commits us to the law of our dignity. Each of these holds us from existence itself.

Let us not lose sight of our goal. We are attempting to discover the content of the imperative essence, in order that we might clarify the moral and spiritual environment. A clarification of this environment, in turn, will clarify our relation to God. This is why it is extremely important to appreciate the power of social relations to acquaint us with data in the imperative mood. The moral sense is a direct product of the moral and spiritual environment. It is not of human devising.

If a person is so foolish as to deny either the law of contradiction or the law of uniformity, that is his private affair. But if he dares to deny the law of our dignity, we instantly abandon our detached attitude. Under no conditions, real or presumed, will we grant him the privilege of deciding whether or not he finds it personally interesting to regard us. This demand is a category of our spiritual life; it is a priori to the moral sense.

Man, in Christian language, is made in the "image of God." As soon as a person enters the circle of nearness, we oblige him to conform to the moral responsibilities that inhere in fellowship. Even as one should not hurl himself over a cliff unless he is willing to accept the physical threats of such a decision, so one should

Moral Self-Acceptance and Social Relations 57

not enter the circle of nearness unless he is willing to accept the spiritual obligations of fellowship. Just as it is foolish to defy the laws of nature, so it is immoral to defy the laws of fellowship.

6. OUR MORAL DEMANDS ON STRANGERS

If one will carefully analyze his actions in the course of a single day, he will see that his moral expectations are governed by the following rather rigid rule: *The more spiritually intimate the relation is, or the more power a person has to threaten or support our happiness, the more we look for evidences that our dignity is being regarded.* "Spiritual nearness" means the place of intimacy which an individual enjoys—enemy, stranger, friend, or kin. Friends must give stronger evidences than strangers; kin must give more intimate evidences than friends. "Power to destroy happiness" means the recognized control over us which another person enjoys. The greater this control is, the more specific the test becomes. Loved ones have spiritual power, while soldiers have physical power.

In order that an experiment may be made of this, let us ask ourselves, "Under what conditions will we trust a stranger?" Since a stranger is not intimately near us, nor is he in possession of any recognized control over our lives, our rule says that only minimal moral demands are exacted. This is surely what experience verifies. We will trust a stranger only to the degree that he shows a want of conscious intention to harm us. Though negative in form, the demand is affirmative in moral quality.

In so perfunctory an act as entering a coffeehouse, we prove our participation in the claims of the moral and spiritual environment. Suppose the waitress removes the cup from some hidden recess, rather than from the clean stack before us. And suppose she nods to a suspicious-looking person in the kitchen—making many superfluous motions before filling the cup. Since she fails to prove that she is moral, we withhold trust and quickly take our leave.

The waitress may inquire how we are, and whether we enjoy the morning, but she is not at liberty to inquire whether we wish to be treated as human beings. Nor are we at liberty to be morally neutral toward her dignity. We would never have entered the coffee-house, nor would she have approached our table, if either had suspected that the other was indifferent to his spiritual responsibilities as an individual.

The negation, thus, is really a disguised affirmation, for the demand that our dignity be regarded is only another way of requiring civility, courtesy, and a gentle walk. It would be an error to conclude that the want of fellowship when passing a stranger implies an equal want of moral obligation, for rich spiritual ties federate even those who, as yet, are merely preparing for fellowship.

Demanding that others spiritually regard us is not an expression of selfishness. It is a sign of a healthy character. An upright man can no more disregard what others do to him than he can disregard opportunities of happiness. We participate in the moral and spiritual environment from existence itself; we cannot divest ourselves of this relation.

And for quite the same reason we participate in the person of God, for in him we live and move and are. This must be stressed, lest it be supposed that a person has no dealings with God until he makes a conscious religious commitment. An ignorance of one's place in God no more excuses him from the obligation to acknowledge God than a skeptic's ignorance of the law of contradiction excuses him from the obligation to acknowledge the law of contradiction. Ignorance is not innocence. Man *knows* what his actions imply because he is morally *responsible* for knowing.

7. MORAL RESPONSIBILITY WHEN ENTERING FRIENDSHIP

The transition from stranger to friend is achieved by a ratifying of the solemn moral pledge that the life of the other person will never be used as a means to some forecasted end. The quality of the pledge is the same everywhere, though the ritual of ratification will, of necessity, vary with the circumstances. Sometimes just

Moral Self-Acceptance and Social Relations 59

living with another person seals the bond, as when employees grow into each other's affections by working together. Each accepts the affable manners of the other as a tacit ratification of the pledge. In most cases, however, some visible sign is required, such as a handshake or the passing of the calumet, according to local custom. The haste and incaution with which individuals enter fellowship must not delude us into thinking that trivial values are being exchanged; for a treaty between major powers could not be framed in more solemn terms. A handshake is like a miniature blossom under the microscope: when carefully examined, magnificent chromatic splendors come into view.

The introductory question, "How do you do?" signifies the following: "I receive you as a person; I willingly bind myself by the obligations of fellowship; no future contingency can release me from this trust." Neither the sculpture of Praxiteles nor the harmonics of Bach can eclipse the beauty of a handshake. No money is exchanged, no forfeit exacted; and yet the greatest of all treasures—that of the heart itself—is gently entrusted to the care of another. A humble demeanor, held in the matrix of a morally honest heart, wins the prize. If friendship were not sealed by sanctions that both parties fear, each would be free to calculate whether or not he finds it advantageous to continue as a friend.

Since a stranger has not been admitted into the privileges of fellowship, no more is demanded of him than gestures of civility and courtesy. But once an offer of friendship has been made—only to be spurned—the invited person vacates the relation of stranger and becomes, to the degree of his malice, an enemy. And before the invitation to fellowship can be spiritually renewed, he must not only give moral signs of accepting the responsibility of friendship, but sincerely and with an eye to inner renovation he must accept the guilt of having spurned the offer of friendship in the first place. Guilt cannot be a mere object of thought. Unless it is morally felt, it is not rationally known. This must be stressed. Knowledge by inference must bow to knowledge by acquaintance. Only a guilty heart can profoundly know guilt.

Hence, though we may be *willing* to forgive one who has rejected friendship—thus showing that we are moral—we cannot renew the offer of friendship until signs are forthcoming that the guilty party has been transformed by an acknowledgment of his guilt. Our refusal to have fellowship with an unrepentant person is just as truly a fruit of the moral and spiritual environment as the original demand that others receive our dignity.

When we speak of one's moral obligation to meet rectitude, we are addressing ourselves to the third type of truth. Truth as personal rectitude comes into being, or goes out of being, in direct proportion to an individual's willingness to be inwardly transformed by the requirements of rectitude. The imperative essence does not exist until one is moral.

As one clarifies the terms of rectitude, he likewise clarifies his relation to the person of God. The purpose of the third method of knowing is to show us how to have fellowship with God. It is necessary to repeat this, lest the supporting arguments befog our general perspective. It indeed is difficult to define our relation to the moral and spiritual environment; but, apart from this labor, we will miss the point of Paul's teaching that we live and move and are in God.

8. MORAL DEMANDS WITHIN FRIENDSHIP

Suppose one friend meets another. Each is instantly obliged by the "cycle of fellowship." This cycle is familiar to all who reflect on the manner of their own lives: an initial greeting, an expression of sustained pleasure, and a token of farewell affection. Let us briefly review these elements.

The initial greeting morally disarms each party. It may be a nod, a handshake, or an embrace, depending on such things as the situation, the intimacy of the relation, and the temperament of the parties involved. But the greeting *must* be morally sincere.

The season of fellowship consists in a spontaneous desire to complete one's own life in and through the life of the other. Fellowship looks for a twinkle in the eye, a cheery word, and a

Moral Self-Acceptance and Social Relations

steady refusal to challenge the other's integrity, even though points of view may differ.

The parting farewell notarizes the relation by a public assurance that nothing will corrupt the purity of this trust. Fellowship is an unconditional obligation.

This may sound academically trite. But when it is weighed by the third method of knowing, it is further proof that man lives and moves in a moral and spiritual environment that he did not create. We participate in, but we do not devise, the terms of fellowship. To prove this, let someone *try* yielding himself without making the demand that others treat him with dignity. "There must be a veracity, a natural spontaneity in forms. In the commonest meeting of men, a person making, what we call, 'set speeches,' is not he an offense? In the mere drawing-room, whatsoever courtesies you see to be grimaces, prompted by no spontaneous reality within, are a thing you wish to get away from."[*]

There is no value in laboring this further. The matter will be lucid to all who submit to the realities that hold them from existence itself. And those who spurn such responsibility would never be convinced, though the world itself were filled with evidences. I repeat: Man's difficulty is not lack of knowledge, but lack of moral courage to act on the knowledge he already has.

9. THE SECOND CRITERION

Let us remember the rule which guides our moral expectations: the more spiritually intimate the relation is, or the more power a person has to threaten or support our happiness, the more we look for evidences that our dignity is being regarded. Having reviewed cases of spiritual intimacy, let us now turn to cases where others have power to threaten or support our happiness. We shall restrict ourselves to two types of demands: the promise and the oath.

A promise is a pledge to do or not to do something specified, as

---

[*] Thomas Carlyle, *On Heroes, Hero-Worship, and the Heroic in History* (Oxford), p. 270.

when a lad assures his friend that he will never betray the secrets of the Treetop Club; or when a bridegroom, in solemn ceremony, vows that he will love and cherish his bride as long as they both shall live. The promise is demanded because of acknowledged power to threaten or destroy our happiness. The demand is grounded in the moral and spiritual environment; it is a contractual expectation. Whenever one shares something very important with another, or whenever one entrusts his safety to another in a rare and unusual way, he looks to the promise as a proof that the privileges of such relations will not be exploited for personal gain. The promise is an assurance that one wholeheartedly accepts the terms of a friendly contract.

The oath is stronger than the promise because the power to threaten or support our happiness is stronger. The oath is a solemn, public appeal to some revered person or sanction for the truth of an affirmation or declaration. Soldiers swear that they will protect the land; rulers vow that they will uphold the constitution. Although classical sources do not always distinguish between a promise and an oath, moral self-acceptance sees at least two reasons why an oath is stronger than a promise. First, it binds parties who are related officially rather than personally. Second, it implicates the swearing party in a more conscious awareness that a violation of this trust casts him on the nemesis of some mutually dreaded power. The ending of the Hippocratic Oath adequately illustrates this: "While I continue to keep this Oath unviolated, may it be granted to me to enjoy life and the practice of the art, respected by all men, in all times! But should I trespass and violate this Oath, may the reverse be my lot!" Although this dreaded power is tacitly implied in both the promise and the oath, it is specifically implied in the oath. It is specific because men under oath have greater power to threaten or support our happiness. A soldier can loot houses, and a president can lend his prestige to laws that bring personal gain.

Since those who make promises are more intimately related, it is not necessary to review the threat of nemesis. Higher and more elevating sanctions are appealed to. But when this intimacy cannot be presupposed, there is no other course than to add a fearful sanction to one's sense of honor. Hobbes well observes that the force of words being too weak to hold men to the performance of their covenants, there are in man's nature but two imaginable holds to strengthen it; and these are either a fear of the consequences of breaking one's word, or a glory or pride in appearing not to need to break it.

10. THE PROBLEM OF ANIMALS

One can effectively divert attention from the present argument by contending that animals likewise participate in the moral and spiritual environment. This is a favorite stratagem of those who refuse to deal with the moral ambiguity of their own lives. Animals, they say, duplicate many human traits: they think, protect their young, and give evidence of the familiar cycles of love, resentment, and jealousy. Therefore, by what right do we say that only man participates in the moral and spiritual environment?

Since I shall address myself to this subject at a later point—and especially as it relates to the Darwinian claims—let me herewith simply say that any present reference to animals is quite beside the point. Only man is under discussion; and until man learns to accept the realities that already hold him, it would hardly be profitable to inquire into the moral status of animals.

But if one is *really* interested in comparing his life with that of animals, he should come at the matter by way of moral self-acceptance. He should ask, "To what truths am I committed as I live and move among animals?" and, "What realities hold me when I have chicken for dinner?" An answer to these questions must be included among the data being considered; otherwise the study will be speculative and academic.

After questions such as these have been raised, let the critic then return to the problem. Let him examine the meaning of his own life when he is confronted by one who treats him like an animal. Animals are used as means to ends; but will he tolerate the use of *his* life as a means to some calculated end? The answer, plainly, is No! If destitution forced others to choose between him or the family dog, he would forcefully resist any who favored sparing the dog. And his response would prove that he is already committed to the assurance that man is of nobler blood than that of an animal. Types of being, let us remember, are revealed by degrees of personal enthusiasm.

It is easy—oh, so easy—to amass academic objections to the assertion that man is spiritually superior to beasts. Captious critics are capable of endless self-deception. They can speculatively argue that the only reason that we eat animals, rather than our own children, is social habit. And the amazing part is that they can make this claim while nonchalantly sipping coffee. What can break down such foolishness? If a person has a poor voice, but obdurately believes he is highly gifted, the greatest voice teacher in the world is powerless to unlearn him. His only hope, like that of the captious critic, is to submit to reality.

A savant who knows more about animals than he does about himself will also know more about animals than he does about God. And the irony of his misdirection is that the image of God in man is the only thing that makes man superior to animals. When man asperses the moral and spiritual environment, he unwittingly asperses himself. And that is bad business.

11. CONSCIENCE AND MORAL RELATIVITY

An even more effective diversion is the claim that conscience does not safeguard fixed moral principles. Rather than monitoring a corpus of absolutes, conscience is simply a guardian of provincial mores. Therefore, even though man *does* participate in a moral and spiritual environment created by God, no fruitful expectations can be grounded on this fact.

Although moral self-acceptance readily recognizes the degree to which the counsels of conscience are a product of social conditioning, the admission in no way damages the findings of the third method of knowing. Notice, if you will, the procedure that sociologists use when reaching their conclusions. Rather than coming at the issue by way of a spiritual acceptance of the realities that already hold them, they come by way of an empirical study of the race. The votaries of science fail to see that neither acquaintance nor inference has access to morals until the data are released by moral self-acceptance. A despiser of the third method of knowing can *never* meaningfully decide the question of morals, for he has no access to the evidences. Conscience's tie-in with cultural conditioning in no way negates one's moral responsibility to accept the realities that already hold him.

There is something ironic about the pretenses of relativists. They are like an individual who, though very much breathing, solemnly repudiates the necessity of breathing. Relativists do not recognize that they could not even lecture against moral absolutes unless they were firmly held by the absolute that those who lecture must say in word what they intend in meaning. Since a decision to rise and speak proves what one really believes, a lecturer on moral relativity contradicts himself; *for that which is indispensable to a given condition cannot meaningfully be repudiated by one who stands within the privileges of that condition.* The bond between lecturer and student would instantly dissolve if the speaker failed to participate in the absolute that one must say in word what he intends in meaning. The classroom is a fellowship, and fellowship is nonexistent unless the participating parties give sincere evidences of not using each other as a means to some calculated end. Deception is one form of such calculation.

If a professor assures his class there will be no final examination in a given course, the students rest in his word because they trust him; and they trust him because they believe he is a man of character. If the professor should terminate the course by announcing a final examination, the students would rise up in wrath. And he could not justify his reversal by saying: "Oh, but you don't understand. You see, I am free to change the meaning of my terms any time I want. When I say I *don't* plan to give an examination, I reserve the private right to mean that I *do* plan to give an examination." Such a reply would not justify him, because significant speech rests on a tacit moral contract. This is one of the main points in Lewis Carroll's delightful tale *Alice's Adventures in Wonderland*. We may not hold idiots morally responsible for a sudden shift in terms, but we do hold normal people responsible.

It is no less foolish of moralists to negate absolute ethical criteria than it is of skeptics to negate absolute truths; for the absoluteness of personal worth antecedes fellowship in the same way that the absoluteness of the law of contradiction antecedes significant speech. Just as skeptics must use the law of contradiction to deny the law of contradiction, so relativists must use a moral absolute to deny moral absolutes. There is why their effort is curiously futile. That which destroys everything has destroyed nothing, for it has already destroyed itself.

12. THE PARADOX OF MORALS

With these arguments provisionally disposed of, we may now proceed with our study. The more we clarify the moral and spiritual environment, the more we clarify our place in the person of God.

Although it is easy to speak about morals, what actually makes up the stuff of moral response? When others enter the circle of nearness, we demand that they show signs of moral sincerity; and yet we are immediately repelled by any affected effort on their part to appear sincere. It seems we are making a demand that cannot be met. A morally inspired act must be both free and necessary. Yet, how can these incompatibles be united?

There is only one possible way to unite them. *Morality consists in choices that are freely expressed through the necessities of the moral and spiritual environment.* A moral act is free because it is natural; and it is necessary because it flows from the moral and

Moral Self-Acceptance and Social Relations 67

spiritual environment. Morality is a fruit, not a work. It cannot be aroused by rational or volitional striving.

A brief review of possible alternatives will convince one that freedom and necessity can be effectively combined in no other manner. Either necessity is recognized and freedom is lost, or freedom is recognized and necessity is lost.

Kant's *Prize Essay* convincingly argues that an action is shorn of moral worth unless it is motivated by impulses that originate in the moral sense. Kant recognized the place of necessity in moral decision. But when he perceived the extent to which conscience can be environmentally conditioned, his regard for the moral sense diminished. In an effort to preserve morality as a science, therefore, he shifted from the moral sense to the self-legislation of reason. This was an extremely regrettable turn, however, for it drained away the very quality of spontaneous necessity which distinguishes truly moral acts from those that are inspired by interest, calculation, or a slavish obedience to law. Therefore, rather than being told what morality consists of, we are simply given a set of rational rules by which to decide whether a particular choice is consistent with all other choices. It we trace Kantian motives back far enough, we discover that they spring from the halls of rational interest, rather than from the moral and spiritual environment. Only those who have a rational desire to be self-consistent are moral.

One can expose the Kantian deficiency by raising this simple question: "Why *should* one be rationally self-consistent?" The question has point because—as we have stressed elsewhere—a rational statement of duty has no moral power to convince a man that he ought to be rational. Kant was on the right trail when he wrote his *Prize Essay*, but the later critiques led him astray. His difficulty lay in the fact that he failed to come at morals by way of the third condition of knowing. His system did not take in the realities that already held him as he taught his philosophy classes in Königsberg. Whenever people receive us because of a respect for rational self-consistency, we are offended. The sheer presence of our person places others under moral obligation, for we are made in the image of God. A spiritual respect for this image—not a calculated desire to be rationally self-consistent—is what we look for.

There is something tragic about Kant's effort to devise a science of morals. Blinded to the place of personal interest in his own life, he failed to see that the canons of rationality can be prostituted in the defense of pride. A tyrant will not find it difficult to argue that the violent destruction of life is a rationally self-consistent act. Whenever one anxiously wants to believe something, there will always be false prophets to counsel him in the art of defense. Machiavelli recognized this, but Kant apparently did not. Kant realized that "radical evil" wars against the counsels of reason, but he did not see that evil also induces philosophers to ground their moral theory in rules of self-consistent conduct rather than in the moral and spiritual environment.

Moral necessity is also qualitatively different from jural necessity. Whenever one is motivated by a desire to conform to law, he is held by a calculated interest to be upright. In such a case, moral worth vanishes, for the sense of necessity has been generated by human striving. The motive behind the act is as autonomously inspired as the Kantian striving for rational self-consistency. One is not responding to the claims of the moral and spiritual environment, for the sheer presence of our person fails to excite moral respect. Law is more highly honored than our dignity. The supposition is that if it were not for law, one would be morally free to decide whether or not it is to his wider advantage to respect us.

Possibly the most perfect analogy to unconscious necessity is the industry and efficiency of the anthill. But it is no more than an analogy, for true morality is a compound of both freedom and necessity. The anthill has instinctive necessity, but not moral freedom. If Rousseau had developed his philosophy from the perspective of moral self-acceptance, he would have recognized that a return to nature would immediately divest man of everything

Moral Self-Acceptance and Social Relations

that makes up his dignity; for dignity *consists* in free moral decision. Man is given a moment-by-moment opportunity to let the claims of the moral and spiritual environment transform him. No animal enjoys the power of moral and rational self-transcendence.

All of this buttresses the assertion that morality consists in "choices that are freely expressed through the necessities of the moral and spiritual environment." This is the only effective way to state the paradox of morals. Whenever we submit our affections to the transforming power of the moral and spiritual environment, the urge for fellowship becomes unconscious, spontaneous, and necessary. But when a sense of necessity must be aroused by a deliberate effort to be moral, unconscious spontaneity vanishes. Man is not able to implant right affections within him; an upright heart is a gift of God.

In an effort to void the claims of the moral and spiritual environment, it might be argued that fellowship can be grounded in practical, rather than moral, motives. If we talk about things that interest other people—taking care to blandish them whenever possible—they will respond by doing nice things for us. This may influence people, but it will never win friends; for the act has no moral value. One's motives must be cloaked with feigned sincerity, which is hypocrisy. One does not dare reveal his true intentions, for he would immediately arouse the judicial sentiment in those whom he seeks to influence.

As we submit to the moral and spiritual environment, God graciously meets our humility by creating right affections in us; and these right affections, in turn, excite a spontaneous desire to be upright. The less conflict there is between duty and desire, the more perfect our actions become. After God has confirmed us in righteousness—an act that takes place beyond the grave—no conflict will remain between what we are and what we ought to be. We will spontaneously do what is right, for the image of God will be fully renewed in righteousness, knowledge, and holiness of the truth. An anticipation of what God has in store for those who love him is a powerful incentive for present moral striving. "Every one who thus hopes in him purifies himself as he is pure" (I John 3:3).

Kant was formally right in his relentless insistence that there is no good but a good will, but he was materially wrong when he defined the good will as a purely rational regard for laws of self-consistent conduct. Not enjoying a vantage point from which to evaluate man's participation in a divinely ordained moral and spiritual environment, Kant was unable to appreciate the fact that love is superior to thought, and that the best in man is not accented until thought yields to fellowship. Although Kant was not always consistent, he nevertheless tended to subordinate the vital man to the rational man, a subordination which the third method of knowing indignantly rejects.

This does not imply a disparagement of the rational faculty, to be sure, for man can only get next to reality's complexity by a full use of all the powers that God has given him. The rational and the vital are too mysteriously interfused for us to expect the complete elimination of either in any act. This is only another way of saying that it is immoral to be irrational. Even as the moral and spiritual environment is the milieu of the heart, so the law of contradiction is the milieu of the mind. Whoever turns against the laws of consistent inference is unwittingly turning against God.*

This complex intermixture of the vital and the rational is one reason that friendship looks for nothing but signs of personal sincerity. Since we do not know the exact causal connections in our own lives, we cannot expect too precise an accounting of the causal connections in the lives of those who enter the circle of nearness. Sincerity is a proof that one is moral. Kant might reject this as too nebulous, but in doing so he would betray his refusal

* The law of contradiction comprises the milieu of the mind because all other laws of logic are analytically included in it—the laws of being and excluded middle, and the general laws governing the syllogism and the square of opposition. This analytic enclosure made it possible for Aristotle to summarize all possible laws of inference. Symbolic logic is no exception to this; it has simply devised a new *application* of Aristotelian logic.

to come to terms with the moral realities that already held him. When Kant surveyed the pupils in his class, he looked for personal sincerity, not for a calculated effort to be rationally self-consistent.

13. THE BALANCE OF MORAL SELF-ACCEPTANCE AS A METHOD

The pleasing qualities in moral self-acceptance can best be accented by contrasting them with the deficiencies that have appeared in classical attempts to draw up a philosophy of life. A balanced world view is made up of three basic ingredients: the facts of experience, the requirements of logical consistency, and the witness of the moral sense. These ingredients correspond to man's fourfold environment: the physical, the rational, the aesthetic, and the moral and spiritual. I feel there are good reasons to believe that only moral self-acceptance unites these elements without falsifying the witness of one in an effort to give an intelligent account of another. Practically every error in the history of thought can be traced back to a faulty emphasis on the facts of experience, the requirements of logical consistency, or the witness of the moral sense.

Empiricism is keenly sensitive to the facts of experience. How can distant things be known if one does not rightly interpret the things that are near at hand? Kant is formally right: concepts without percepts are empty. But empiricism so restricts its data to the witness of sense perception that knowledge is reduced to knack, judgment to personal opinion, and duty to emotive suasion. Cratylus cannot even wave his hand to express his philosophy, for all is in flux. This is why Plato's *Theaetetus* is one of the really majestic documents to emerge from classical thought. Unless the mind participates in a rational environment which antecedes sense perception, no knowledge is possible. The forms of thought cannot be acquired by sense perception.

Rationalism's merit is that it comprehends the requirements of logical consistency. Sense data yield no meaning unless they are ordered by criteria not found in experience. Kant again is formally right: percepts without concepts are blind. But rationalism is tempted to confuse reason as a *test* of truth with reason as a *source* of truth. Whenever one yields to this temptation, the fluidity and plurality of reality are Procrusteanized to fit the abstract requirements of logical consistency. Nature is a boiling caldron of change; it cannot be tamed by man's a priori desire for consistency. Evidences of rationalism's error are easy to adduce: Gorgias' diaphanous being, Plotinus' mysterious One, Spinoza's geometrized nature, and Hegel's identification of nature with the *Weltgeist*. Each one falsifies the real in his own particular way: Gorgias by denying motion, Plotinus by negating the soul's separation from the World Soul, Spinoza by universalizing the finite modes, and Hegel by absorbing the individual into the absolute. As can be detected, these are simply intriguing variations of one error. "The plays are all the same; the cast only is changed!"*

Since most philosophical efforts are a complex blend of both empiricism and rationalism, however, they cannot be classified as purely this or purely that. But the point is that one can mix experience and validity in any manner one chooses, and the result, of necessity, will be conclusions limited to the descriptive mood. Neither knowledge by acquaintance nor knowledge by inference can escort the mind into the moral and spiritual environment. Rationalism can define the conditions of validity, but it is powerless to communicate a sense of moral duty. This is why it is always embarrassed by the question, "Why *should* a man be moral?" When only a dread of inconsistency induces one to be moral, one can easily find reasons for preferring to be inconsistent. Classical thought has never really appreciated the extent to which man enjoys spiritual freedom over rational form. The persistence of this error is due, in large part, to the refusal of philosophers to develop their view of life in conjunction with the realities that already hold them as living individuals. If they would give closer heed to the manner of their own lives, they would immediately see that

* Marcus Aurelius, *Thoughts*, X, 27.

Moral Self-Acceptance and Social Relations

a rational statement of duty has no power to convince a man that he ought to be rational. Duty is never felt until one stands inside duty itself. The content of morals is acquired by a humble participation in the moral and spiritual environment. Knowledge by inference may validly order the data of the moral sense, but it cannot authorize such data.

Moral self-acceptance is able to make peace with the moral sense because it has the courage and the consistency to begin there; and it is able to work out from this without doing violence either to the facts of sense perception or to the requirements of logical consistency.

14. KIERKEGAARD

To my present knowledge, only Socrates, Pascal, and Kierkegaard made any real attempt to relate the moral sense to the wider problems of philosophy. But only Kierkegaard went on to develop his convictions into the rough outlines of a complete world view. Socrates remained maieutic and cautious, while Pascal died before his fragments of thought could be gathered up into a system.

Whoever has worked through the basic writings of Sören Kierkegaard will agree, I feel sure, that no previous thinker has more energetically tried to interpret reality from the perspective of the free, ethical individual. From one end of the literature to the other he releases a scorching negation of detached philosophies of life. If the existing individual is to *be*, he must passionately mediate eternity in time. Duty is never rightly felt until it transforms one. The real man is expressed through ethical decision.

I must say, it is easy to follow the very one who wanted no followers. Without the stimulation of the Danish gadfly, I probably would never have learned how to ask questions from the perspective of inwardness. It is a pleasure to acknowledge my indebtedness to Kierkegaard.

But this does not mean that I uncritically endorse the existential approach, for as one studies the fine print in the literature he finds that Kierkegaard's method suffers from a serious structural flaw. And this flaw, ironically, resulted from Kierkegaard's own effort to avoid the excesses in detached thinking.

Let us work into this by way of the familiar ingredients of a consistent world view: the facts of experience, the requirements of logical consistency, and the witness of the moral sense. Does Kierkegaard adequately blend these ingredients? Although it is a bit difficult to establish the charge, the answer is in the negative.

There is no doubt but what Kierkegaard does reasonable justice to the facts of experience, for he never wearies of insisting that individuality is not accented until one passionately answers to the whole of experience, inward and outward. It was this keen sensitivity to life's plurality that gave him a point of vantage from which to launch his attack on Hegel. Since logic structures necessary relations, while much of life is threatened by fortuity, Hegel erred in trying to comprehend reality by a dialectical ordering of logical categories. His "finished system" excluded the possibility of ethics, for ethical decision mediates either-or, not both-and.

Rather than developing a pedantic refutation of the Hegelian approach, however, Kierkegaard brandished the rapier of irony. He heaped ridicule on the system which eliminated the possibility of free, moral decision. Decision confronts contingency, not necessity.

Kierkegaard also does reasonable justice to the witness of the moral sense. In my opinion, his power as an ethicist peers that of Socrates, Plato, or Augustine. The Christian community has yet to penetrate the profundity of his book *Works of Love*. Using the cold steel of relentless dialectic, Kierkegaard chisels away at the very foundation of formalistic ethics. He persuasively proves that eternity is mediated in time, and the task of individuality is met, by passionate, ethical decision. *Thinking* about duty is not the same as *doing* one's duty. Thought must yield to action.

When one examines Kierkegaard's attitude toward the requirements of logical consistency, however, there is good reason to believe that he flagrantly violated this axiom: *that a man corrupts his own dignity, and thus lessens the possibility of knowing truth, if his passionate, ethical life is developed in defiance of a calm and unclouded intellect.*

Kierkegaard, to be sure, frequently invests the rational life with a measure of the same dignity conferred on it by Aristotle and Aquinas, thus making it risky to universalize. Furthermore, it is not always easy to tell just what Kierkegaard is attacking. Is he simply contending that detached thinking is refractory to ethical decision? If so, he is only saying that one cannot know the meaning of an ethical truth until he humbly submits to the moral and spiritual environment. Or, is he going beyond this to argue that passionate, ethical response must stoutly *defy* the authority of rational consistency? If so, he dooms ethics as a science; for although only knowledge by moral self-acceptance has access to the moral and spiritual environment, it is powerless to interpret this environment without the help of knowledge by acquaintance and knowledge by inference. Ethical passion may invest moral conduct with a sense of duty, but it cannot codify a science of morals. Defining and defending rectitude are tasks which belong to the intellect; and whoever denies this is consigning the passionate life to subjectivity. The question "What should I become passionate about?" cannot be answered within passion itself. The question belongs to the domain of the intellect. But the intellect is stripped of its precision whenever it is clouded by subjective passion.

Kierkegaard became so intoxicated with his vision of overturning Hegel that the error in rationalism was exchanged for the error in existentialism. To make sure that a dispassionate use of the intellect would never be confused with ethical decision, a polarity tension between objective certainty and subjective faith was defended. The objectively repellent becomes a measure of the corresponding inwardness of faith. Faith must choose in defiance of the intellect, for without risk there is no faith. Inwardness decreases as objective certainty increases. "The absurd is precisely by its objective repulsion the measure of the intensity of faith in inwardness. Suppose a man who wishes to acquire faith; let the comedy begin. He wishes to have faith, but he wishes also to safeguard himself by means of an objective inquiry and its approximation-process. What happens? With the help of the approximation-process the absurd becomes something different; it becomes probable, it becomes increasingly probable, it becomes extremely and emphatically probable. Now he is ready to believe it, and he ventures to claim for himself that he does not believe as shoemakers and tailors and simple folk believe, but only after long deliberation. Now he is ready to believe it; and lo, now it has become precisely impossible to believe it. Anything that is almost probable, or probable, or extremely and emphatically probable, is something he can almost know, or as good as know, or extremely and emphatically almost *know*—but it is impossible to *believe*. For the absurd is the object of faith, and the only object that can be believed."* This is very clear language. Its intent cannot be mistaken.

Defending a polarity tension between objective certainty and subjective passion is not only a needless alternative to Hegelianism, but it is pre-eminently contrary to good sense. If one wonders why Kierkegaard is so repelling to scientists and philosophers, it is chiefly this doctrine that ethical passion does not come into being until an individual rallies courage to act in defiance of logical consistency. Faith is supposed to be challenged by claims that are repugnant to the canons of science and philosophy. But thinking individuals will not outrage their dignity by defying the verdict of a critically disciplined understanding. Whatever else faith may be, it is at least a "resting of the mind in the sufficiency of evidences." The extent of this sufficiency is measured by a cool and dispassionate use of reason. An upright man cannot violate the rational environment; he cannot believe logical contradictions. If a dispassionate use of reason assures him that he has no money

* Kierkegaard, *Concluding Unscientific Postscript* (Princeton), p. 189.

Moral Self-Acceptance and Social Relations

in his pocket, all the existential heat in the world cannot induce him to act on the firm assurance that he is rich. "Can we, by any effort of our will, or by any strength of wish that it were true, believe ourselves well and about when we are roaring with rheumatism in bed, or feel certain that the sum of the two one-dollar bills in our pocket must be a hundred dollars? We can *say* any of these things, but we are absolutely impotent to believe them."*

Nor can Kierkegaard rescue his case by arguing that the leap of faith in defiance of objective certainty is only necessary when one is confronted by the paradox that God came into time as a man. Such a suggestion violates two fundamental rules of praiseworthy response.

First, *Passion should be guided by the seriousness and truth of the object, and not by its rational offensiveness.* A religious zealot may be correct in believing that personal commitment to the will of God is the highest possible act, but before he yields himself in passion he should be objectively certain that it is God, and not the devil, he is committing himself to. "I bear them witness that they have a zeal for God, but it is not enlightened" (Romans 10:2). The pages of religious history are filled with the tragic account of those who were so anxious to get on with the business of commitment that the intellect did not take time to define its goals. "The good of mankind requires that nothing should be believed until the question be first asked, what evidence there is for it."† Enthusiasts not only have zeal without enlightenment, but they tend to make the Kierkegaardian mistake of thinking that the quality of religious commitment improves when one rallies courage to believe against the understanding. Zealots must learn that faith is not based on a risk; it is not an alternative to knowledge. "Beloved, do not believe every spirit, but test the spirits to see whether they are of God; for many false prophets have gone out into the world" (I John 4:1).

* William James, *The Will to Believe*, II.
† John Stuart Mill, Speech on "The Church," in *Autobiography* (Oxford), p. 322.

Second, *Worthy faith should be aroused by a joint cooperation between the nature of the object and the sufficiency of the evidences that support it.* If it is claimed that a destructive hurricane is on the way, passionate commitment should be proportioned to the intellect's critical satisfaction that such a storm is actually coming. Suppose the reality of the storm is objectively in doubt. Perhaps those who report it are known to be habitually mendacious. If one were then to act on the reality of such a storm, those who observe his preparations would justly wonder whether he had taken leave of his senses. They would know that the native person —the one who has never read Kierkegaard—is at his best, and thus is most obedient to everything that comprises human dignity, when the ethical life follows, rather than passionately defies, the verdict of a critically disciplined understanding. The stuff of generic faith is formed of a whole-souled, rational satisfaction with truth, not a passionate leap in the face of paradox.* Sound generic faith always rests on *warranted* belief. This is what justified God's decision to send false prophets among the people of Israel. He wanted to see if the Israelites proportioned subjective commitment to objectively sufficient evidences. "If a prophet arises among you, or a dreamer of dreams, and gives you a sign or a wonder, and the sign or wonder which he tells you comes to pass, and if he says, 'Let us go after other gods,' which you have not known, 'and let us serve them,' you shall not listen to the words of that prophet or to that dreamer of dreams; for the Lord your God is testing you, to know whether you love the Lord your God with all your heart and with all your soul" (Deuteronomy 13:1-3). Kierkegaard has no final way of crediting the true prophet because he has no final way of discrediting the false prophet.

Kierkegaard's existential approach puzzles me greatly, for nearly all his goals could have been reached without setting the rational self against the moral self. Why this penchant for paradox? The

---

* Bear in mind that we speak only of *generic* faith. The problem of *saving* faith will be dealt with at a later point. There are degrees of faith, even as there are degrees of knowledge; or better, generic faith and knowledge are the same thing—a resting of the whole man in the sufficiency of the evidences.

Moral Self-Acceptance and Social Relations 79

problem is interesting, but unanswerable, for its resolution calls for information to which the third method of knowing has no direct access.

Now that I had to part company with the Dane, I felt somewhat like a wayfarer who, having come a long distance by himself, is suddenly joined by one going to the same country; only to find that when they unexpectedly confront a fork in the road, each adamantly defies the judgment of the other. In the end they must go their separate ways, for each tenaciously clings to his own convictions. Though keenly regretting the loss of fellowship, each must courageously venture the hope that wisdom is on his side. Johnson rightly observes that we never do anything consciously for the last time without sadness of heart.

Chapter Five

MORAL SELF-ACCEPTANCE AND THE JUDICIAL SENTIMENT

1. A TRANSITION THROUGH KANT'S PRACTICAL IMPERATIVE

Although I have repeatedly asserted that a knowledge of the imperative essence can be gained by a humble submission to the realities that hold us when we enter social relations, I have not proved that this is the case. We yet do not know the pith and marrow of the imperative essence. Determined to get on with it, therefore, I returned with Socrates to the market place, there to drink the full cup of moral experience.

I met instant disappointment, however, for my resolution to proceed did not bring me to the desired goal. Although I exposed myself to people from all levels of life, the third method of knowing yielded no new conclusions. My difficulty, I soon found, was that I had no norm to guide me. Hitherto I had applied the rule that "types of being are revealed by degrees of enthusiasm." This was a fruitful standard, but it now needed refining. Mingling with people would be pointless until I knew what to look for.

With the hope that deliberate mental exercise might stimulate such a criterion, I began to reflect on Kant's "practical imperative": So act as to treat humanity, whether in thine own person or in that of any other, in every case as an end withal, never as means only.

I stumbled right from the start. The imperative sounds convincing, but it does not stand up under careful rational analysis. Kant seems to say that, since all people are part of humanity, a man would be inconsistent if he asked them to treat him by a norm that he rejected when treating them. Judged from the perspective of moral self-acceptance, this is a very poor way of going at the matter; for duty is drawn from a calculated respect for rational consistency rather than from the moral and spiritual environment.

Furthermore, the necessity to regard others is not a logical consequence of our demand that they regard us. This can easily be illustrated. Although animals are never authorized to eat the flesh of man, it certainly does not follow that man is never authorized to eat the flesh of animals.

And even if Kant's argument were formally valid, it would in no way enlarge our knowledge of the imperative essence; for moral information is not rationally comprehended until it is spiritually apprehended. A rational knowledge of the practical imperative communicates no sense of moral responsibility. Knowledge by moral self-acceptance must release the data of the moral life. Otherwise, man will participate in a moral and spiritual environment without being conscious of either the fact of such a participation or the vital responsibilities that flow from it.

A utilitarian might reply that, though the practical imperative is formally fallacious, its substance is true; for it is to our *advantage* to will the greatest good of the greatest number. If we kill, we may be killed in return; if we steal, our goods may be plundered. Such arguments may please utilitarians, but they disgust moral self-acceptance. Since reciprocity is a fruit of enlightened self-interest, rather than the moral sense, it is as void of moral force as Kant's rules of self-consistent conduct. Neither Kant nor a utilitarian can invest the practical imperative with moral worth because neither is in contact with data in the imperative mood.

Some might argue that it is *selfish* to expect others to answer to a higher rule than we ourselves follow. Whatever sentimental force this argument may have, it has no moral force. When others enter the circle of nearness, we level our demands in the name of the moral and spiritual environment. If we were motivated by a rationally inspired calculus of interests, we indeed would be acting selfishly. But this is not the case.

Selfishness, of course, seldom overlooks an opportunity to take shelter under the aegis of the moral sense. It is extremely difficult to keep our affections pure. When we think we are acting from moral motives, it often occurs that we are held by egoistic interests. But our best conduct is always somewhat inspired by impulses that flow from the moral and spiritual environment. The validity of this will be established in due time.

2. AN EMPIRICAL TRIAL OF THE PRACTICAL IMPERATIVE

But despite the academic objections to the practical imperative, our hearts remain warmly attracted to its substance. And how could this be otherwise, when the practical imperative is merely a philosophical counterpart to the golden rule? "So whatever you wish that men would do to you, do so to them; for this is the law and the prophets" (Matthew 7:12). To defend a lower view of duty than that of Kant would hardly comport with the spirit of Christ. "Love your enemies and pray for those who persecute you, so that you may be sons of your Father who is in heaven; for he makes his sun rise on the evil and on the good, and sends rain on the just and on the unjust" (Matthew 5:44-45). If we expect to establish the validity of the practical imperative, however, we must do it by a patient application of moral self-acceptance.

Some might reply: "Well, why not simply quote the Bible? Why go to all this apologetic effort? If Scripture is true, it certainly will not be improved by the strategies of human reason." The answer is that we are *commanded* to give a reason for the hope that lies within us—I Peter 3:15. The choice is not optional. And one of the most effective ways of discharging this duty is by the apologetic labor of showing that Christ's gospel is consistent

Moral Self-Acceptance and the Judicial Sentiment

with the claims of man's fourfold environment—physical, rational, aesthetic, and moral and spiritual. If the Christian world view were repugnant to the faculties that God has given us, how could one commit himself to it? A man of character can believe nothing until it is established by sufficient evidences.

In any event, the duty to defend Christianity is part of Christianity. We cannot evade our responsibility. The fact that some do not feel the force of this obligation in no way releases the conscience of those who do.

When verifying the practical imperative, however, one must use the same approach that was followed when the conditions of fellowship were verified. If the necessity of regarding others is part of the moral and spiritual environment, we ought to detect traces of this obligation whenever we mingle with men. So we ask, "When we stand in the presence of others, do we sense an obligation to regard their dignity?"

Judged by the unknown masses in distant lands, the practical imperative is *not* part of the moral and spiritual environment, for a knowledge of remote peoples arouses no measurable moral sentiments in us. Unknown individuals are mere statistics—quantities to be added or subtracted, like sheep or walnuts. Our own headache gives us more concern than the vague report of a distant tidal wave.

More patient reflection proves, however, that this reference to unknown, distant people is, strictly speaking, irrelevant. Others are powerless to arouse the moral sense until they enter the circle of nearness. Our interests must first be penetrated. We should not lose sight of this important distinction.

At the other extreme are our loved ones. Experience proves that whenever we are near those we love, an irresistible sense of moral necessity is aroused in us. If we try to be objective toward a loved one, we violate our own dignity. Love completes itself through the beloved.

Standing between distant nations and our own loved ones are the crowds of people we meet on the street, at the opera, and in church. And here, I believe, is what moral self-acceptance teaches in their case: regardless of where we meet an individual, and regardless of how physically attractive or repulsive we find him, if we draw sufficiently near to look into his eyes, or if we let him reveal the intimacies of his heart, some sense of moral obligation, however faint, is kindled within us. But it is necessary to draw near to him; otherwise this feeling of moral obligation is not aroused. If we keep our distance, it might be more in accord with reason to defend an obedient Dalmatian or a useful beast of burden. Man can rise higher, and sink lower, than any animal.

At this point in my experiment, however, I quickly caught myself, for, rather than preparing the way for the practical imperative, I was merely reviewing the effects which others happen to have on us; just as I might decide whether dampness causes asthma or whether coffee disturbs sleep. These were interesting, but irrelevant, pieces of information. If one had the years of Methuselah in which to roam the market place, he could never establish the practical imperative by empirically exposing himself to others. Empiricism can only assert the following: "These people, whom I now name, aroused a moral feeling the last time they were in my presence. Whether they will arouse a similar feeling the next time I meet them cannot be established." Hence, it is obvious that the practical imperative will never be verified by an empirical review of how others affect us.

This trial and error may seem pointless, but I include it to help ensure an appreciation of the uniqueness of moral self-acceptance. If empiricism could lead us to the moral and spiritual environment, we would not need to develop the third method of knowing. But empiricism cannot; therefore, we may proceed.

3. A FURTHER CLARIFICATION OF PROCEDURE

Rather than provisionally accepting the practical imperative, and then looking for ways to justify it, I decided to let duty name its own content by once again yielding to the moral and spiritual environment. If it is necessary to repeat it, then let me repeat it:

Moral Self-Acceptance and the Judicial Sentiment

The only way to recognize duty is by morally submitting to the duties that already hold us. One cannot work into duty from data in the descriptive mood. He must let duty spell out its own essence.

In simplest terms, this meant that I had to stand in the center of a duty already established. If the practical imperative belongs to the claims of the moral and spiritual environment, I ought to detect its force whenever I cordially yield to such claims. Even as the oak is included in the acorn, so new duty is included in the duty that already holds us.

Once I finished cleaning the signposts, it was not hard to decide what road to take. Since I had previously asked, "To what moral realities am I committed when others enter the circle of nearness?" I now decided it would be in accord with good procedure if I simply extended the question and asked, "To what moral realities am I committed when those in the circle of nearness refuse to show signs of fellowship?" If the first question yielded such a harvest of information, there was every reason to believe that the second, if raised with equal care, would do the same.

It took no time at all to answer the second query. *Whenever others offend my dignity, I judge them guilty.* Judgment flows with instantaneous spontaneity; I simply cannot look with moral indifference on acts of inconsideration; I hold court a hundred times a day. And I suspect that what is true in my experience is true also in the experience of others.

Try as we may, we are morally powerless to arrest our habit of judging other people. We withhold fellowship from ingrates and boors with a necessity that inheres in character itself. Even as we cannot think or speak without reliance on the law of contradiction; and even as we cannot act without reliance on the law of uniformity; so we cannot entrust ourselves to others without a reliance on both our own personal dignity and the moral obligation of others to respect it. These elements of reliance hold us from existence itself.

Although this was a gratifying discovery, I did not know

whether to rejoice or lament over it; for although I *claim* that inconsiderate individuals arouse judicial feelings in me, how can I prove that this is really the case? How can I answer a critic who asserts that such responses are nothing but evidences of personal disgruntlement? Rather than mirroring the moral and spiritual environment, they may betray only the degree to which we are excessively preoccupied with ourselves. Possibly we do not *like* those who are unfriendly, even as we do not like spinach. But what bearing would this have on truth?

Even this was not the end, however, for I soon found that the most trivial frustrations can arouse sentiments of indignation. A stalled automobile or a dripping faucet can cause volcanic eruptions in the soul, the ashes of which are similar to those left by individuals who outrage our dignity. This was a very discouraging observation.

Thinking that a clarification of terms might help, I decided to define the meaning of "personal dignity." After several elaborate attempts, however, I concluded that dignity, like personality, is a given that is known only as it is felt. Knowledge by inference cannot comprehend its essence. The meaning of dignity must be apprehended by direct experience.

The only public way to represent personal dignity is by a review of its social manifestations. Dignity expresses itself in the form of human rights. That is why one is justified in speaking of either dignity or rights. Even as dignity comprehends the secret essence of personality, so rights comprehend its social expression. Dignity is a name for our spiritual essence, while rights are the field on which this essence stretches its limbs. The accepted poetic redundancy, "life, liberty, and the pursuit of happiness," sums up our indefeasible rights as creatures made in the image of God. Moral freedom is the stuff of personality, even as life, liberty, and the pursuit of happiness are the stuff of human rights. Freedom to express ourselves is not an adventitious element that can be added or subtracted without altering the essence of our dignity. It is as indispensable to our essence as the beating of the heart. An attack on our rights is an attack on our person.

This was a rewarding discovery, for it meant that our procedure would henceforth be more manageable. The mysterious inner core of dignity could now be translated into socially measurable terms. The rights of an individual are public; they can be debated in court.

4. HUMAN RIGHTS AND MORAL SELF-ACCEPTANCE

Since it is easier to speak of human rights than of human dignity, let us alter our question and ask, "To what moral realities are we committed when our rights are violated?" Suppose we are unexpectedly catapulted into a society where our basic rights are removed by force. On what evidence would we rest our final protest? Would we cry with Epictetus that a tyrant cannot chain us, for Zeus has set us free? The kind of answer we give would be an index to our real convictions.

Plato, for example, stratified the Republic on the assumption that rational skill, not spiritual dignity, decides one's place on the social ladder. Beginning with the philosopher as king and ending with slaves as living possessions, Plato developed a socio-political application of his assumption that the real man is the rational man and that man is at his best when he is thinking.

I am not unaware that the Republic embodies Plato's ideal, archetypal society, and that it probably was never his intention to actuate such a scheme on the plane of history. But this observation does not mitigate the difficulty. Since an ideal ought to represent the outside possibilities of perfection, Plato's defense of a communistic state all the more betrays his pathetic comprehension of human nature.

Identifying the real man with the faculty of thought is, I believe, one of the most dreadful fruits of classical philosophy. "But such a life would be too high for man; for it is not in so far as he is man that he will live so, but in so far as something divine is present in him; and by so much as this is superior to our composite nature is its activity superior to that which is the exercise of the other kind of virtue. If reason is divine, then, in comparison with man, the life according to it is divine in comparison with human life. . . . And what we said before will apply now; that which is proper to each thing is by nature best and most pleasant for each thing; for man, therefore, the life according to reason is best and pleasantest, since reason more than anything else *is* man."* Aristotle seriously misunderstood the nature of man. And the source of his difficulty was his refusal to come at the problem by way of moral self-acceptance.

When a man has courage to develop his view of life from within the realities that already hold him, he will quickly perceive that his dignity is *not* measured by intelligence quotient. The whole man sometimes thinks, sometimes chooses, and sometimes weeps; but the whole man is neither thought, will, nor emotion. Man is the mysterious interpermeation of all his faculties; he is an unfathomable unity of spiritual freedom. Let others enter the circle of nearness: whether our ability to think is advanced or retarded, we immediately oblige them to give signs that they accept the dignity of our person.

We need not search long to explain why Plato abolished private property in the interests of state primacy. Negatively, he did it for the same reason Marx did. Although Plato argued from the perspective of rational consistency, while Marx appealed to the immanent dialectic in class struggles, both developed their philosophy of social rights without consulting the realities to which they themselves were committed. The Socratic approach witnesses against both Plato and Marx, for Socrates at least had the moral integrity to limit his assertions by the spiritual quality of his own life. Samuel Butler is right in contending that each man's work is always a portrait of himself. The more one tries to conceal himself, the more clearly will his character appear in spite of himself.

Since no tyrant has ever tried to retrench my liberties, however, I decided that reference to such a highly contrary-to-fact

* Aristotle, *Nicomachean Ethics*, X, 7, 1177b-1178a. Despite all his Christian insights, even Augustine was betrayed into this dreadful error. "I say: Who can doubt that the best element in man is nothing else than that part of the mind to which it behooves all the other parts in man to conform as to a master? And that part—lest you should request another definition—may be called the understanding or reason." *Contra Academicos*, I, 2, 5.

Moral Self-Acceptance and the Judicial Sentiment

condition as Plato's Republic did not advance the argument. If a violation of our free rights is immoral, then *any* instance of such a violation ought to arouse judicial feelings within us. This proved to be the case.

One afternoon I happened to be in a local nursery, patiently waiting to buy a pound of grass seed. When the unhurried clerk finally rang up the sale and it was my turn to be waited on, to my utter dismay he turned to assist a young couple that had just entered the store. I did not need Plato's Republic to realize what it means to have my rights violated, for all the elements were right there.

Determined to make a deliberate study of this incident, I went to the rear of the nursery and sauntered through the rose gardens. When I examined the ingredients in my moral response, I found a strange and conflicting fact. Since I had been defrauded of just rights, my feeling of judicial indignation witnessed to the claims of the moral and spiritual environment; but since I wanted to take personal revenge on the careless clerk, not all of my zeal was thus inspired. I had to find some way to defecate the impurities. I soon found this way.

After a short time I returned to the nursery and the clerk waited on me. Once again I took a careful reading of the realities to which this experience committed me. I found that though my passion to seek revenge had abated, there was no subsiding of my moral conviction that the indolent clerk had violated my rights. This immediately showed me how to separate egoistic responses from the claims of the moral and spiritual environment.

In the rear of the rose garden was a mound of fresh fertilizer. When I smelled the fetid odor, and moreover when I saw that some of the dung was stuck to the side of my shoe, I experienced feelings of indignation which looked the same as those the careless clerk had aroused. This gave me a perfect opportunity to conduct an experiment on my own soul. Both responses excited me; both kindled feelings of indignation; and both could be morally justified by a skilled use of rationalization. How, then, could they be separated?

The answer came when I returned to the store and once again confronted the young clerk. Whereas nothing but a strong sense of personal timidity kept me from complaining about my unjust treatment, I found that only by outraging my own soul could I defend my indignant attitude toward the fertilizer. Here, then, was the long sought-for clue: *A morally provoked feeling can be defended with the consent of our nobler faculties and the praise of men of character.* A defense of justice edifies the soul, while a defense of peevishness deteriorates it. I could not stand in the nursery and shout: "I can't stand this smell! . . . Do you understand? . . . This smell irritates me!" Oh, I could *do* it—that is, I was free to do it; but I could not do it without feeling aftereffects of shame and regret. My nobler faculties would be in revolt.

Let me illustrate this principle. Illicit love, for example, has a peculiar attraction to it. It even answers to aspects of the self which are left unappeased by licit love. "Stolen water is sweet, and bread eaten in secret is pleasant" (Proverbs 9:17). But since illicit love offends our nobler faculties, it cannot be freely engaged in by the whole self. It must be indulged in secret; it deteriorates our dignity; it cannot be urged on our children and loved ones; it is repugnant to men of character.

At this point some may cavil: "But who *are* men of character?"—the insinuation being that we are resting our case on some asserted, but quite unproved, standard. Whoever comes at this by way of the third method of knowing will see why the charge is pure cavil. When a person willingly entrusts his possessions or his family to the care of another, his actions prove that he already knows what character is; for he could not release his treasures unless he were morally certain that the one being trusted *is* a man of character. And being committed to this knowledge, he ought to have the mettle to acknowledge it. Character is moral steadi-

Moral Self-Acceptance and the Judicial Sentiment

ness. It is the kind of life which has received its dye from the moral and spiritual environment.

Morally aroused indignation can be analyzed and accepted by the whole man; it can be brought to the attention of upright hearts without leaving deposits of spiritual insecurity on our memory. A pursuit of justice suffuses the soul with feelings of moral cleanness. We cannot make a moral issue out of personal tastes. But if we are given dill pickles, after paying for sweet pickles, a hesitation to speak would not be due to any want of conviction that an injustice has been done. We may hesitate because we are afraid, or because we think the matter is too trivial; but not because we are uncertain of the evil.

5. THE JUDICIAL SENTIMENT

Now that this criterion has been clarified, we can answer our question. Having asked, "To what moral realities are we committed when our rights are violated?" we answer, "We are committed to the assurance that those who do this are guilty, for we can defend our sense of indignation with the consent of our nobler faculties and the praise of men of character." It should not be supposed that we are merely reviewing subjective attitudes. We are probing into the foundational claims of the moral and spiritual environment. We can no more cease judging those who violate our rights than we can alter our concreated sense of personal dignity. Unless this point is clearly understood, our case will look like nothing but an egoistic review of personal disgruntlement. The problem must be evaluated within the moral realities that hold us when others outrage our dignity. Whoever refuses to meet this condition will never recognize the claims of the moral and spiritual environment. The third method of knowing must be applied. Charging inconsiderate individuals with guilt is merely the reverse side of our demand that our dignity be respected.

I have no fear of critics who say that moral indignation is simply the daughter of selfishness, personal disgruntlement, or a vague desire to ensure self-preservation; for whether we are cheated by misrepresented merchandise; whether we are by-passed when privileges are distributed; whether our property is invaded; whether others take advantage of us when we are in a position of weakness—whether any of these overtake us, or a thousand other situations familiar to this or any other culture, we are immediately held by the conviction that those who instigate such acts are guilty. We are committed to a moral absolute. Not only is there no escape from the conviction that wrong has been done, but any attempt to try would constitute a sure sign of character deterioration. Let us hereafter refer to the offended moral faculty as the *judicial sentiment*.

Our participation in the moral and spiritual environment has now been clarified from two diffcrent sides. First, we are created with a sense of our own spiritual dignity. "For no man ever hates his own flesh, but nourishes and cherishes it, as Christ does the church" (Ephesians 5:29). God has ensured that a man of character will never take a light view of the image of God in him. Only complete moral degeneration can release one from a sense of his own spiritual dignity. The second greatest of the laws in the Christian faith—that we must love our neighbor as ourself—is rooted in this divinely implanted sense of personal sanctity. Second, we are created with the responsibility of defending our dignity and our rights before violators. The judicial sentiment deputizes us to judge all who enter into the circle of nearness. We must determine whether a just relation obtains between our own life and the responsibility of others to respect it. There is no praiseworthy way to escape this task.

Of course, if one were to evaluate this without taking in the realities to which he is committed when he drives his car or shops for oranges, there is no limit to the suggestive, but irrelevant, questions he could raise. For example, he could ask, "What right have we to judge a neighbor?" or, "Who has given us authority to probe into another's life?" Such questions cannot be answered until one proceeds to the matter through moral self-acceptance. A spiritual defense of our dignity, and the judicial condemnation of those who violate it, are complementary claims of the one moral and spiritual environment. We cannot block the flow of these claims without atrophying character. Man is free to blind himself to this, of course, but that is neither here nor there. *Nothing about rectitude can be learned until one humbles one's self before the real.* Whether one will admit it or not, it so happens that an upright man cannot be morally neutral when others break covenants, when they compete unfairly, when they destroy rights, or when they violate the terms of fellowship.

But does this not run contrary to the counsel of Christ? "Judge not, that you be not judged. For with the judgment you pronounce you will be judged, and the measure you give will be the measure you get" (Matthew 7:1-2). How, then, can we say that the third method of knowing successfully leads to a defense of the Christian faith? Although more will be said about this at a later point, let us now venture a provisional answer. The ambiguity is in the word "judge." Some judgment is valid; some judgment is invalid. For example, we must decide whether or not a man is a cheat or a murderer. We cannot have fellowship with good people unless we are able to decide who are, and who are not, good.

Jesus is saying at least this: *We have no right to administer the law in personal relations.* Any attempt to do so is sullied by sentiments of revenge. God has lodged the powers of administration in duly appointed officials—the father, the elder, the civil magistrate, and finally the divine tribunal itself. We cannot administer justice in personal relations without taking the law into our own hands; but Christ expressly forbids this. He knows that once our prejudices are aroused, we are unable to separate justice and revenge. ". . . for, though the spirit of revenge is so pleasing to Mankind, that it is never conquered but by a supernatural grace, revenge being indeed so deeply rooted in Humane Nature, that to prevent the excesses of it (for men would not know Moderation) Almighty God allows not any degree of it to any man, but says, *Vengeance is mine*: And, though this be said positively by

God himself, yet this revenge is so pleasing, that man is hardly perswaded to submit the menage of it to the Time, and Justice, and Wisdom of his Creator, but would hasten to be his own Executioner of it."*

6. THE JUDICIAL PREDICAMENT

Since we are custodians of the law, it is our solemn moral responsibility to decide whether a just relation holds between the demands of rectitude and the willingness of others to be upright. Those who enter the circle of nearness must show signs of friendship; otherwise they are guilty.

The moment we grant this, however, we are immediately cast into a judicial predicament. Here is the difficulty: whereas our participation in the moral and spiritual environment deputizes us to guard our dignity, this participation gives us no authority to enforce the law against the guilty. We cannot ignore inconsiderate acts in others; yet we cannot execute the penalty of law. We have no right to complete the moral cycle. This is why we are in a judicial predicament. We are custodians of the law, but who enforces the law?

Some think they can dissolve this predicament by asserting that guilt is only a subjective dialogue between our higher and lower selves. It has no reference to external sanctions and penalties. But such an attempt must be rejected by one who spiritually accepts the realities that hold him when he reports a theft or accuses a fellow employee of perjury. Liability before law is the only element which distinguishes guilt from a vague feeling of personal unhappiness. Petty feelings of guilt may be nothing but unorganized sentiments in the heart; but essential guilt—guilt in the presence of law—is not. A person who cheats us ought to feel guilty, for he has fallen from rectitude. Restoration cannot be made until an account is given before a lawfully appointed tribunal. This will

---

* Izaak Walton, *Lives* (Oxford), p. 222.

be perspicuous to all who come at the question by way of moral self-acceptance.

Since guilt implies culpability, an admission of guilt implies the accompanying admission that one is liable to law. Strip away the element of "liability to law" and one destroys the essence of guilt, for guilt means that a person is subject to the just consequences of law. There is no need to labor this further. Those who are honest with their own hearts already realize the truth, and those who refuse to be honest would not realize it even if further evidences were adduced.

Before we develop the implications of the judicial predicament, however, it is necessary to pause for a moment. Unless we clearly see that we have no native rights to administer the law against a neighbor, the force of the judicial predicament will escape us. There is no doubt but that we are never wholly free from a desire to take the law into our own hands. But this is a work of pride, not character. We already know enough about morals to realize that we cannot pretend to be the administrator of justice without disgracing our nobler faculties. Although we sense no spiritual inhibition when crying out against injustice, the purity of our moral life deteriorates the moment we attempt to administer justice. We have never tried, nor would we now try, rushing into the street and shouting, "We administer justice in the name of an authority that inheres in us by natural right!" Not only would others scorn our pretense, but in the silence of our own chamber we would scorn ourselves.

Our sense of unworthiness would be a sign of guilt, for the right to administer justice is not a fruit of the moral and spiritual environment. If we lose control of passions and strike another person, a proof of our shame is the care with which we confine any ensuing discussion to the guilt of the other. We never encourage a serious investigation into the authority by which we administered justice in the first place. This is added proof that the essence of guilt includes a spiritual obligation to accept the punishment of law, for a dread of penalty makes us hesitant to confess guilt.

After we have offended another person, we are afraid to face him. We fear the consequences of law, not the other person. Or better, we fear the law as it is revealed through him.

Whenever we inflict punishment on another individual, we are acting on sentiments that are only faintly judicial. Because we are powerless to act from purely judicial interests—as any presiding jurist strives to do—we prove that our urge to administer justice is partly a covert urge to take revenge. This, as we have suggested, is one reason that Christ says we are not to judge one another. We cannot complete the moral cycle when dealing with a neighbor, for any attempt betrays us into vindictiveness. The fact that we are powerless to execute judgment without venting revenge shows, once again, that we are guided more by power than by mind; for neither mind nor will can nullify our proneness to take revenge.

We have now reached one of the critical turning points in the argument. Unless the force of the judicial predicament is felt, much of what follows will lose its relevance. Here, then, is a brief review of this predicament: our participation in the moral and spiritual environment deputizes us to name the evil in those who outrage our dignity; but it does not empower us to exact the just consequences of transgression. Although we cannot arrest our habit of judging those who mistreat us, we have no authority to administer the law against them. We are never permitted to complete the moral cycle in man-to-man relations.

The significance of this predicament, and especially its place in the Christian apologetic, will be traced shortly. But before this is done, a supporting phase of the argument must be developed. The more information we have before us, the richer will be our perspective from which to evaluate the judicial predicament.

7. HARMONIZING DUTY AND DESIRE

The Christian ethic, let us remember, is premised on the self's love for the self. Nothing motivates us unless it appeals to our

Moral Self-Acceptance and the Judicial Sentiment

interests. Both Old and New Testament refer to our concreated sense of spiritual dignity when defining the zeal and consistency with which we must respect a neighbor. "You shall not take vengeance or bear any grudge against the sons of your own people, but you shall love your neighbor as yourself: I am the Lord" (Leviticus 19:18). Whenever others offend us, the judicial sentiment is aroused. This means that the regard for our dignity, and the judgment of those who outrage it, are but two sides of the same moral force. Even as God releases no one from an omnipresent sense of his own dignity, so he makes it impossible for one to look with indifference on acts of inconsideration and injustice.

If a system of ethics fails to blend self-love and duty into one vital unity, it is large with the elements of its own destruction. Man is made in the image of God; no worldly wisdom can alter this. Even as we natively love ourselves, so we natively protect our life from those who threaten to injure it. The love is desire, while the protection is duty; but both flow from the moral and spiritual environment.

Ethicists usually make one of two capital errors. Either they deny man's concreated sense of dignity, and so end up with a formalistic ethic that outrages the heart; or they recognize the omnipresence of self-love, but fail to anchor it in a sense of duty. Both options destroy the possibility of a consistent ethic. Kant's "categorical imperative" illustrates the first error, while William James's essay *The Will to Believe* illustrates the second. Let us examine them in this order.

Kant thought that the banishment of self-love from morals was a very inconsequential thing. But he soon faced an impasse from which there was no easy retreat. The mind is asked to act only on that maxim whereby it can at the same time will that it should become a law universal, the presumption being that human reason has plenary power to develop and obey self-consistent rules of conduct. But how can a limited rational perspective be sure that its verdict *is* harmonious with a hypothetical universal judgment? Suppose we want to walk through an alley. Our act is not moral unless we can will the maxim of our conduct to become a law universal. But we cannot will this, for a healthy economy not only confines many to sedentary tasks, but the complex involvements of others would make it difficult to decide whether or not it is wise for them to walk. This is not to mention the fact that there would be insufficient room in the alley for everybody. This may sound like very trivial talk, as if we have missed the profundity of the categorical imperative (and we may have). But it at least illustrates some of the prima facie difficulties that common sense encounters whenever it tries to be moral on Kantian terms.

In another place Kant said that one is not moral unless he takes in the happiness of all men. Once again, it is impossible to act. Suppose we try to apply this principle to so simple a procedure as buying a pound of butter. The more we try to be obedient, the more deeply we are quagmired in difficulties. Possibly local farmers are happy if we buy the butter, while distant farmers, equally anxious to move their dairy products, are not. Possibly the grocer is delighted with the business, while organized labor, now picketing the store, is offended. Before we can be rationally certain of the moral quality in the act, we must have an exhaustive knowledge of its place in the total economy of all men everywhere; which would only mean that we must be God. And all of this is a fruit of Kant's refusal to ground ethics in our concreated sense of spiritual dignity. Self-love is the foundation of any consistent ethic.

When Kant finally located a workable application of the categorical imperative, the instance did not illustrate what it was supposed to. Kant argued that if lying were universal, it would defeat itself. But this is the counsel of prudence, not duty. It is a warning against the prospect of certain disagreeable consequences. It was not without reason, thus, that Mill unmasked the empirical foundations of the Kantian ethic. A universal adoption of lying would lead to consequences that no prudent man would want to incur. I doubt if Mill's criticisms apply to all of Kant, for his earlier efforts were more to the point. But the criticisms certainly fit the

Kant who tried to develop a rational ethic in defiance of man's concreated sense of spiritual dignity. Moral self-acceptance may never enjoy Kantian precision, but it at least defends a view of ethics which succeeds in harmonizing the vital and the rational selves.

Once we admit that a sense of our own spiritual dignity belongs to the fabric of selfhood, however, we must likewise come to terms with the judicial predicament. Those who abuse either the self or its rights are guilty before law. They must give an account to a lawfully appointed tribunal. And so we are cast back on the judicial predicament. We are custodians of the law, but who administers the law? This predicament may be difficult to deal with, but the Kantian impasse is far worse.

Having shown what happens when one defies self-love in an effort to safeguard duty, let us now show what happens when one defies duty in an effort to safeguard self-love. Pascal's "wager" will serve as our point of departure.

Pascal based his wager on a forced option. Since we are committed to the inevitability of death and eternity, a decision for or against God *must* be made. And since wisdom favors deciding for God, a refusal to believe in God would be consummate foolishness.

In his celebrated essay *The Will to Believe,* James caught up the forced option and invested it with philosophical dignity. Arguing with usual lucidity and warmth, James asserted that whenever an individual faces problems that cannot be resolved by mind alone, it is entirely in accord with empirical procedure to cast the self wholeheartedly on that alternative which seems most in harmony with known truth and accepted moral opinion—the one, in short, that is most congenial to self-love, everything considered. Since circumstances force us to act, a decision, of necessity, must be made. If one waits and waits, determined to withhold action, even *this* decision is freighted with perils all its own. James skillfully lampoons rationalists who try to delay decision until the evidences are fully compelling. He shows that those who deny the lawfulness of voluntarily inspired faith are all the while chock-full of some kind of faith or other. They cannot escape commitment.

I have never read *The Will to Believe* but what I want to say of James, as Socrates said of Euthyphro, "Rare friend! I think I can do no better than be your disciple!" James shows such a sweet spirit of humble devotedness to the whole of reality that one is easily drawn to his side.

Further reflection shows, however, that though pragmatism verifies many practical things in life—and to this extent it is an indispensable negative test for truth—it nevertheless is inspired by enlightened self-interest. James spoils the limited validity of pragmatism by absolutizing its claims.

After majestically analyzing forced options, James entrusts their resolution to affections that are more easily charmed by selfishness than by the moral sense. Forced options are overcome by a prudential balance of better and worse. A sense of compulsion, proceeding from the moral and spiritual environment, is conspicuous by its absence.

Let me illustrate this. James says that voluntarily inspired faith is justified whenever the mind faces a complete disjunction. Here, in truth, is such a disjunction: when others enter the circle of nearness, they either give evidence of accepting our spiritual dignity or they are guilty. James would resolve this by his code of pragmatically inspired prudence, for even the very question of having moral beliefs at all or not having them is decided by our will. The third method of knowing rejects this as unworthy and immoral. It is unworthy because it fails to mirror the realities to which James himself was committed when he argued with Royce in Cambridge, and it is immoral because it sanctions the subordination of life to calculated interests. Duty is not felt until one stands in the center of duty itself.

Kant and James illustrate the impasse one faces when he refuses to blend self-love and duty. Either self-love is driven from morals, as in Kant, or options are resolved by enlightened self-interest, as in James. In neither instance is a truly rigorous philosophy of morals possible.

8. THE REALITY OF THE ADMINISTRATOR OF JUSTICE

From the very beginning we have asserted that the person of God forms the moral and spiritual environment in which man lives and moves and is. We are attempting to clarify the elements in this environment, in order that we might clarify our relation to God. Although man subsists in God from the first moment of moral self-consciousness, he remains unaware of this relation until self-sufficiency yields to a humble walk. One must submit to the moral realities that already hold him. There is no way that a knowledge of man's life in God can be directly communicated. Each person must pursue the matter for himself. The third method of knowing aids one in this pursuit.

We certainly do not mean to imply that man does not know God until he makes a conscious effort to find God. He is not yet in *fellowship* with God, of course, and thus has no knowledge by acquaintance. But he can, and does, know God in another sense; for knowledge is "man's systematic contact with the real." Conscious awareness is not essential to knowledge. One may be systematically in contact with God without realizing it. But his lack of consciousness in no way negates the reality of the knowledge.

This will be puzzling unless we recall that there are three conditions of knowing: direct experience, a conceptual account of the real, and moral responsibility. We refer to the third condition of knowing. Man subsists in God from the first moment of moral self-consciousness, for God completes the moral cycle by answering to the judicial sentiment. This is why we say that man is already systematically in contact with God, and thus knows God. Other things being equal, man can become rationally conscious of this relation whenever he wills to.

We have reached a point in the argument where it is necessary to give a reason for our hope. We believe, on Scriptural authority, that we live and move and are in God. Now it is incumbent on us to show how this faith successfully blends the basic ingredients of a world view: the facts of experience, the requirements of logical consistency, and the witness of the moral sense. Let me develop the apologetics of this question by setting down a series of propositions. Like children's boxes nested one within another, each new proposition is analytically included in the one that precedes. All ensuing propositions are implied in the first. This harks back to the third method of knowing: we *know* we live and move and are in God because we are morally *responsible* for knowing. The third method of knowing yields no synthetic a priori judgments. Each new conclusion is analytically part of a conclusion already established. We start with realities that hold us from existence itself.

Proposition One: Man is not the author of his own existence. This was the first truth to be proved by moral self-acceptance. Since we are held by powers greater than ourselves, we have no assurance that we will live from one day to the next. We are dependent creatures.

Proposition Two: Analytically included in the relation of dependence is the moral and spiritual environment. We are held by a consciousness of duty from the first moment of moral self-consciousness. It is impossible to stand in the presence of another person without being confronted by the claims of this environment.

Proposition Three: Analytically included in the moral and spiritual environment is the moral cycle: a concreated sense of our own spiritual dignity, the obligation of others to accept this dignity, and the guilt of those who abuse or offend us. An aroused judicial sentiment is proof that inconsiderate people are culpable.

Proposition Four: Analytically included in the moral cycle is the judicial predicament. Although we are custodians of the law, we have no authority to enforce the law. But since we continue judging others, we reveal our belief in their culpability. And analytically included in culpability is the obligation to answer to a lawfully established tribunal. This is why we assert that the very manner of our conduct commits us to the reality of the administrator of justice.

In sum: Those who injure us are guilty; but the cycle of guilt

Moral Self-Acceptance and the Judicial Sentiment

is incomplete unless they are morally answerable for their transgression. Whenever we judge others, therefore, we reveal our belief in the administrator of justice; for, apart from the obligation to appear before a duly authorized tribunal, there is no meaning to culpability. All of this is analytically included in our original admission of dependence.

If one admits that he participates in the moral and spiritual environment, but denies that his participation simultaneously implies the reality of the administrator of justice, he is consciously or unconsciously untrue to the real. His actions contradict his words. The real, let us remember, defines the limits of the true. And it is the duty of a free creature to bind himself to what is true. If there is an apple tree in the yard, it would be immoral to fly in the face of the facts and deny it. It makes no difference how personally interesting one may find falsehood, or what losses he might incur by admitting that it is an apple rather than a peach tree.

We are no more free to question the reality of the administrator of justice than we are to question the validity of either the law of contradiction or the law of uniformity. Each truth is analytically included in the realities that already hold us. *Even as meaningful speech implies the law of contradiction, and even as meaningful action implies the law of uniformity, so meaningful moral judgment implies the administrator of justice.* Realities to which we are committed by existence itself need only be impressed, not proved.

Since guilt means "liability for the transgression of law," it would of necessity follow that if unjust and inconsiderate people were not answerable to a lawful tribunal we could never with moral propriety judge them. We might empirically describe their foul deeds; we might walk up and say we do not like what they are doing; but unless the moral and spiritual environment authorizes us to be custodians of the law we could not meaningfully say that those who disregard us are culpable. So, we are confronted with a forced option. Either we must once for all desist from the habit of judging those who mistreat us, or we must spiritually adjust ourselves to the reality—*not just the possibility*—of the administrator of justice.

But even this is an unacceptable way of putting the matter, for it faintly suggests that we remain spiritually free to decide whether or not we will continue to judge inconsiderate individuals. Let it be said again and again; let it be shouted from the housetops; let it be etched in bronze for all future generations to read: We judge thoughtless people by a necessity that is woven into the fabric of our lives by creation itself. There is no way to escape this—no moral way, that is.

It would be the simplest thing in the world for one to *pretend* that he is not held by the moral and spiritual environment. He might even gain academic notoriety for his pretense. But in so doing he would only illustrate man's pathetic powers of self-deception. If one does not have the intellectual honesty to accept both the reality of his own dependence and the moral responsibilities analytically included in it, he at least ought to give up his pretenses to scholarship. His profession is contradicted by his life. The first mark of scholarship is a sensitive willingness to be led wherever the facts point. A scholar must face the whole of life.

In sum: If we claim that the reality of the administrator of justice is *not* analytically included in the moral cycle (arguing, perhaps, that the judicial sentiment is only a conditioned moral habit that withers under more mature scrutiny), we immediately contradict ourselves; for we are repudiating the very conditions to which we instinctively appeal whenever others mistreat us. But if we accept the moral basis of dignity, we must also accept the full implications of the moral cycle. This cycle is made up of law, transgression, and accountability before a duly authorized moral tribunal.

9. THE ELIMINATION OF FALSE ALTERNATIVES

Now that the reality of the administrator of justice is known to be analytically included in the realities that already hold us, no other course is open than to clarify the nature of this administrator. To assist us in this, let us return to the question which grew out of the judicial predicament: "To what, or to whom, are guilty individuals responsible?" If guilt implies the necessity of answering to a moral tribunal, to what, or to whom, should this account be rendered? The cycle of guilt must be completed.

To eliminate the possibility that guilty individuals are answerable to a *thing*, we need only briefly clarify the meaning of responsibility. To be responsible means "to be liable to give an account to"; as when a college student, entrusted with a large sum of money, renders an account of his stewardship. He is responsible *for* the money, but not *to* the money. If he mismanages his trust, and thus incurs guilt, he appears before his benefactor, not the money. This is so clear that it would be pointless to dilate it further. Since only a living person is spiritually free to hear and evaluate evidences, it follows that whenever others violate our dignity they are morally answerable to a person, not a thing.

But may not the *offended person* have power to enforce the law? No, for an honest acceptance of life shows that although pride would be delighted to mete out justice, one cannot exercise such a right without offending his own nobler faculties and those of men of character. If one were to cry, "I am the administrator of justice; I have inherent powers to enforce the law; I therefore ask you to step forward, that your conduct may be reviewed," his hearers would justly wonder whether the spirit of Don Quixote had been reincarnated. It is true that we must appear before those whom we have offended and apologize for our mistakes, but we do not look to them as the fountainhead of law. They are our metaphysical equals. We simply realize that unless we apologize, our souls will never be forgiven by a moral tribunal greater than man. The offended party merely provides an occasion for a very mysterious moral transaction. If his word of forgiveness does not issue in spiritual relief, he is at wit's end; for he, no less than the offender, is held within a moral and spiritual environment over which he has no personal control.

And it is no less certain that *people in general* enjoy no natural rights to enforce the law against us. Were we to establish this empirically—listing reasons, perhaps, why first this man, then the next, has no inherent rights over us—we would saddle ourselves with an altogether hopeless task; for human beings are born faster than we can acquaint ourselves with their possible power over us. Perhaps right now in India there is a bearded recluse who has authority to slap us if we fail to smile the right way. How can science possibly tell?

The marvelous feature of moral self-acceptance is that in the space of a moment it can prove what empirical procedures could never in eternity do. Bring the hypothetical recluse into the circle of nearness! Whether he be of high or low caste, we will withhold fellowship until he gives mutually acceptable signs of receiving our dignity. And if such signs are not forthcoming, the judicial sentiment is aroused and we judge him guilty. The same holds true for all people, past, present, and future. We will trust only those who give evidence of participating in the moral and spiritual environment. If a civil officer arrests us, he acts on delegated, not inherent, authority. The moment he steps outside his office, he has no right to administer law; and he becomes guilty if he tries. He cannot search our home without a warrant.

Some have argued that we are responsible to the state, but they only betray their own ignorance. The state is an impersonal entity, and it is meaningless to render an account to a thing. This may not flatter dictators, but it is nonetheless the truth. Fortunately, oppressive rulers have no power to change the character of reality.

If a tyrant pretends that he is both custodian and administrator of the law, his claims are rendered nugatory by the fact that we appeal to law when reflecting on his political worth in the first place. Rulers are good or bad, depending on the degree to which they conform to imperatives that are higher than both themselves and their subjects. A tyrant may break our limbs, but he cannot bind our conscience; for the duty to obey a lawless tyrant is not analytically part of any duty to which we are already committed.

I am not unaware that many will barter their freedom for the transient security of bread and circuses. That is their responsibility, not mine. Whenever a clan owns no allegiance to a moral and spiritual environment higher than itself, it ends up making the ridiculous claim that the true, the good, and the beautiful are settled by party interests. Whether a person should say in word what he intends in meaning is determined by the prevailing climate at the time. There are no moral absolutes written into the world by creation itself. "Morality" is but a bourgeois term for expediency.

If Rousseau had paid closer attention to his own moral commitments, he would never have defended the fantastic notion that there was a hypothetical time when men surrendered their rights to the state. Men cannot surrender what they do not have. Freedom is a privilege accorded by God; it is not a natural right. Furthermore, covenants are always made in the name of a higher power. Men swear by God. A neglect of this truth inspired the French Revolutionists with their romanticized version of "liberty and equality." The end was anarchy. No wonder Edmund Burke called the "age of reason" the "age of ignorance." When a social contract is cut loose from the moral order that comes from above, it is not a contract at all; for it has no moral foundation. It is simply a shrewd extension of selfish interests, binding on a signatory only as long as his preferences are safeguarded.*

10. THE PERSON OF GOD AS THE ADMINISTRATOR OF JUSTICE

Once I realized that we are committed to the reality of the administrator of justice from existence itself, I was shattered by a knowledge of my own ingratitude. Although our search for the administrator of justice has been somewhat prolonged, it now appears that the ground of our being and the administrator of

* The framers of the Declaration of Independence were prudent enough to recognize this: "We hold these truths to be self-evident, that all men are created equal; that they are *endowed by their Creator* with certain unalienable rights; . . ." The 1954 Act of Congress likewise shows the nation's consciousness of its theistic foundations. When we pledge allegiance to the flag, we now say "one nation, *under God*, indivisible, with liberty and justice for all."

justice are one and the same. Hence, there is good reason to be shattered by a knowledge of ingratitude. It is as if we were to make elaborate preparations to meet one who has given us generous financial assistance over a long period of time; only to discover that our unknown benefactor is really the gardener: the same individual who has silently observed our self-centered ways during the very time we were being saved from destitution. What language can we borrow to conceal our evil ways? To be sure, we knew him only as gardener, not as benefactor, but does this excuse us?

Twist and turn though we may, a spiritually sensitive individual cannot elude the fact that the person of God completes the moral cycle by answering to the judicial sentiment. I define person as *freedom expressed through moral self-consciousness*. I define God as *that person to whom violators of our dignity must give an account*. The omnipresence of God completes the moral cycle by answering to the judicial sentiment.

Since we have passed to the reality of God by way of human experience, however, some might question the validity of our procedure. How can we be sure that our standards are the same as the standards of heaven? This objection can easily be met, for the critics reverse the true order of things. Civil courts are patterned after the heavenly exemplar, not the other way around—as in the inscription on Harvard's Langdell Hall: *Non sub homine sed sub Deo et lege*. The oath is the foundation of all accepted testimony; and the oath is taken in the name of God. The moral cycle exists because man participates in a divinely ordained moral and spiritual environment. If man were morally autonomous, juridical decisions would be an expression of personal interest, not of law and the right. But this would spell the end of all jurisprudence, for morality would be nothing but expediency.

Hence, let speculative, detached arguments reach Himalayan majesty; let skeptics make sport of the claim that the person of God forms the environment of our moral and spiritual life. These efforts fail to corrode the confidence of one who approaches the

Moral Self-Acceptance and the Judicial Sentiment

question by way of the third method of knowing. Since we cannot even walk through a drugstore without appealing to a tribunal higher than man, we can only repudiate the administrator of justice by reducing life to either a lie or an illusion. Even as skeptics must use the law of contradiction when attacking the law of contradiction, so critics must stand within a divinely ordained moral and spiritual environment when attacking the reality of this environment. In each case the objection destroys itself. As we stated at an earlier point, *That which is indispensable to a given condition cannot meaningfully be repudiated by one who stands within the privileges of that condition.*

A detached critic cannot address himself to the question, however, for a spiritual sense of one's own limitations is the moral prerequisite for knowing any person, whether God or man. Personality can never be perceived until one is humble.

I have said from the very beginning that I have no interest in proving the existence of God. This resolve has not changed. The third method of knowing is a method, not a proof. It is merely a procedure by which one acquaints himself with the realities that already hold him. And the fact that man lives and moves and is in God is one of these realities. Man is held in the person of God from the first moment of moral self-consciousness—though he will never meet God until he is spiritually transformed by this relation.

Possibly this is what Kierkegaard meant by his cryptic assertion that freedom is the truly wonderful lamp; and that when a man rubs it with ethical passion God comes into being for him. I cannot be sure, for it is such a strange way to put the matter. But if he means that man dwells in the person of God from the dawn of moral self-consciousness—though he remains unaware of this relation until he humbly accepts the ethical task of becoming an individual—I once again rejoice at the sagacity of the Dane. And if this is not what he meant, I can only reply that it is what he should have meant.

11. KANT'S APPEAL TO CONSCIENCE

An approach to the person of God through moral self-acceptance can be set in sharper relief if we contrast its success with one of the failures of Kant. Sometimes we do not appreciate a given position until we recognize the inadequacy of its maturest alternatives.

Kant developed an approach to God which, at first glance, seems to be identical with that of moral self-acceptance, but which on closer inspection proves to be radically different. Kant argued from conscience's power to render a moral verdict against the soul. Conscience delivers accusations from a moral tribunal that cannot be identified with the self being accused, for no man will deliberately condemn himself. And since this voice of accusation judges all our free actions, we must conclude that conscience is the subjective principle of responsibility for one's deeds before the divine tribunal. Only God has power to probe into the secret parts of man with the force of an all-obliging judgment.

It is easy to see why this argument is outwardly similar to the third method of knowing, for it seems to draw its force from the judicial sentiment. But since the judicial sentiment and conscience are two separate faculties, agreement is more verbal than real.* Whereas conscience accuses the *self*, the judicial sentiment accuses *others*. The direction of accusation is the important thing. Conscience monitors one's own moral conduct, while the judicial sentiment monitors the moral conduct of others.

Furthermore, conscience is subject to social and cultural conditioning, whereas the judicial sentiment is not. All normal men, past, present, and future, experience an aroused judicial sentiment whenever they are personally mistreated. The self's love for the self is woven into the very cloth of the soul. No man has a right to use us as a means to his own calculated ends.

---

* This is a provisional judgment. At a later point we will review one instance where the judicial sentiment functions *through* conscience. But it would be highly imprudent to inject such an exception at this point, for nothing is so insipid as the answer to a question which has not yet been raised.

Conscience cannot conveniently lead us to God because of its chameleonic tendencies. Notice the mass of evidence adduced by Darwin. "A North-American Indian is well pleased with himself, and is honoured by others, when he scalps a man of another tribe; and a Dyak cuts off the head of an unoffending person, and dries it as a trophy. The murder of infants has prevailed on the largest scale throughout the world, and has met with no reproach; but infanticide, especially of females, has been thought to be good for the tribes or at least not injurious. Suicide during former times was not generally considered as a crime, but rather, from the courage displayed, as an honourable act; and it is still practiced by some semi-civilised and savage nations without reproach, for it does not obviously concern others of the tribe. It has been recorded that an Indian Thug conscientiously regretted that he had not robbed and strangled as many travellers as did his father before him. In a rude state of civilisation the robbery of strangers is, indeed, generally considered as honourable."*

Darwin's evidences strongly *suggest* that remorse can be explained without reference to a divinely implanted moral faculty. Does God allow in one tribe what he expressly forbids in another? Is God the author of confusion?

If I understand Darwin correctly, he is saying that man experiences compunction because of his powers of rational self-transcendence. Man can reflect on the past and anticipate the future. If an individual follows one natural impulse, rather than another, the choice of an inferior impulse leaves deposits of moral insecurity on his soul. He remembers an imprudent decision; he realizes that he ought to have followed dominant instincts. Conscience, thus, is nothing but a dialogue between the free and involved selves. If birds had powers of self-transcendence, they would likewise experience remorse when they disobey dominant instincts.

Darwin's approach has plausibility, of course, for conscience, in some sense, *is* a dialogue between the free and involved selves. But I do not think the last word has been said on the subject—

* *The Descent of Man* (Britannica), pp. 314-315.

not by a long shot. Although chameleonic in nature, the accusations of conscience are somehow connected with the moral and spiritual environment.

But I must confess that I do not know what this connection is. Moral self-acceptance has given no hints along this line. All we can do is let the question linger on the edge of consciousness, with the hope that new insights will be found as the inquiry proceeds.

Darwin's attack is to the hurt of Kant, however, and not of the third method of knowing. Kant made the capital mistake of trying to pass from earth to heaven on the ladder of contingent experience. Darwin shows that he does not even get off the ground. The third method of knowing avoids Kant's difficulty by starting *within* the moral and spiritual environment. Our approach is analytical, not synthetical—an extremely important difference to observe.

Since we are held by a sense of our own spiritual dignity from existence itself, it follows that the roots of our moral life go deeper than cultural conditioning. The intuition of our dignity is drawn from the moral and spiritual environment; it is not an acquired characteristic. An aroused judicial sentiment is merely heaven's warning that the image of God is being outraged. Cultural conditioning may alter the *direction* of the judicial sentiment, but it does not alter the faculty itself. Our participation in God issues in a spiritual intuition of our own dignity, on the one hand, and the guilt of those who violate it, on the other.

This is not to be construed as a salute to the superiority of Darwin, however, for he, no less than Kant, appealed to conditioned experience. Whenever Darwin is judged by moral self-acceptance, his identification of compunction with offended social instincts is unvarnished foolishness. It illustrates what happens when one takes a method of science and transfers it to morals. Although Darwin professes to be faithful to all the facts, he neglects the most important facts of all. He tells us many interesting things about the far-flung tribes of the world—their relative

Moral Self-Acceptance and the Judicial Sentiment

moral standards, their strange rites and customs, and their conflicting mores and taboos—but (to my knowledge) he fails to tell us anything about the moral realities to which he himself was committed as a passenger on the *Beagle*. It would be interesting to learn whether, when others were inconsiderate of his person or careless of his rights, he was able to say, in all sincerity and honesty, that his sense of indignation was nothing but a self-transcendent reflection on an imprudent balance of dominant instincts; and that if he had been conditioned by another society it might have been a matter of moral indifference whether others regarded his life with malice and incivility.

Before Darwin can establish his thesis, therefore, he ought to name at least *one* tribe whose members (in the honesty of their heart) are not held by an intuition of both their own spiritual dignity and the moral duty of others to regard it. But this has not been done.

"My dear sir," the devotee of Darwinian relativism retorts, "get a hold of yourself, for what you ask is beyond our tether. Science has no access to the intimacies of the heart." Quite true, quite true. So, would it not be in accord with good empirical procedure if scientists tempered their assertions somewhat? Darwin cannot judge the meaning of compunction until he stands in the center of the moral and spiritual environment. Let savants recognize, once for all, that methods in physics and biology are inappropriate in morals. Empirical procedure is limited to what *is*, while duty deals with what *ought to be*. Two different spheres of being are in purview. This is why I unshrinkingly assert that neither Darwin nor his classical defenders have touched the outer garment of the imperative essence. Duty is never felt until one cheerfully submits to the duties that already hold him. A voyage on the *Beagle* is no substitute for moral self-acceptance.

I protest against pedants in endowed university chairs who encourage students to believe that man's sense of compunction results from a refusal to follow dominant instincts—as if man is of the stuff of an animal, rather than a free, moral creature made in the image of God. And I base my protest on the realities to which both student and professor are already committed by life itself.

12. A FINAL WORD ABOUT KANT

Kant is literally a library of conflicting arguments for and against the existence of God. Leibnitz might have enjoyed portions of the *Critique of Judgment*, for here Kant sought to establish the reality of God from an erudite survey of all experience. God must be postulated as the necessary condition of a teleological union of the intelligible and sensible worlds. It is hard to say just what all this accomplished.

I find Kant's most curious effort in the *Critique of Practical Reason*; for after developing a method that might have outflanked both Aristotle and Aquinas, he made such an inconsistent use of it that he drew the scorn of Jacobi, Fichte, and Herder. Let me develop this briefly.

I shall not comment on the dubious distinction between "theoretical" and "practical" reason, except to note that, in my opinion, it creates more problems than it solves. Nor will I inquire why Kant thought that regulative ideas are of the stuff of faith, rather than knowledge.* Is not *all* critically tested belief a resting of the mind in the sufficiency of the evidences? And what name do we give this, if not knowledge? Knowledge, let us remember, is man's systematic contact with the real. Kant speaks academic double talk when he asserts that though we must postulate a priori conditions for practical action, the mind's resting in the validity of these conditions is not knowledge. If regulative ideas mirror man's critical apprehension of the real, then they, no less than the axioms of geometry, belong to man's ever enlarging body of knowledge.

Kant argued that the manner of our lives obliges us to postulate three "regulative" ideas: freedom, immortality, and God. I feel

* Knowledge and generic faith are synonyms—a resting of the whole man in the sufficiency of the evidences.

that if Kant had used the same method in defending the idea of God that he used in defending the idea of freedom, his theological effort would never have been dismissed as a historical curiosity.

Unless the profundity of Kant escapes me, the reality of human freedom is established by what is formally similar to the third method of knowing. After granting the reality of the moral sense, Kant then inquired into what conditions must be presupposed for such a fact to be meaningful. And so he concluded, "Thou canst, for thou oughtest." Freedom makes moral responsibility possible. Unless man is free, he cannot meaningfully be called moral.

Since there are good reasons to believe that one may be obliged by laws greater than he can meet (a matter that will be developed at a later point), I do not think that the Kantian argument can be accepted without an important proviso. But such a proviso, for the time being, is beside the point. Kant at least was shrewd enough to see that the reality of personal freedom is analytically included in the reality of the moral sense. Whoever admits the one has already admitted the other. Man must be free to know the obligation, and free to do something about it. I deem this Kantian proof no less valid than Aristotle's negative demonstration of the law of contradiction. If a person challenges moral freedom, he asks his hearer to evaluate his arguments in moral freedom; and thus his objection, like a critic's objection to the law of contradiction, destroys itself.

This is splendid thus far. But when Kant went on to establish the regulative idea of immortality, he shifted to an arid academicism. Since the analysis of a moral command implies no guarantee that a man will choose to be moral, the idea of happiness is imported as an *ad hoc* support. And since the highest good is enjoyed only when the sensuous demand for happiness and the ethical demand for virtue are harmonized in the one individual, one needs ad infinitum opportunity to complete the union of virtue and happiness. Such an argument, it can be seen, is quite void of force. The Stoics were content to believe that virtue is its own reward, and Spinoza regarded mortality as part of the general perfection of reason and nature. It may be nice to believe we are immortal, but the Kantian defense does not ground this hope in rationally sufficient evidences.

The regulative idea of God is no less inconclusively established. Rather than arguing that the reality of God, like the reality of freedom, is analytically part of commitments that already hold a man of character, Kant postulated God as the supreme intelligence who overcomes our inadequate control of sensible nature. This might be pious to believe, but it is hardly the conclusion of good argument. It gives every appearance, in fact, of wishful thinking.

Kant's moral confusion is a direct result of his overly generous empirical concessions in the *Critique of Pure Reason*. This is why the Kantian system keeps coming apart at the seams. The theory of knowledge in the first critique nullified the possibility of a consistent theory of morals in the second critique. Modern man would do well to reflect long and hard on this Königsberg predicament.

Part Three

BECOMING ACQUAINTED WITH THE PERSON OF GOD

Chapter Six

PREPARATIONS FOR MEETING GOD

1. GOING BEYOND SPINOZA

If one were content to know the *existence* of God, rather than pressing on to an acquaintance with God's *person*, this would be the logical place for him to stop; for the probe from here on will seem pointless to all who do not appreciate the fact that personality can only be known as one either introduces himself or is introduced. If we want to enjoy a rich knowledge of God, deliberate steps must be taken to become acquainted with his person. To refuse acquaintance is to refuse knowledge. An inferential knowledge of God's existence is without value until fellowship is gained by an acquaintance with God's person. In person-to-person relations, knowledge by inference must yield to knowledge by acquaintance.

Spinoza, however, would deny that the heart *has* a right to expect satisfactions which go beyond those enjoyed by mind. He contends that when ideas are perceived "under the form of eternity," man is already in possession of the richest conceivable satisfaction. To search for anything beyond this is to quest after the Holy Grail. We enjoy an intellectual love for God whenever knowledge is accompanied by the idea of God as cause; and this love, in turn, works pleasures in us that are supreme and unending.

Only the satisfactions of thought rest on immutable foundations. All other pleasures plunge the soul into the deepest sadness.*

Spinoza's position would be acceptable if two controlling presuppositions were granted: first, that God is an abstract force, not a person; second, that the real man is the rational man, and that man is at his best when he is thinking. But we will never grant these. The first presupposition must be rejected because of the moral cycle. Those who disregard our dignity are morally responsible; but they are answerable to a person, for only a person has organs to hear and evaluate evidence. The second presupposition is refuted by a spiritual submission to the realities that already hold us from existence itself. If others merely *think* about us, rather than vitally engaging us in fellowship, we judge them guilty. They must pass from an inferential knowledge of our existence to an acquaintance knowledge of our person; and if they are not attracted by this higher knowledge they transgress law. They are guilty of violating our dignity. The real man is not the rational man; the real man is the moral and the loving man.

Spinoza errs, furthermore, in supposing that a resting in right rational relations is equivalent to moral virtue. He argues that a good person is one who is held by knowledge that is accompanied by the idea of God as cause. This assumes that a wise man is a virtuous man, which is not necessarily true. A wise man may be morally wretched, even as an ignorant man may be a model of rectitude. There is a *toto caelo* difference between the quality of thought and the quality of virtue. The terms of one sphere cannot be credited to the other. The imperative essence is met by freely initiated moral behavior, not by taking thought. Rectitude is a quality that inheres in right affections; it is not simply a name for consistent reflection. Thought anticipates the good as a hypothetical possibility, but only moral decision can actuate it.

---

* This is a seventeenth century version of the classical Greek notion that reason is the divine element in man. "The man who follows reason in all things is at once leisurely and active, cheerful and composed." Marcus Aurelius, *Thoughts*, X, 12a. Man is most harmonious when he is in accord with universal reason.

2. GOING BEYOND ARISTOTLE

This leads to another problem. Why should it be supposed that fellowship with God fills the heart with consolations that are not experienced when one is warmed by the rays of the sun? God completes the moral cycle, while the sun completes the physical cycle. But though we are dependent on the sun for life, we certainly do not expect an acquaintance with the sun to issue in spiritual consolation. Why, then, should spiritual consolation be expected from an acquaintance knowledge of God?

Aristotle would reply that even as it is natural for the sun to illuminate the universe, so it is natural for God to move the universe; and that just as it is quite without meaning to expect spiritual consolations from an acquaintance knowledge of the sun, so it is equally without meaning to expect such consolations from an acquaintance knowledge of God.

Aristotle's position is as faulty as that of Spinoza, for the "unmoved mover," no less than Spinoza's "substance," is impersonal. Aristotle simply did not have an accurate understanding of God's nature. The being who answers to the judicial sentiment is a person, not an abstract, metaphysical center of eternal self-knowledge. A person, let us remember, is "freedom expressed through moral self-consciousness." Were we to dignify the idea that God is related to the world in the way that Aristotle argues, not only would we negate God's person, but we would have to argue that God does not even know that the world exists. A knowledge of mutable things would introduce change in God, and any change in God would be a change for the worse. But this would throw our lives into complete spiritual consternation, for it would efface the claims of the very environment from which we draw the intuition of our own dignity. Apart from our participation in the moral and spiritual environment, we would simply be saying that we do not *like* it when others treat us uncivilly, just as we might say that we do not like garlic. But no moral information would be communicated.

Preparations for Meeting God

The tragic error of classic philosophy cannot be appreciated until this is grasped. The very manner of our existence commits us to the reality of a God who is occupied with what is vastly more dignified business than eternal self-knowledge. God is the author of the moral and spiritual environment; he is the sleepless monitor of our dignity; he completes the moral cycle by answering to the judicial sentiment. He is, in short, our only reason for believing that human values, and the ultimate values of the universe, are metaphysically continuous; and that we are not alone in our moral stand.

This is not to be construed as a veiled defense of personal immortality. Quite the contrary. Nothing in the third method of knowing has proved that the soul will survive the shock of physical death. All I say is that whether in Aristotle's Greece or Spinoza's Holland, one is already held by the terms of the moral cycle. It would be easier to give up breathing than to be released from the claims of the moral and spiritual environment. God completes the moral cycle by answering to the judicial sentiment. This is why it is entirely in accord with good procedure to expect that an acquaintance knowledge of God will invest the heart with satisfactions that surpass a rational contemplation of God's existence. Therefore, until fellowship with God is enjoyed, it is clear that we do not rightly know God.

3. EXTENDING THE CYCLE OF FELLOWSHIP

From the very beginning I have argued that the nearness of God makes it difficult to develop a perspective from which to decide what conditions must be met if we are to enjoy fellowship with God. Such a difficulty is clearly illustrated at this point in the argument. How can we go about acquainting ourselves with the person of God? Where shall we begin?

At an earlier point we asked the question, "Under what conditions shall we trust another individual?" And we answered, "We shall trust him only to the extent that he shows signs of receiving the dignity of our person." This query led to what we called the "cycle of fellowship": an introductory word, the sustained pleasure, and a warm gesture of farewell. Let us now extend this cycle by adding a new element.

Suppose we are walking along the bank of a muddy river, when suddenly we notice that a young mother's rowboat has slipped its knot and is drifting out into the current. Without calculating consequences, we dash into the water and reach for the line, only to soak our clothing and be inconvenienced for the rest of the day. When we finally recover the boat and return it to the woman, does our participation in the moral and spiritual environment oblige her to meet any new terms?

There can be no doubt, as we ponder this and similar illustrations, that *whenever we do a large favor for another, the person helped is morally obligated to express a spontaneous word of thanks.* By large we mean measurable, out of the way, not legally expected. Whoever is faithful to the manner of his own life will immediately recognize that there is no exception to this rule. Not to look for evidences of spontaneous gratitude is as clear a sign of character deterioration as an indifference either to one's own dignity or to the moral demand that others respect it.

I do not mean to imply that we fail to look for evidences of gratitude when we do small favors, for experience teaches that *any* act of kindness, however small, excites this expectation. Whether we merely open the door for another, or go so far as to save a life, the judicial sentiment is somewhat aroused if our effort is taken for granted. "It is observed, that a desire of glory or commendation is rooted in the very nature of man; and that those of the severest and most mortified lives, though they may become so humble as to banish self-flattery, and such weeds as naturally grow there: yet they have not been able to kill this desire of glory, but that, like our radical heat, it will both live and dye with us; . . ."* I simply confine the discussion to large instances of gratitude, in order that the likelihood of captious objection might be lessened.

* Izaak Walton, *Lives* (Oxford), p. 77.

Preparations for Meeting God 123

Let us not be troubled by the critic who charges that expectations of appreciation are merely projections of an overweening ego. Such a claim is based on the tacit Kantian assumption that nothing is moral unless it is done out of a regard for law. But such a view of morals is unacceptable to the third method of knowing. Self-love forms part of the base of any consistent ethical theory. Whether we will it or not, the manner of our own existence commits us to the cycle of fellowship; and included in this cycle is the sense of indignation which arises whenever others take our sacrifices or favors for granted.

Not *all* expectations of appreciation flow from the moral and spiritual environment, of course, but some do; and it is only of the latter that we speak. If we cut the hedges, we look for tokens of appreciation from the family; but our expectation has a different quality to it than our moral demand on a neighbor whose dog we have rescued from a deep well shaft. If our family fail to commend us for cutting the hedges, they have simply missed a splendid opportunity to add to the world's happiness. We cannot make a public issue out of the matter without offending our better faculties. But if we return the dog to the neighbor, only to be met with icy indifference, this *can* be openly discussed without offending either our own nobler faculties or those of men of character. Nothing arouses the judicial sentiment quicker, even as nothing holds it at attention longer, than deliberate ingratitude.

It is quite in harmony with good procedure to assume that an arousing of the judicial sentiment by ingratitude is as much a proof of our participation in the moral and spiritual environment as an arousing of the judicial sentiment when our dignity is offended. Name any illustration you want. If the judicial sentiment is genuinely aroused by an act of ingratitude, certain things follow. Suppose we go out of our way to push a stranger's car. In doing so, we unexpectedly bend the chromium grille on our own car. But just as we look for signs of sincere thanks, the stranger speeds away in a cloud of dust, not even bothering to wave his hand. Here is what follows: we can reflect on the incident long after our temper cools; we can use it as an illustration without injuring our reputation; we can review it before men of character; we can recount it to our children; we are not ashamed of our judicial response, either now or when we devoutly recommend our soul to its Maker.

Close analysis reveals that ingratitude is nothing but a refusal to accept the dignity of our person. It is an unartistic way of announcing that one is quite willing to use us as a means to his own calculated ends. The grossness of the disregard makes the offender all the more liable to the judgment of God. If a person enters the circle of nearness and openly rebuffs our overtures of fellowship, we know where we stand; but if he covertly feigns fellowship, in order that he might gain certain benefits from the relation, a discovery of his fraud swiftly arouses the judicial sentiment. He is guiltier—vastly more so—than one who does not want to be a friend at all. Were we to choose between two people who are ungrateful—one who openly admits his indifference and another who tries to conceal it—we would unhesitatingly choose the first; for, despite his want of rectitude, he at least is decent enough to be honest. The second is guilty on two counts. Not only is he distant from rectitude, but he compounds his guilt by pretending that he is righteous.

In special circumstances an act is so heinous that an aroused judicial sentiment assumes the form of what is known as "righteous indignation." The experience of righteous indignation is further proof that man's soul is held within the claims of a divinely ordained moral and spiritual environment. The unique feature of such indignation is that it morally justifies anger. It arises whenever a man of character confronts situations where holy or extremely intimate matters are exploited for base ends; as when a war widow is bilked out of her savings by one who pretends to have information about her husband's dying words.

The sum of the matter is this: if we expect to approach the person of God, our effort will be presumptuous unless we are held by spontaneous feelings of gratitude for all God has done. This much is clear. But words of gratitude can only be exchanged within

Preparations for Meeting God

fellowship itself. So, this leaves us just about where we started. An enlargement of the cycle of fellowship has solved no problems. Our plight, in fact, has even worsened. The more we know about the good, the less able we are to be good.

4. SPIRITUAL PREPARATION AND THE PERCEPTION OF TRUTH

Classical thought has seldom appreciated the fact that one can "know" another person only after definite spiritual preparation. Philosophers assume that, regardless of what phase of reality one may probe, the preparations for knowledge are quite the same. This simply is not true.

Take the trivial matter of knowing a pear, for example. There are at least three different approaches to the pear, each requiring a different quality of preparation: Is it a pear? How does the pear taste? May I take the pear? Knowledge by inference establishes the reality of the pear; knowledge by acquaintance the taste; and knowledge by moral self-acceptance our ethical relation to the pear. If a person confuses this order, he confuses knowledge; and if he negates any one method he negates his chances of knowing a part of reality. Knowledge by inference answers to mind; knowledge by acquaintance answers to perceptive faculties; and knowledge by moral self-acceptance answers to the moral sense. Rational inference may decide the existence of the pear, but it cannot tell how a pear tastes; and general experience may decide the taste, but it cannot tell whether it is right to make off with the pear. Each method answers to some specific aspect of man, and this aspect, in turn, answers to the whole individual.

As we shift from one method of knowing to the next, a shift must likewise be made in the spiritual tone of the heart. And just as there are three methods of knowing—each answering to a particular aspect of the real—so there are three grades of spiritual preparation.

Knowledge by inference asks for nothing but a desire to construe one's judgments consistently. This calls for a modicum of spiritual preparation, but the amount is too insignificant to be identified. An arrogant individual can excel in logic and mathematics. Perhaps this is why philosophers restrict themselves to knowledge by inference, for pride is left untouched.

Knowledge by acquaintance asks one to relate the content of experience to what he publicly professes. Since one can easily deny what he experiences, a measure of real humility is presupposed. The less public the data are, the more convenient it is for ignorance and pride to deny them. A guilty person can stand before the court and plead, "Not guilty." A severely injured person can reply, "Pain has no reality; it is an error of the material sense." Because knowledge by acquaintance asks for a correlation of experience and profession, it calls for much greater spiritual preparation than knowledge by inference.

Knowledge by moral self-acceptance asks for a spiritual willingness to be morally transformed by the realities that already hold one. The content of experience must be related to the total self, not simply to what one professes. Thus, the spiritual preparation is the greatest. The third species of truth—truth as personal rectitude—has no existence until one closes the gap between what he is and what he ought to be. The whole person must be spiritually drawn into the task. This means that one cannot even begin the third method of knowing until he has won a decided spiritual victory in his heart. One will not recognize the content of the moral and spiritual environment until he is humble, for duty is not known until one stands within the center of duty.

No profound truth can be perceived until all three methods are effectively blended. One cannot say, "I know my neighbor," let alone, "I know God," until he submits to the witness of the fourfold environment—physical, rational, aesthetic, and moral and spiritual. To know a friend calls for the verdict of sense perception ("the friend is warm"), the faculty of judgment ("the friend is Norwegian"), and the moral sense ("the friend is kind"). The assertion, "This is my friend," cannot be established either by logic or by science. There is no straight-line way to prove the reality of personality. Even as others do not know us until they are humble, so we do not know others until we are humble. The meaning of personality must be spiritually intuited. Whenever one attempts to establish our reality by speculative techniques, he arouses the judicial sentiment and we judge him guilty. He is guilty because he violates the claims of the moral and spiritual environment. He has no right to treat us as an object.

If we cannot approach one another without satisfying the claims of the moral and spiritual environment, how can we avoid these claims when approaching God? Is it easier to know God than a fellow citizen? We certainly dare not treat God as an object; he cannot be regarded as the conclusion to a rational argument. God must be spiritually experienced; he must be encountered in the dynamic of fellowship.

God, it seems, is always just beyond the reach of our interests. Although the dignity of our life is safeguarded by the divine vigil, we tend to transact all business in the impersonal corridors of the judicial sentiment. After the dignity of our lives has been vindicated, rather than seeking out God and thanking him, we turn to other interests.

Since it is advantageous to have God complete the moral cycle by answering to the judicial sentiment, it might appear that we are guilty of using God as a means to our own calculated ends. But such is not the case. Although we look to God to complete the moral cycle, we are held in this necessity from existence itself. Since we are made in God's image, we cannot be indifferent to those who abuse us. We can more easily flee from the universe than we can flee from the presence of God, for in him we live and move and are. "If I ascend to heaven, thou art there! If I make my bed in Sheol, thou art there! If I take the wings of the morning and dwell in the uttermost parts of the sea, even there thy hand shall lead me, and thy right hand shall hold me" (Psalm 139:8-10). Therefore, if the charge of culpability is to be leveled anywhere, this is not the place. God has made certain that the whole human race shall look to him for spiritual as well as physical and rational well-being.

Some might despair of ever enjoying fellowship with God. They err. We *know* the preconditions of fellowship because we are morally *responsible* for knowing—thus decrees the third condition of knowing, a condition that holds us from existence itself. Since we are able to discover that God is a person, we are equally able to discover the terms of fellowship; for the second piece of information is analytically implied in the first. If one admits that God is a person, but despairs of ever knowing God through acquaintance, he contradicts himself.

5. THE MORAL PREDICAMENT

From the very beginning we have admitted that we depend on powers greater than ourselves. These powers, we now know, center in God. All we have and are is a gracious gift. "What have you that you did not receive? If then you received it, why do you boast as if it were not a gift?" (I Corinthians 4:7). Even our ability to strive and get gain is from God. Without him we can do nothing. "Beware lest you say in your heart, 'My power and the might of my hand have gotten me this wealth.' You shall remember the Lord your God, for it is he who gives you power to get wealth; that he may confirm his covenant which he swore to your fathers, as at this day" (Deuteronomy 8:17-18). This means that if we fail to be held by spontaneous sentiments of gratitude toward God, we sin.

Since this is the case, it would seem that we ought to get on with it. But this is easier said than done. Though we may sincerely *want* to be held by expressions of gratitude for all God has done, we have no power to make good this intention. We simply cannot convert our affections. "Can the Ethiopian change his skin or the leopard his spots? Then also you can do good who are accustomed to do evil" (Jeremiah 13:23). The more we consciously strive to arouse sentiments of spontaneous gratitude, the more we are

Preparations for Meeting God

betrayed into what I call a "moral predicament." Each effort to escape this predicament draws us all the more deeply into it. We are like wretches in a pool of quicksand: our very determination to escape lowers us all the deeper into the liquid death.

Here is a pithy summary of the moral predicament: *Although it is evil to be morally indifferent to those who do us favors, not only are we not held by a spontaneous sense of gratitude when we contemplate the divine favors, but we have insufficient moral resources to convert ourselves.* The more we *try* to be grateful, the more affected, and thus the less moral, our attitude becomes. We may wring our hands, meditate with our faces toward heaven, or drone out holy desires to have fellowship with God; but at the end of each religious exercise we end as spectators who acknowledge a moral task greater than we can meet. We cannot thank God unless we have fellowship with God; but our very want of thankfulness is itself a barrier to fellowship. Which way can we turn?

It would be very easy for one to *pretend* that he has feelings of spontaneous gratitude to God, but this surely would conduce to folly. "If we say we have no sin, we deceive ourselves, and the truth is not in us" (I John 1:8). Carlyle observes, in this connection, that the greatest of faults is to be conscious of none. Since an omniscient God forms the environment in which man lives and moves and is, holy eyes scrutinize our every thought and intention. "O Lord, thou hast searched me and known me! Thou knowest when I sit down and when I rise up; thou discernest my thoughts from afar. Thou searchest out my path and my lying down, and art acquainted with all my ways" (Psalm 139:1-3). A resolution to be transparently honest before God may not secure fellowship, but it at least provides a clean moral platform on which to build. We cannot deceive God.

I must confess that no fruit of the third method of knowing has proved more puzzling than the moral predicament. We admit we ought to be held by spontaneous sentiments of gratitude, yet we have no moral resources to convert ourselves. If we were grateful by nature, we would fulfill rectitude out of unconscious necessity.

The moral predicament is serious because it throttles the very possibility of fellowship. Fellowship is a daughter of spiritual spontaneity; it is not brought into being by legal or rational striving. But until we are personally acquainted with God, we really do not know God, for personality must be experienced to be known.

Although we speak of God as "personal," William James would be quick to point out that, functionally and pragmatically, we *mean* the same thing that Aristotle meant by the unmoved mover. God is an ultimacy who explains areas in our life that we happen to call important. We postulate God to explain our participation in the moral and spiritual environment, while Aristotle postulated God to explain motion and rest in nature. But what is the functional difference between these two efforts? Until we know God by acquaintance, there is none.

6. THE CHARACTER OF GOD

One phase of the moral predicament must now be carefully examined, for it may help us resolve our difficulty. Suppose the moral predicament *does* exist. Are we culpable for this fact? Can we be blamed for failing in what we cannot do? Blind people cannot see color, and we cannot arouse spontaneous sentiments of gratitude; but may either of us be meaningfully blamed? It would seem not.

As I meditated further, I discovered that an important phase of our relation to God has not yet been explored. What if it can be shown that God completes the moral cycle from a necessity that is immanent in his own character? Would this not immediately relieve the moral predicament? Just as God exists of necessity,* so he completes the moral cycle of necessity; and just as we need not

---

* In asserting that God exists of necessity, we are not appealing to the ontological argument. Kierkegaard has given the *coup de grâce* to the Anselmic dream of passing from the idea of God to the existence of God. (See Kierkegaard, *Concluding Unscientific Postscript* [Princeton University Press], p. 298.) We here argue from within the Thomistic-Kantian tradition. If *anything* exists, something exists of necessity. This necessity is God. The argument from contingency is dialectically more compelling than that drawn from the idea of an all-perfect being.

Preparations for Meeting God

thank God for his existence, so we need not thank him for completing the moral cycle. If this accords with truth, the case is closed.

Some may charge us with probing into the secret things of God: "We have no present right to look into God's essence, for that privilege is reserved for the beatific vision. We must *believe*, not question." This is all well and good, but what should we believe? Unless we can spell out the terms of fellowship, we cannot prepare to meet God.

The truth is, we already know the essence of God. God is perfect rectitude. God unfailingly defends our dignity by answering to the judicial sentiment. To argue otherwise would be repugnant to truth. Were we to assert that God is *not* held by a necessity to judge those who mistreat us, we would obscure the clearest element in our moral experience; for our reliance on God is woven into the very fabric of existence itself. It is impossible to have fellowship with wicked people. But it is not we who judge the wicked; it is God who judges them through us. We are only vessels through which a duly authorized moral tribunal works. We have no native rights to judge one another. "For there is no authority except from God" (Romans 13:1). This is why we cannot avoid believing that God completes the moral cycle out of a necessity that resides in his own character. We are only saying, in more elaborate language, that God is God. God and an upright man are held by similar attitudes toward justice and injustice, for the moral and spiritual environment is common to both. The more perfect man is, the more like God he becomes.

But some may ask, "Are we not limiting God? Isn't a sovereign God free to do whatever he wants?" Certainly God is free—absolutely free. Freedom means that one acts in accord with his nature; and it *is* in accord with God's nature to see to the judgment of those who abuse us. This in no way impedes sovereignty.

It is not we who limit God, but God who limits our power of apprehending him. We perceive God in and through the claims of the moral and spiritual environment, for we live and move and are in God.

Others may add, "But if we cannot trust a fellow human unless he shows signs of receiving our dignity, neither can we trust God unless he shows similar signs; in which case we place an abstract rule above God, and God is no longer sovereign." The objection fails to respect our true relation to God. We do not turn God's standards back on God, for it is God himself who judges immoral people through us. A house divided against itself cannot stand. Were it not that we live and move and are in God, we should never know what duty is. We should be brutes. Dissolve our confidence that God completes the moral cycle, and the very meaning of rectitude collapses.

The moral and spiritual environment admits of no exceptions. Whenever a person enters the circle of nearness—be he God or man—we *cannot* extend fellowship until he shows signs of receiving the dignity of our person. This necessity is not subject to the control of our will, for we are held by an a priori expectation. But this expectation in no way justifies the charge that we judge God by a standard higher than God. A discriminating mind will see that when we look to God for evidences that he is God, we are already piously submitting to God; for God himself, as we have shown, makes up the claims of the moral and spiritual environment. *This means that the character of God is the norm by which we test for the character of God.* If a cosmic being appeared before us, but showed no signs of truth and justice, we would know that he was not God. The devil is the father of all lies. False religions deserve their title because they appeal to a supreme being whose character is not continuous with the claims of the moral and spiritual environment.

Christian theologians are usually more chary of this structure than secular philosophers. This is explained by their zeal to safeguard the sovereignty of God. I commend them in this, for their caution reflects a genuine respect for the divine integrity. But their attitude ceases to be praiseworthy when it dulls the mind to see and defend truth. Suppose a religious prophet said, "God delights in those who commit murder." Would a morally upright theologian assign this to God? The answer is plain. He would not because he

Preparations for Meeting God

could not, and he could not because the claims of the moral and spiritual environment would be violated. This shows that the theologian, down deep in his heart, really believes the position we are defending. And believing it, he ought to acknowledge it.

Thus, it is wide of the mark to say that we judge God by a rule that is metaphysically more ultimate than God. We test for God, to be sure, but God himself is the author of our expectation that God will show signs of rectitude. If one looks to fellowship with God, he must know what kind of evidences to expect when God reveals himself. A moral man honors God by resolutely refusing to worship non-God. Plato elevated the Good above God, but the Christian does not. The Christian judges God by God.

This accounts for both the purity of the standard and our immutable right to apply it. Those who mistreat us are guilty; this is a moral absolute. Night or day, now or at the hour of our death, we are calmly confident that God answers to the judicial sentiment by a necessity that is immanent in his own character. We are relieved of any fear that the intrinsic value of our life will be revised in the light of shifting standards, for the character of God is the fixed point for defining our spiritual dignity. Were it not for this unassailable truth, the meaning of decency would immediately collapse.

One is not rightly related to God, and thus does not rightly know God, unless he recognizes that the very character of God issues in a moral guardianship of those who are made in his image. Either we ground our hope in the person of God, or we are betrayed into a capital error from the very start.

Rather than unworthily intruding into the counsels of God, therefore, our contention that God necessarily defends human dignity is simply another way of saying that God is God. He is perfectly held by the same moral necessities that hold an upright man imperfectly. Rectitude consists in a spontaneity that is unconscious of lawful necessity; and God enjoys perfect rectitude.

If we cannnot believe that our dignity is grounded in God, there is no way of disproving the extreme charge that man's moral standards are so different from those of God that what man calls good, God calls bad. In this event, our very effort to clarify the relation between time and eternity would be nullified. We would be agnostic regarding the divine standards. It would be meaningless to speak of "moral preconditions when approaching God," for we would be devoid of any norm by which to anticipate the nature of such conditions.

One may strongly disagree with what William Ellery Channing finally did with his assertion, but it is difficult to deny the truth of the assertion itself; namely, that if we have no moral equipment with which to judge what agrees or disagrees with the character of God, then what we *think* is consistent with perfect rectitude may, when the scrolls of eternity are unrolled, be found consistent with malignity and error.

But back to what originally brought on this discussion. Let us not lose sight of the problem before us. We inquired whether we might be relieved of the moral predicament on the ground that God must defend our dignity out of a necessity that is immanent in his own character. Having shown that it is both spiritually decorous and rationally consistent to believe that God *does* defend our lives out of such a necessity, we may now proceed with the question: "Does this necessity relieve us of the moral predicament?"

When one judges the issue by the third method of knowing, the answer is decidedly in the negative. Even though an act of kindness is performed out of necessities that flow from moral character itself, the one benefited is in no way exempt from the necessity of expressing spontaneous feelings of gratitude. Suppose we risk our lives to save a friend from a burning building. Although we are borne along by uncalculated, spontaneous courage, this absence of forecast in no way nullifies the fact that, at a convenient moment, a word of gratitude must be given. And if such an expression is not forthcoming—when opportunities to do so exist— the one we have rescued is culpable.

There is no reason to believe that any other principle holds in the case of our relation to God. Even though God completes the moral cycle by a necessity that is immanent in his own character, we are morally culpable if we fail to be held by spontaneous sentiments of gratitude for all God has done. And so, we are cast back on the moral predicament; for even though we may *desire* to be held by a natural love for God we lack the power to convert ourselves. We are not free, for there is discord in our affections.

7. THE UNIVOCAL POINT OF IDENTITY BETWEEN TIME AND ETERNITY

Although the problem of time and eternity is common to both philosophy and theology, the labors of the theologians are generally less profound than those of the philosophers. This is due to their refusal to acknowledge a univocal point of identity between time and eternity. The theologians make two separate mistakes. They err in thinking that the problem of time and eternity *can* be solved without affirming a point of identity, and they err in thinking that the affirming of such a point would either anthropomorphize God or deify man.

Since man is made in the image of God, man shares in the life of God whenever he makes contact with ultimate elements in either the rational, aesthetic, or moral and spiritual environment.* The true, the beautiful, and the good find their metaphysical status in God. And man comprehends each sphere through a specific point of contact: the law of contradiction, the law of proportion, and the law of life respectively. God is truth; God is beauty; and God is love. But since the third method of knowing has restricted itself to the claims of the moral and spiritual environment, it is

---

* We omit the physical environment because it is the field on which elements in the other environments express themselves. For example, by our transcendental participation in the law of proportion, we perceive beauty in nature; and this perception, in some way, is a perception of God. Knowing God, we are reminded of him in nature. Cf. Psalm 19:1 and Romans 1:20. At this point Plato and the Pythagoreans were not far from the kingdom. Augustine properly affirms that not only is God the light by which we see truth, but he is also the truth seen.

only right, in the interests of economy, that we limit our inquiry to this one point of contact.

We may conceive of this point of contact in either the *broad* or the *narrow* sense. The total claims of the moral and spiritual environment make up the broad point of contact between God and man, for God himself forms the very stuff of this environment. The narrow point of contact is the judicial sentiment. It is narrow because it focuses our attention on one particularly pure aspect of the moral transaction between God and man. And because it is narrow, it is also more precise. Once we see why the judicial sentiment is the point of contact in the narrow sense, we shall also see why the moral and spiritual environment is the point of contact in the broad sense.

The judicial sentiment is the guardian of our dignity. When right moral conditions prevail and our life is respected, it blends into the background and is dormant. But when our dignity is violated, it rushes forward to defend the life. It remains rigidly alert until the offending party propitiates it by meeting the right moral conditions. We have no active part in either the arousing or the subduing of the judicial sentiment. The entire transaction occurs without authorization from our will. The judicial sentiment is deaf to everything but an immoral act. We have no power to awaken it, and we have no power to placate it. This is only to say, as we have said before, that valid judgment of another life is the judgment of God working through us. Whoever offends the image of God offends God. Only God can judge, and only God can forgive. This is why the judicial sentiment is our most precise point of contact between time and eternity. A man is in contact with God, and thus should acknowledge it, whenever he entertains an aroused judicial sentiment; for the voice of the judicial sentiment *is* the voice of God. The significance of this will develop as we proceed.

This justifies a further word about Christ's counsel, "Judge not, that you be not judged." An aroused judicial sentiment, when morally pure, is not our own judgment; it is God judging others through us. Hence, the counsel of Christ is not offended until we sully the purity of the judicial sentiment by unlovely feelings. But the moment we do this, we become sinners; for we try to complete the moral cycle without help from God. Either we wait on God to complete this cycle, or we violate rectitude. And there are three ways—and only three—that God does this. First, by our going to the offending party and in a friendly tone asking him to apologize. Second, by summoning a duly appointed officer. Third, by submitting to the ambiguity of history and waiting for the final judgment. But sinners are tempted to reject all three alternatives. Suppose they have been offended while riding in their car. First, they are too cowardly to confront the other driver. Second, the incident is too small to be reported to an officer. Third, they are too anxious for settlement to wait for the final judgment. So, they take the law into their own hands. They think or say unkind things about the other driver. At this instant they violate the counsel of Christ, for they usurp a prerogative that belongs to God alone.

I am not unfamiliar with the clamant protests of those who say that if God and man have anything in common, the Creator-creature relation is effaced and God no longer rules man with a sovereignty that is metaphysically discontinuous with creation. But do these zealots realize what they are asserting? Unless God and man have something in common, it is impossible to make meaningful judgments about God. Hence, if one elects to guard God's sovereignty by denying that God and man share some point of identity, he should prepare for the fact that nothing significant can be known or said about God—not even that there is a God, let alone that God is a person. God and man cannot meaningfully be compared unless they have something in common. This is true of all analogies. If we say, "The mind is to the soul as the eye is to the body," the univocal element is "light" or "guide." And if we say, "A steamship is like a canoe," the univocal element is "force-propelled conveyance for water transport." But what element could God and man possibly have in common, save the moral and spiritual environment?

And when I say common, I mean common, for the issue is too

critical to be obscured by a slippery use of language. *I now mean, even as I shall continue to mean, that the moral and spiritual environment on the finite level is precisely of the same stuff as the moral and spiritual environment on the divine level; and that it is not improper to say that God is perfectly held by standards that hold an upright man imperfectly.** God's moral nature issues in a praise of the good and a condemnation of the bad; and so does that of an upright man. God defends justice and condemns injustice; and so does an upright man. "Thus says the Lord God: Enough, O princes of Israel! Put away violence and oppression, and execute justice and righteousness; cease your evictions of my people, says the Lord God. You shall have just balances, a just ephah, and a just bath" (Ezekiel 45:9-10). This is only another way of saying that God and an upright man share the same moral and spiritual environment. When our affections are transformed by the claims of this environment, we become good. But God is good by nature.

I realize how blasphemous this will sound to those who cower before Feuerbach's charge that man has made God in his own image and that all theology is nothing but anthropology. I can only say, in reply, that it is foolish to correct one error by introducing a new one. If the meaning of God's character cannot be anticipated by information drawn from our own conception of decency, what significance is conveyed by the term "God"? And how can God be distinguished from other unknowables? These are extremely serious problems.

Our position does not imply pantheism. We speak only of a common *environment*, not a common essence. Beings of incompatible orders can share the same environment without sharing the same essence, as when human beings and brutes breathe the same air. Man's essence consists in personality expressed

---

* This is only a manner of speaking, of course, for the divine life confronts no outside environment. An upright man completes his life in God, while God completes his life in himself. God is held by affections that inhere in his own character. But this distinction in no way alters the truth that God and an upright man have identical attitudes toward good and evil, justice and injustice.

through moral and rational self-transcendence, while that of the brute does not. God is uncreated, self-generating essence, while man is created, dependent essence. Yet, both share the same moral and spiritual environment. Man lives, and moves, and is in God. The defense of life, and the condemnation of those who mistreat it, are spontaneous moral sentiments that make up the characters of both God and an upright man. The third method of knowing safeguards God's transcendence not only by showing that creation is dependent on God for its being, but also by showing that creation is judged by a norm which flows from the very substance of the divine character.

Since man lives and moves and is in God, at least two analogical predications about God can be made. First, "God is a person." A person, let us recall, is "freedom expressed through moral self-consciousness." Second, "God praises justice and condemns injustice out of a necessity that resides in his own character."

If modern theologians would only heed the realities that already hold them, they would immediately perceive that most of the debate about "point of contact" is mere sophomoric quibbling. God is "wholly other" only in a very special sense. One cannot even walk down the street without participating in a moral and spiritual environment that is common to both God and an upright man. God is immanent as well as transcendent. Theologians ought to recognize that when others are unkind to them, or when their rights are violated, the judicial sentiment is aroused; and that the judicial sentiment, on analysis, is the voice of a moral tribunal that outreaches human authority. Inconsiderate people are responsible to God. If one nullifies this point of contact, the entire significance of the moral life collapses. Man is left with nothing but tastes and feelings to guide him through social tensions.

Possibly no student of moral philosophy has expressed the matter more effectively than John Stuart Mill. His language is as beautiful as his arguments are persuasive. "Here, then, I take my stand on the acknowledged principle of logic and of morality, that when we mean different things we have no right to call them by the same name, and to apply to them the same predicates, moral and intellectual. Language has no meaning for the words Just, Merciful, Benevolent, save that in which we predicate them of our fellow-creatures; and unless that is what we intend to express by them, we have no business to employ the words. If in affirming them of God we do not mean to affirm these very qualities, differing only as greater in degree, we are neither philosophically nor morally entitled to affirm them at all. . . . If in ascribing goodness to God I do not mean what I mean by goodness; if I do not mean the goodness of which I have some knowledge, but an incomprehensible attribute of an incomprehensible substance, which for aught I know may be a totally different quality from that which I love and venerate . . . what do I mean by calling it goodness? and what reason have I for venerating it? If I know nothing about what the attribute is, I cannot tell that it is a proper object of veneration. To say that God's goodness may be different in kind from man's goodness, what is it but saying, with a slight change of phraseology, that God may possibly not be good? To assert in words what we do not think in meaning, is as suitable a definition as can be given of a moral falsehood. Besides, suppose that certain unknown attributes are ascribed to the Deity in a religion the external evidences of which are so conclusive to my mind as effectually to convince me that it comes from God. Unless I believe God to possess the same moral attributes which I find, in however inferior a degree, in a good man, what ground of assurance have I of God's veracity? All trust in a Revelation presupposes a conviction that God's attributes are the same, in all but degree, with the best human attributes."*

If David Hume were here to speak, he doubtless would say that our discussion is quite void of meaning. To speak about a "point of contact with God," when we have no information about God, is mere prattle. Since we are empirically closed up to the condi-

* *An Examination of Sir William Hamilton's Philosophy* (Longmans, Green and Co.), pp. 127-128.

tions of time—while God presumably is not—we cannot make meaningful predications about God.

As might be suspected, Hume's difficulty stems from his failure to take a close look at the realities that already hold him from existence itself. The moral and spiritual environment is *not* subject to the limitations of time. It is of the stuff of eternity. Hence, we forthrightly reject the theory of knowledge which inspired Hume's philosophy. We proceed to God by way of an intuitive participation in the moral and spiritual environment, not by way of Lockian percepts. This is an extremely important difference to observe.

Others believe that the problem of predication can be solved on the faith that God has authorized a book, church, or priestly caste to witness to his will; and that if one will only submit himself to such authority he will assuredly gain fellowship with God.

The third method of knowing does not for a moment *deny* that God may have elected one, or several, of these means to bridge the gap between time and eternity. This can only be settled by a patient examination of relevant evidences. But if God and man are not analogically related, one can posit as many mediators as he wants, and we yet are left with moral skepticism.

If we submit to a particular book, church, or priestly caste, does it mean that we no longer need to make decisions that decide our destiny? If so, the counsel of Kierkegaard is again germane. Whenever individuals rely on objective security as an escape from moral decision, they jeopardize their own individuality. It would hardly be appropriate to repeat Kierkegaard's incisive arguments here. We need only say, as has been said before, that individuality *consists* in ethical decision; for the real man is the moral man. Neither book, church, nor priestly caste can relieve us of the responsibility of closing the gap between the descriptive essence and the imperative essence; and any attempt to do so would rob us of selfhood.

Or is it meant that if we yield to a book, church, or priestly caste, we shall gain information about God that would otherwise remain inaccessible? If so, it is all the more necessary that the problem of meaningful predication be faced. If we cannot anticipate the character of God by using elements drawn from the moral and spiritual environment, then by the same token we have no way of judging the character of God's representative, since this decision, though one step removed, involves the same difficulty. Unless we can meaningfully anticipate God's standards of rectitude, it may turn out that the book, church, or priestly caste that is least moral on human standards is most moral on divine standards; and we are once again left with skepticism.

Some may rise to a final defense by asserting that it *is* our religious *duty* to submit to God's representative, whether we understand the reasons or not; for faith is a venture, a leap of the will in the face of paradox and objective uncertainty. To look for evidences is a sign of unbelief. Any delay will only increase our chances of losing eternal happiness.

This is a specious claim. Nothing is our duty unless it is analytically part of a duty to which we are already committed; and in all time it will never be a rational man's duty to submit to demands which outrage larger elements in our fourfold environment—physical, rational, aesthetic, and moral and spiritual. God addresses us as intelligent creatures; his word is never discontinuous with truth.

8. THE PROBLEM OF GOD'S FINITUDE

Since the moral and spiritual environment forms the broad point of contact between time and eternity, we now have a fruitful norm by which to decide between true and spurious preternatural powers. Since God completes the moral cycle by answering to the judicial sentiment, it follows that whoever or whatever arouses the judicial sentiment is not God; for God is not divided against himself.

This is a gain of no small importance. Whenever we are confronted with doctrines or practices which outrage our sense of decency, we can be negatively assured that they do not originate in God; for the God of the judicial sentiment, by nature and by choice, is committed to the praise of justice and the condemnation of injustice. Whenever God deals with us, he respects the sanctity of our individuality; he never offends his own image.

Let us not be unhinged by those who charge that if God defends our dignity from moral necessity, he is finite in power. When such a charge is evaluated by moral self-acceptance, we quickly see why it is invalid. We are finite creatures, for example, but what makes us finite? We are finite because we cannot actuate our desires. We do not have power to resolve the moral predicament. We experience a conflict between what we are and what we ought to be.

In the instance of God, however, conformity in every area of his being is perfect. Completing the moral cycle by answering to the judicial sentiment is not an onerous task. It is an activity born of interests and affections that reside in the divine character itself. God is not finite unless conditions prevent him from doing his will. But God *wills* to defend our dignity, for we are made in his image. Therefore, such a necessity does not imply finitude.

The God of Plato is really finite. Held by an earnest desire to meet the conditions of the Good, God struggled to inform nature with the perfection of the world of Ideas. But he was frustrated by a refusal of matter to yield to the creative overtures. The time-space receptacle is the passive cause of evil. Since God did the best he could, natural evil must be assigned to a deficiency in matter, not a deficiency in God's character. "Then God, if he be good, is not the author of all things, as the many assert, but he is the cause of a few things only, and not of most things that occur to men. For few are the goods of human life, and many are the evils, and the good is to be attributed to God alone; of the evils the causes are to be sought elsewhere, and not in him. . . . Let this then be one of our rules and principles concerning the gods, to which our poets and reciters will be expected to conform—that God is not the author of all things, but of good only."*

* Plato, *Republic*, 379-380.

9. THE PROBLEM OF EVIL

No sooner has this been said, however, than we face another serious charge. If God's character commits him to the defense of justice and the condemnation of injustice, and if God is sovereign over even matter itself, how can we explain the many evils in nature? Who can reflect on the tragedy of idiocy without wondering whether God is deficient in power, and thus is finite; or whether he takes pleasure in creating idiots, and thus arouses the judicial sentiment in us? If God is perfectly held by the same standards that hold an upright man imperfectly, why does natural evil outrage our sense of fair play?

The ancients formulated the problem very succinctly: Either God wants to prevent evil, and he cannot do it; or he can do it and does not want to; or he neither wishes to nor can do it; or he wishes to and can do it. If he has the desire without the power, he is impotent; if he can, but has not the desire, he has a malice which we cannot attribute to him; if he has neither the power nor the desire, he is both impotent and evil, and consequently not God; if he has the desire and the power, whence then comes evil, or why does he not prevent it? "Thou who art of purer eyes than to behold evil and canst not look on wrong, why dost thou look on faithless men, and art silent when the wicked swallows up the man more righteous than he?" (Habakkuk 1:13).

Since we shall say more about the problem when we reach the end of the book, our word at this point must, of necessity, be provisional. I do not believe that the difficulty can be fully resolved until we have fellowship with God; and fellowship cannot be had until we are confronted with the claims of Jesus Christ. But more about this later.

Although the third method of knowing assures us that God is good, this assurance does not contain a catalogue of ways that the divine life must express itself if the works of God are to be harmonious with what we ourselves consider good. Moral self-acceptance has only proved that God defends justice and condemns injustice by a necessity that is immanent in his own character. But this is insufficient to serve as a detailed revelation of the ways and manners of the divine life.

The significance of one's actions cannot be accurately inferred from an external review of conduct. "For many acts are merely means to some hidden end, and, in general, much is to learn before one man can pronounce with certainty on the action of another."* *Full* explanations come by personal revelation. "Dr. Adams told me that Johnson, while he was at Pembroke College, 'was caressed and loved by all about him, was a gay and frolicksome fellow, and passed there the happiest part of his life.' But this is a striking proof of the fallacy of appearances, and how little any of us know of the real internal state even of those whom we see most frequently; for the truth is, that he was then depressed by poverty, and irritated by disease."†

Suppose we refuse to greet a friend as we walk into a bank. From the point of view of the friend, it surely seems that we are violating the conditions of fellowship; but this need not, in fact, be the case. We may possibly be followed by a gunman who would do bodily harm to any whom we might salute. In such an event we prove our loyalty by not speaking. And so in the instance of God. The presence of idiots may seem to suggest that God is not on the side of human values; but when the counsels of eternity are revealed, and we become fully acquainted with the immanent Logos in the divine wisdom, we then may be given ample reasons why the decreeing of this type of universe is quite harmonious with the claims of the moral and spiritual environment.

I do not rest my case on this approach, however, for it is too easily abused. Theology can be used as an engine in the defense of pride; it can justify "moral holidays." When religious enthusiasts want to sanctify their own acts of injustice, they simply point out that inequality is part of the mystery of the divine decrees.

---

* Marcus Aurelius, *Thoughts*, XI, 18.
† Boswell, *Life of Samuel Johnson LL.D.* (Britannica), pp. 15-16.

This relieves them of any duty to bring the social order into conformity with perfect justice—a wretched outcome, indeed.

We by no means imply that history will ever actuate perfect equality, for some men are born to lead, others to follow. Samuel Johnson never wearied of pressing home this point in his defense of aristocracy. But Johnson failed to appreciate the normative power of the ideal. Ideal equality must judge actual inequality; otherwise the *inevitability* of inequality will convert to the *necessity* of inequality. The ideal and the real must be kept in constant moral tension. By struggling for the ideal, Marx was wiser than Johnson; but by being sensitive to the limits of the real, Johnson was wiser than Marx.

Thus, there is another, and far more important, consideration. Those who see evil in nature, but not in themselves, are guilty of projecting their own moral optimism into metaphysics. They think that a great "chain of being" links time and eternity in one logical or ontological plenitude. "The order and connection of ideas is the same as the order and connection of things."* This chain is forged on the optimistic negative assumption that no causal relation exists between evil in nature and sin in the heart. But what if the world is under the judicial displeasure of God? What if men are sinners? Evil in nature would then be a partial proof that the present order is subject to God's wrath. Nature must be redeemed. "For the creation waits with eager longing for the revealing of the sons of God; for the creation was subjected to futility, not of its own will but by the will of him who subjected it in hope; because the creation itself will be set free from its bondage to decay and obtain the glorious liberty of the children of God. We know that the whole creation has been groaning in travail together until now" (Romans 8:19-22). Although critics are quick to see evil in nature, they seldom see evil in themselves; and because of this oversight they do not consider the possibility that nature is federally involved in the sin of man. "Cursed is the ground because of you; in toil you shall eat of it all the days of your

---

* Spinoza, *The Ethics*, Part II, Proposition 7.

life; thorns and thistles it shall bring forth to you; and you shall eat the plants of the field" (Genesis 3:17-18). Philosophers ought to inquire whether God's judicial sentiment is aroused when *philosophers* fail to humble themselves. The problem of evil would then be seen from a new perspective.

Since man stands in a created relation to God, his dignity as an individual is a derived virtue. It has no per se status. When man effaces the Creator-creature relation, therefore, he separates himself from the source of his dignity. In trying to become everything, he becomes nothing. Mingling his identity with the flux of time, he is immediately plagued by the threat of nothingness. All sorts of anxieties and neuroses are excited within him. And his difficulty always traces back to the same error: pride transmutes *derived* dignity into *inherent* dignity.

Egoistically inflated by a contemplation of his own goodness, man thinks it is perfectly decorous to press moral demands on God. Only the blindness of personal sin could induce such arrogance, for a humble person will recognize that he is held in the relation of dependence from existence itself. God sustains human life from grace, not necessity.

This does not give us a direct answer to the problem of idiots, of course. But it does, at least, aim the inquiry in the right direction. Rather than confining oneself to an academic discussion about "mud, hair, and filth," a humble philosopher will be shattered by the terrible fact that he judges others for doing the very thing that he does to God. He judges ingrates guilty, while he himself is an ingrate.

I solemnly charge that until a person stands in a right moral relation to God, he is not in a spiritual position to probe into the delicate details of how an aroused judicial sentiment in God will express itself toward a disobedient creation; and as long as he is ignorant of this expression, he cannot decide whether it is wrong for God to afflict nature in a way that cannot be justified by human wisdom. "But, who are you, a man, to answer back to God? Will what is molded say to its molder, 'Why have you made me thus?' Has the potter no right over the clay, to make out of the same lump one vessel for beauty and another for menial use?" (Romans 9:20-21). In other words, a solution to the problem of evil must wait until we discover how a moral God will dispose of immoral man. And this can only be discovered by becoming acquainted with God. God must reveal the conditions of justice from the divine side.

Hence, only one really valid question may be raised: *Can we trust God?* Once we are satisfied that the one before us is actually God, the character of God becomes the standard by which we compare, and correct, our own finite notion of the good. In due time we shall complete this cycle of evidences. But just now we have insufficient data, for "grace and truth came through Jesus Christ" (John 1:17).

This Calvinistic emphasis may seem to conflict with our earlier endorsement of Mill's assertion that we can trust no one, terrestrial or celestial, who fails to show signs of goodness. The conflict is superficial. In proving this, let us distinguish two types of attitude. When we approach a person for the first time, we impose critical tests on him that are inappropriate when we learn to know him better; *for introductory standards are of a different quality than standards of intimacy.* When we appealed to Mill, we confined ourself to the qualities of character that the true God must evince if we are to be sure that he is the true God. Whether on earth or in heaven, we are powerless to trust a person unless he show signs of receiving the dignity of our person. If a cosmic being were to *claim* to be the true God, but support this with no evidence of rectitude, we would be assured by the moral and spiritual environment that we were doing business with other than the true God. Therefore, when we look for evidences which assure us that the person before us is really God, we glorify, rather than offend, the divine nature. Our refusal to yield to non-God is an honor to God. "I the Lord your God am a jealous God" (Exodus 20:5). Jealousy symbolizes God's displeasure with idolatry. If a man loves God, he proves it by the holy caution with which he directs his worship.

But once introductory tests have been met and the heart is assured that it *is* being confronted by the true God, one either shifts from introductory tests to the intimacy of fellowship, or he becomes an enemy of God. There is no middle ground. A person who prolongs critical tests proves he does not believe that he stands in the presence of God; or at least he proves that he is not spiritually interested in being transformed by the responsibilities of this relationship. To look for credentials higher than the will of God is an affront to God. This is where Plato made his capital mistake. He could not worship God because he placed the Good above God.

Mill erred in prolonging his critical attitude. Valid introductory tests never gave way to the pleasures of fellowship. This, I take it, accounts for the moral emptiness of his life. Mill was a giant in matters of the mind, but a child in matters of the spirit.

10. MORAL SELF–ACCEPTANCE AND THE TERMS OF FELLOWSHIP

If God and man share the same moral and spiritual environment, not only are we able to make meaningful predications about the divine nature, but we are supplied with a rather decisive way of going about the task of finding fellowship with God.

Since God and man are both persons, it is quite in harmony with good procedure to assert that a knowledge of how to have fellowship with God is analytically included in a knowledge of how men have fellowship with one another. If the moral and spiritual environment joins God and man in one lawful order, then the analogy between God and man ought to hold in all its pivotal points.

Once we approach the question by way of moral self-acceptance, it is not too difficult to name the condition that must be met before fellowship is born. A *person entering the circle of nearness must humble himself.* I do not mean that he must bow and scrape, as if we are his metaphysical superiors. I mean only that we are not at liberty to release the warmth of our personality until he stands in a right relation to the dignity of our lives. Regardless of how willing we may be to extend fellowship, our participation in the moral and spiritual environment makes it impossible to do so until proper moral conditions prevail. A proud and overweening attitude blocks the flow of fellowship as effectively as insulation blocks the flow of electricity.*

If this is an accurate representation of truth, it follows that from this point forward we may meaningfully speak of God's self-revelation; for fellowship exists only in revelation. Even as no one can extort fellowship from us (for we share our hearts as a free gift), so we would depart from right procedure if we supposed that one can extort fellowship from God. Fellowship is either cheerfully released or it does not exist at all. There is no third, or middle, condition. And if humility provides the occasion for men to reveal themselves, humility ought also to provide the occasion for God to reveal himself. But revelation must come from the divine side; otherwise we shall never have an acquaintance knowledge of God's person.

This leads us back to the meaning of moral rectitude. Whenever others are humble in our presence, and thus meet the terms of fellowship, we become guilty if we refuse to complete the cycle of moral response by revealing ourselves. It is evil to answer humility with pride. Fellowship is a solemn contract; neither party is at liberty to violate its terms without incurring guilt. Just as it is morally wrong to withhold goods from those who have paid for them, so it is morally wrong to withhold fellowship from those who humble themselves. This is clearly proved by the third condition of knowing.

Confident that I have not unduly pressed the univocal point between God and an upright man, I have no hesitation to venture the belief that even as God's character obliges him to defend

---

* This is not the *only* attitude that blocks fellowship, of course. Modern psychiatry and psychotherapy have found several others. But I choose this one as my paradigm because it most fruitfully gets us on with the job of discovering how to gain fellowship with God. A selection must be made in the interests of economy.

the dignity of our lives, so his character obliges him to reveal himself whenever the right moral conditions prevail. This will sound blasphemous to those whose theological and apologetical convictions have ossified. But to all who remain docile before the witness of God in the moral and spiritual environment, the assertion is but another way of enforcing the truth that God is God. He enjoys perfect rectitude.

This does not imply that an immanent attribute of benevolence releases God from an interest in the moral condition of those who look to him for fellowship. To the contrary. Our first encounter with the moral and spiritual environment established God's justice; for God completes the moral cycle by answering to the judicial sentiment. Therefore, *no* man can be received by God until right moral conditions prevail. " 'With what shall I come before the Lord, and bow myself before God on high? Shall I come before him with burnt offerings, with calves a year old? Will the Lord be pleased with thousands of rams, with ten thousands of rivers of oil? Shall I give my first-born for my transgression, the fruit of my body for the sin of my soul?' He has showed you, O man, what is good; and what does the Lord require of you but to do justice, and to love kindness, and to walk humbly with your God?" (Micah 6:6-8). To say that God can have fellowship with those who refuse to humble themselves, what is this but to say that God is not good? Neither God nor an upright man can extend fellowship until right moral conditions prevail.

In sum: *The minimal elements in fellowship oblige us to believe that God is under the same necessity to extend his life to the humble as he is to withhold it from the proud; and that his eternal approval of the humble is but the reverse side of his eternal disapproval of the proud.** "God opposes the proud, but gives grace to the humble" (James 4:6). Our right to believe this stems from the assurance that the claims of the moral and spiritual environment hold both God and man; and that the difference

---

* Reasons will be given to show why this assertion gives neither aid nor comfort to the spiritual complacency, *"Dieu pardonnera; c'est son métier."*

between rectitude in God and rectitude in man is (*mutatis mutandis*) one of degree and not of quality. God is the standard for measuring rectitude in man. Since we are made in the image of God, we must strive to conform ourselves to the will of God. "You, therefore, must be perfect, as your heavenly Father is perfect" (Matthew 5:48). "You shall be holy, for I am holy" (I Peter 1:16). Such admonitions would be pointless unless God and man shared the same moral and spiritual environment.

If a person shies away from the assertion that a univocal point of identity binds God and an upright man in like attitudes toward justice and injustice, he should prepare to deal with the live rational possibility that God may reveal himself under conditions that an upright man cannot anticipate—an eventuality that would spell complete moral disaster. If God does not extend fellowship in ways that can be named by a patient study of the manner in which we extend fellowship to one another, we have no sure way of answering those who say that God may confront man on terms which, when judged by our highest norm of rectitude, are contrary to goodness; in which case the lecher and the saint are equal authorities on how an individual may become acquainted with God. Whether men ought to be humble or proud could never be established in advance of the decision.

This seems to clinch the conviction that a refusal to meet the terms of fellowship is the only thing that stands in the way of a reconciliation between God and man.* If we fail to enter into fellowship with God, the third condition of knowing warns that the fault is solely ours. We *know* the terms of fellowship because we are morally *responsible* for knowing. "Humble yourselves before the Lord and he will exalt you" (James 4:10). To be humble before God means to conform ourselves to the total fact that

---

* This sweeping universal is premised on information gathered *up to this point*. The reader will err if he thinks this is the whole story. The terms of fellowship are more complex than we may suspect. The cross of Christ stands between sinful man and a holy God. But it would be apologetically imprudent to plunge into this complexity without working up to it by a patient application of the third method of knowing.

he is the sovereign author of all we have and are. Humility is proof that we see and accept this relation.

We can establish the point by a carefully directed application of moral self-acceptance. If we humble ourselves before others, and yet our act is not honored by their release of trust, the judicial sentiment is aroused and we judge them guilty. To refuse to extend fellowship, when the right conditions prevail, is a sure mark of character deterioration.

11. THE ANATOMY OF HUMILITY

Two things have now been established: first, that humility is the universal precondition of fellowship; second, that although there is no way of measuring quantities of humility, one yet can be confident that if he purifies his affections long enough a place will be reached where fellowship is enjoyed. The problem now is to decide how to go about making ourselves humble.

We cannot become humble by deliberate rational effort, of course, for artificially induced humility is as repugnant to moral self-acceptance as artificially induced gratitude. Nothing is moral unless it freely springs from the imperative essence. Humility before God, like sorrow for acts of evil toward one another, must be a free product of the unfree necessities of the moral and spiritual environment. But what can we do? Shall we simply sit by and wait for God to create feelings of humility in us?

Fearful that this might lead to indolence, I turned to a patient study of the anatomy of humility. At the end of this rewarding probe, I concluded that even as duty is enlarged by showing that new duty is analytically part of a duty already felt, so new experiences of humility can be released from an already existing body of humility. Humility, strangely enough, is its own father and mother. It cannot be sired by either volition or thought. Yet, without both volition and thought one will not place himself in the right condition for humility to extend itself. This is the paradox of humility.

My confidence in asserting this stems from experiences already reviewed. On at least two separate occasions new humility grew out of a quantity of humility that already held me.

The first experience was the honest admission that I am not the author of my own existence. The moment I had the mettle to submit to my own limitations, I was humbled by the realization that I am held by powers over which I have no direct control. Whether I shall continue to live from day to day cannot be established with certainty. The stuff of my existence is very tenuous. "What is your life? For you are a mist that appears for a little time and then vanishes" (James 4:14).

The second experience was a result of the first. The more I contemplated the place of my life in God, the more I recognized that a knowledge of God's benefits does not stir up feelings of spontaneous gratitude in my heart. A submission to the reality of metaphysical dependence made me humble before the reality of the moral predicament.

This was sufficient to assure me that humility is generated by a species of spiritual fission. Although we are powerless to make ourselves humble, we *can* take those steps which release humility into other areas of the life.

Humility increases itself in roughly this order: first, a native willingness to be honest; second, a critical review of the realities that already hold us; third, a moral submission to the claims of these realities. As each new step is taken, the eyes of the understanding behold aspects of the real which remain hidden to pride. Each new insight intensifies our humility. If one will not be honest, he will never recognize that he is a dependent creature; and if he will not submit to the reality of dependence he will never know that he is held by God; and if he will not submit to God he will never know the terms of fellowship. Each submission lays new deposits of humility on the heart; and these deposits, in turn, clarify the nature of the real. This again illustrates the truth we have stressed from the beginning: *One cannot perceive*

Preparations for Meeting God

ultimates until his affections *are in harmony with the moral and spiritual environment.*

Thus, there seemed to be no good reason to deny, and several good reasons to affirm, that if we let humility grow by spiritual fission a point would be reached when God would say, "It is enough!" If God's character obliges him to release fellowship whenever proper moral conditions prevail, it would seem that nothing but man's obdurate refusal to meet these conditions stands in the way of our experiencing the person of God. This appeared to be a valid conclusion. In any event, I determined to launch on it until evidences strong enough to challenge its claims could be found.

Chapter Seven

THE ADMISSION OF GUILT

1. A REVISION OF PROCEDURE

It had been my expectation that if I continued to lay new deposits of humility in my heart, the accumulation would eventually equal the quantity needed to release God's fellowship. But it did not take long to recognize that in following this procedure I was being untrue to the moral and spiritual environment. I had forsaken the consistency of my own method.

When a person enters the circle of nearness, we never look for a quantity of humility—as if the accepting of our dignity is a piecemeal affair, like adding twigs to make a fagot. There is no situation where a person is almost humble enough, though not quite. No time lapse is needed before the issue is drawn to a decision. We classify an individual with an immediate moral intuition, for in a flash we can sense whether he is in or out of fellowship. And there is no third possibility; he is either a friend or he is not.

Therefore, were we to say that God looks for a quantity of humility, while upright men look for a quality, we instantly should negate our assertion that God and man share the same moral and spiritual environment. Fellowship between persons is based on an analogy. But an analogy must hold in all of its pivotal points. Since men look for a particular quality of humility, we must argue that God likewise looks for this same quality. Fellowship between

The Admission of Guilt

men, and fellowship between God and man, are not comparable unless the two realms can be conceived in an analogous relation.

2. THE PARADOX OF HUMILITY

But a man is not humble until he sincerely, and with an eye to moral responsibility, denies that he is humble. Whoever makes humility an object of calculated interest is not the man he professes to be; for humility, like all other moral states, cannot be speculatively comprehended. A right expression of humility includes the swift spiritual denial that one is humble. "And as he was setting out on his journey, a man ran up and knelt before him, and asked him, 'Good Teacher, what must I do to inherit eternal life?' And Jesus said to him, 'Why do you call me good? No one is good but God alone'" (Mark 10:17-18).

Viewed academically, the paradox of humility is only a curiosity; but, viewed as an obstacle to be overcome before we can enjoy fellowship with God, it is an extremely serious matter. Although humility before God is the precondition of fellowship, the moment we deliberately strive to be humble we negate the very possibility of becoming humble. Whichever way we turn, we are defeated. Unless we are held by spontaneous sentiments of humility, we do not conform to rectitude; but the instant we make humility a calculated goal of striving we are betrayed into self-sufficiency.

As a possible way out of this paradox, I decided to argue that our inability to become humble is nothing but a more delicate expression of the moral predicament; and that just as we are impotent to arouse spontaneous sentiments of gratitude to God so we are impotent to arouse spontaneous expressions of humility. If the one issues in no culpability, neither does the other.

But I was too far along in moral self-acceptance to believe that such an expedient could relieve our difficulty. The paradox of humility cannot be included in the moral predicament for the obvious reason that becoming humble *is* within our power. We prove this every time we enter into fellowship, for humility is the very matrix of pleasant relations.

If humility is the universal precondition of fellowship, then such a condition, we must assuredly believe, holds in the instance of our having fellowship with God. Just as we are able to humble ourselves before one another, so in some way we are able to humble ourselves before God.

3. DIRECT AND INDIRECT FULFILLMENT

At an earlier point I said that Kant's dictum, "Thou canst, for thou oughtest," was acceptable only if a very important proviso were allowed. Let us now analyze and apply this proviso.

Kant restricted himself to what I call "direct fulfillment." A law cannot bind us unless we have resident moral ability to fulfill it. Such an approach is unacceptable, however, for it contradicts one of the most patent parts of our moral experience—that of "indirect fulfillment." Judged from within moral self-acceptance, an individual can satisfy rectitude in two different ways: either by spontaneously doing what is right or by spontaneously expressing sorrow for having failed. The gentle life is direct fulfillment, while the penitent life is indirect fulfillment. Both satisfy the claims of the moral and spiritual environment. Kant made the Pelagian mistake of thinking that man can only be held responsible for laws that he can directly meet.

Moral self-acceptance is not so naïve, of course, as to assert that a person can metamorphose his own character by moral or rational effort. Although we should have natural affections for God, and although we energetically strive to arouse such affections, neither knowledge nor striving can alter the core of our character. After every strategy of mind and will has been expended, we end with the admission that our affections are not naturally inclined toward humility. We are proud by nature and by choice. Mutinous impulses hold sway in our members.

But surely a despair of direct fulfillment does not justify a despair of indirect fulfillment. A moral defense of inactivity would be regrettable. Although we lack spiritual resources to stir up natural affections for God, we have ample native power to be sorry for our lack of such affections. A knowledge of what we *cannot* do should stimulate a search for what we *can* do.

The meaning of indirect fulfillment is perhaps no more beautifully illustrated than in the rare, but nonetheless real, instances where an act is unlawful as direct fulfillment, but lawful as indirect fulfillment. Suppose a weary, disheveled father has just returned from a long journey. As the children outdo each other in acts of love, the smallest one finally decides to get his father a glass of cool water. But as he brings the water into the living room, he has his thumb inside the glass, and the dirt from the day's play is slowly settling to the bottom. Judged as a direct fulfillment of law, the act is unworthy; but judged as indirect fulfillment the act is perfect. And the glint of joy in the father's eyes proves it.

Kant thought that if one wants to be moral, the procedure to follow is very simple. All he has to do is conform his life to canons of self-consistent conduct.

But in at least the instance of becoming humble, the individual who is too attentive to procedure will not only never be humble, but his chances of even recognizing rectitude will vanish. One is not humble unless he despairs of all lawful attempts to become humble. This is the irony of morals. Humility has no existence until the heart gives up all deliberate efforts to become humble.

A Kantian might say that this leads to moral inactivity, as if those who are indifferent to the ethical task have a greater chance of being moral than those who strive toward the mark with earnest devotion. The full truth is that neither the spiritually indolent nor the rationally ambitious can complete the terms of duty, though for opposite reasons. A careless person will never be humble because he does not try, while a legalist will never be humble because he tries improperly. The moral task, when done in the right way, is urgent, exciting, and intensely personal. But it must be done in the right way.

Let us put the matter to the test of moral self-acceptance. If an individual enters the circle of nearness and tries too hard to accept us, he becomes guilty to the degree that his effort is deliberate. The more he tries, the more affected his overtures become, and the more the judicial sentiment is aroused. An upright person does not look on fellowship as a prize for either rational or moral striving. He meets the conditions of fellowship without consciously trying.

Fellowship comes into being the instant one's affections are converted by the moral and spiritual environment. An overrationalized demeanor drives out fellowship. Fellowship exists only as one "lets himself go." One must walk up to another person and ask, "How are you?" Once the aura of humility is created, personality is free to flow.

4. THE TWO QUALITIES OF MORAL RESPONSE

Let us now distinguish between the two qualities of moral response. An individual may enter the circle of nearness and say, "I must respect you," and mean that he is compelled to do so out of legal or personal interests; or he may say, "I must respect you," and mean that he cannot turn aside from the obligation without outraging his own sense of dignity. These qualities of moral response are mutually exclusive. The first is born of autonomously inspired action: a desire to be accepted by others, a fear of legal sanctions, or a rational respect for rules of self-consistent conduct. The second is born of affections that receive their tone from the moral and spiritual environment.

Only the second quality of response has moral value. This is immediately proved by the third method of knowing. If an individual accepts us because he finds it to his interest, he arouses the judicial sentiment and we judge him guilty. He is guilty of interposing secondary considerations. The sheer presence of our person should place him under moral obligation.

Suppose a husband asks his wife if he *must* kiss her good night.

The Admission of Guilt

Her answer is, "You must, but not that kind of a must." What she means is this: "Unless a spontaneous affection for my person motivates you, your overtures are stripped of all moral value."

Let us give names to these two types of moral response, that we may henceforth refer to them with convenience. If one enters the circle of nearness and accepts us because of a fear of law, he is held by the *law of legal necessity*. But if he accepts us out of a moral compulsion that is unconscious of lawful necessity, he is carried away by the *law of the spirit of life*. The law of legal necessity may imply anything from mere rational assent to a groveling sense of enthrallment. The law of the spirit of life knows no such range, for it always is informed with a sense of cordial pleasure in doing what is right.

Quite the reverse of Kant, therefore, the third method of knowing contends that motives diminish in moral worth as one acts out of a conscious regard for law. An act done out of a fear of law is better than a deliberate transgression of law, to be sure, but an act with no consciousness of law is the best of all. Motives are impure unless they are fathered by a cordial participation in the moral and spiritual environment. A person who does the right out of a fear of law is not held by affections that flow from this participation. If he were moral, he would be moved by the same unconscious necessity that moves the stomach to perform digestion. Rectitude would be natural.

Let me illustrate this by another reference to the marital bond. Suppose a husband celebrates a wedding anniversary by bringing home a dozen dew-laden, American Beauty roses. His elated wife throws open the door and cries: "Honey, you remembered! Oh, thank you—thank you *very* much!" To which he dryly responds, "Don't mention it; it's my duty." With this single word, all moral worth vanishes. He instantly arouses the judicial sentiment in his wife; for, rather than being pleased with the flowers, she is morally offended. She knows that he does not love her; otherwise he would never place a higher value on an abstract duty than on the dignity of her person.

Lest there be misunderstanding, however, we are not suggestting that one can be moral without meeting the terms of law. Nothing is moral unless it is at least lawful. We call the imperative essence *imperative* for the very reason that, as the mainspring of our sense of duty, it has power to impose lawful demands on the soul. The issue before us is simply the quality an act must have if it is to be moral. One may enter the circle of nearness and make deliberate attempts to receive us. But since he is not held by a spontaneous sense of spiritual necessity, his effort is immoral. Unless an act fulfills law, it cannot be moral; but an act done out of lawful interests is not necessarily moral. It may be done in selfishness, malice, and so on. For example, children may apologize to each other because they are forced to do so. They meet the letter of the law, but their act is void of moral worth.

5. A CLARIFICATION OF DIRECTION

Once we recognize that humility before God has no moral value unless it is borne along by the law of the spirit of life, it is obvious that any calculated effort to meet the preconditions of fellowship is self-defeating; for it supposes, after the manner of Kant, that morality is formed of a chain of legal responses that can be anticipated with tolerable rational precision. When others enter the circle of nearness, they remain immoral unless they forfeit rational calculation. They are either held by unconscious spontaneity or they are culpable. The sheer presence of our person forces this moral disjunction.

As each major truth unfolds, a greater burden is placed on us to accept the realities that already hold us. Three such truths have been established: first, that humility is the universal precondition of fellowship; second, that humility is a quality, not a quantity; third, that this quality does not and cannot exist apart from the law of the spirit of life.

Comprehensive though these truths are, they are insufficient to direct us to an acquaintance with God. Much more information is

The Admission of Guilt

needed if we are going to know how to have fellowship with the ground of our being.

Thinking that I might have overlooked some important clue, I decided to hark back over the argument as I had developed it thus far. This proved to be a very helpful gesture, for my eye was soon drawn to an illustration that I had used. It pertained to the recovering of a young mother's rowboat from a muddy river. The illustration was not much in itself, but it did at least turn the discussion in the right direction; for soon afterward we were able to develop such crucial insights as the moral predicament, the univocal point of identity between God and man, and the insight that humility is the universal precondition of fellowship. But there was something about the illustration that made me wonder whether the best use had been made of it.

Now that I was back on familiar territory, I felt it would be rewarding if I deliberately reversed my question. Formerly I asked, "If a person receives a large favor, what responsibility does the moral and spiritual environment place on him?" And I answered, "He must show evidences of being held by spontaneous sentiments of gratitude." Let me now reverse this and ask, "If an individual is ungrateful for gifts and benefits, what moral conditions must he meet before he can be received back into fellowship?"

Suppose we have recovered the young mother's rowboat from the muddy river, only to have our act of sacrifice rebuffed with icy indifference. What moral conditions must the woman meet before she can be received into fellowship? The answer is obvious to all who accept the realities which already hold them when they encounter ingratitude. *She must offer a sincere apology.**

This truth can be illustrated in so many different ways that one

---

* This should not be pressed too mechanically, for we do not always demand an apology. At times we simply forget about the matter. At other times we recognize that we were at fault. And in rare cases the offended party disarms us by new acts of friendship. The details of moral conduct are not crucial for our study. An aroused judicial sentiment stays aroused until right moral conditions prevail; and *ordinarily* this calls for a word of apology.

is baffled by the abundance of available evidences. Suppose we are awakened late at night by a ringing telephone or a loud rapping on the door, only to find that some other party was sought. A knowledge of this careless intrusion immediately arouses the judicial sentiment. And thus it goes. An unjust accusation, an offense of protocol, a discourtesy, an embarrassment of our life, a ridicule of our dress or manners, or any minor invasion of our person or our rights—all of these oblige us to look for sincere signs of apology. This is only another way of saying that the laws of courtesy have a moral foundation. "Give no offense to Jews or to Greeks or to the church of God" (I Corinthians 10:32). Since human dignity is expressed through the nobler elements of culture, an offense against these elements is an offense against the person. "Let your speech always be gracious, seasoned with salt, so that you may know how you ought to answer every one" (Colossians 4:6).

Since an apology is a personal acknowledgment of guilt, it must be a spontaneous fruit of the moral and spiritual environment. Guilt has no existence outside of a subjective sense of shame. Guilt is the voice of an offended duty; it can only be felt as one stands within duty itself. This was an exciting insight, for it suggested a way to the heart of God.

6. THE ANATOMY OF AN APOLOGY

When one individual comes to another and apologizes, he heartily acknowledges two things: first, that fellowship has been violated; second, that this violation is sufficiently of his own doing that he is willing to accept the blame. Whether his word is brief or prolonged, precise or general, depends entirely on the situation. If a person happens to bump another, the moral and spiritual environment is satisfied by the conventional, but sincere, "Oh, I'm dreadfully sorry!" But if a more serious violation of fellowship occurs, a more detailed response is necessary.

The Admission of Guilt

An apology can only be given when the involved parties are either in rapport, or when no history of strained relations prevents the easy creation of rapport. Unless the deck is relatively clear of moral obstacles, an apology can neither be offered nor accepted. Those whose relations are marred by continued incivility do not apologize for any particular act in the series. Restoring fellowship through an apology is the privilege of those who, in fact or presumption, are in rapport. This much is clear.

As one examines the anatomy of an apology, however, he finds this very striking feature: *One can apologize within reasonable legal security.* There are at least two separate reasons why this is so.

First, when a man apologizes for a given indiscretion, he knows in advance that only this particular incident will be investigated. Suppose he disturbs a woman's hat while making his way to an opera seat. He immediately apologizes. But his word does not authorize the woman to probe into other evidences of guilt in his life. And if she tries, she arouses the judicial sentiment and he judges her guilty. This means that a person can be grieved about trifles, while remaining unmoved about murder and theft. A confession of gross sins would implicate the self in more guilt than pride will tolerate.

Second, although it is not easy to offer an apology, a man knows that his word will eventuate in a moral security whose outcome can be anticipated with surprising precision. It makes little difference whether the apology is accepted or rejected, for the security of the confessing party is assured in either case. Since an apology satisfies the claims of the moral and spiritual environment, it puts the offended party in the perilous position of either forgiving or becoming guilty. If the apology is accepted, the guilty party is released and fellowship is restored; and if the apology is rejected, guilt passes from him to the other. Whatever the outcome, therefore, the one who apologizes ends with reasonable legal security. And this outcome is known in advance of the act.

7. WHY WE CANNOT APOLOGIZE TO GOD

This does not mean that our problem is solved, however, for an apology is appropriate only when the parties involved are either in rapport or when nothing systematic prevents the easy creation of rapport. But God and man are not in rapport. Our want of natural affection is the very *cause* of the moral predicament. Although God's solicitude is our only reason for believing that human values are continuous with the values in the universe, we remain spiritually aloof from God. We are powerless to arouse spontaneous sentiments of gratitude.

We cannot apologize, furthermore, because it is impossible to name any particular incident that has caused our rupture with God. Our affections are essentially self-centered. Although we look to God to complete the moral cycle, we do not return any of the warmer affections that accompany fellowship. And since this want of gratitude interpermeates all our faculties, it is impossible to explain our separation from God on the ground of a given act or a series of acts. Therefore, until we spiritually recognize that our affections are out of harmony with the divine character, we can neither comprehend nor meaningfully respond to our moral task as individuals.

We are not herewith denying that one must grieve over the evil in his life. We simply argue that an apology, as one expression of moral sorrow, is inappropriate unless the right conditions prevail; and such conditions do not prevail in our relations with God. If our life were marked by a rather consistent delight to do God's will, it *would* be meaningful to apologize. Spasmodic instances of evil can be accurately listed. But since the sweep of our life is so ambiguous that pride and ingratitude tincture every thought and action, a word of apology is not appropriate.

As we continue our odyssey to the person of God, it is well to bear in mind that moral response must be appropriate to the prevailing conditions. Who will pay in gold, when he thinks silver will do? Cervantes sagaciously observes that he who has no intention of paying does not trouble himself about difficulties when he is striking the bargain.

8. THE ANATOMY OF REPENTANCE

Once we come at the matter from the correct point of view, we quickly see that if a person spurns our favors, not once or twice, but as a habit, *only a sincere act of repentance can satisfy the moral and spiritual environment.* And if such a person refuses to repent, he arouses the judicial sentiment. Regardless of what situations we may imagine—whether that of a neighbor who for years has rebuffed our acts of kindness, or that of a fellow employee who takes an egoistic delight in making us miserable—the demands of the moral sense are exactly the same. We cannot extend fellowship until the guilty party is so awed by the spread of his wickedness that he repents.

When I turned to name the exact difference between apology and repentance, I decided that whereas an apology can list the precise incidents that have ruptured fellowship, repentance confronts such a long series of acts that it simply throws a moral cover over the whole.

But this certainly was not a very profound explanation of the difference, for unless one knows what he is being asked to forgive he is morally unable to decide whether a word of sorrow is enough or whether amends must be made. A jury cannot be appointed until the corpus delicti is established. Judge the following from within moral self-acceptance: "Will you please forgive me for something I would rather not mention?" A refusal to name the evil makes it impossible for a just verdict to be rendered.

This led me to reflect once again on the anatomy of an apology. Let us remember that an apology forces the offended party into the moral disjunction of either freely forgiving or becoming guilty himself. This element of anticipated legal security is always present. Even when an apology is insufficient to satisfy justice, the principle remains unaltered. Suppose a neighbor expresses sorrow for damaging his friend's automobile. Whether an apology suffices, or whether damages must be redressed, depends upon the circumstances involved. But the apology at least forces the friend to negotiate the matter on a personal rather than a legal basis. If he charges a disproportionate sum to have his automobile repaired, the judicial sentiment in the neighbor is aroused. This is known long before the neighbor rallies moral courage to confess his wrong.

It is precisely at this point, I decided, that the essential difference between an apology and repentance appears. *Repentance does not exist until the guilty party despairs of finding a legal way out.* Even though both apology and repentance are acts of contrition, repentance confronts such an ambiguous series of relations, and such a conflict of voluntary and involuntary causal connections, that it abandons all hope of forecasted legal security. The key to forgiveness is one's sincere willingness to bear his guilt without the hope of negotiating the issue on the plane of give-and-take. Repentance allows guilt to be escorted through the moral sense without arousing the judicial sentiment. This is the marvelous feature of the moral and spiritual environment. From the legal, it demands a legal settlement; but to those who despair of finding a legal settlement it gives pity and mercy.

As long as we approach the problem from the center of moral self-acceptance, we always end up at the same place. Whereas an apology can be offered within comfortable legal security, repentance can cling to nothing but the spiritual hope that the offended party will look upon him with pity and mercy. If hope converts to a legal demand, either the nature of guilt has not been comprehended or one believes that some mutually satisfactory arrangement can be worked out. In either event, one is not really repenting.

Repentance is the most shattering admission of guilt. But like any form of guilt, it has no objective existence unless it is subjectively felt. Guilt implies a cordial spiritual willingness to accept the consequences of transgression. Despairing of a *quid pro quo* settlement, a repentant soul throws himself on the mercy of the court.

The Admission of Guilt

If these elements are combined in the right way, and if the suppliant is willing to yield to the claims of the moral and spiritual environment, his transgression can be escorted past the judicial sentiment on the wings of pity and mercy. But if any shade of insincerity or dissimulation appears, pity and mercy take their flight and law re-enters. Law and mercy are incompatible. "For all who rely on works of the law are under a curse" (Galatians 3:10).

Although an apology cannot be rejected without transferring guilt from the penitent to the offended, no such security can be anticipated in repentance. If the suppliant learns that his evil is too heinous to be forgiven, he cannot claim that an injustice has been done. Regardless of how personally grieved he may be when he learns that resources of pity and mercy do not exist, he has no legal ground of complaint. If he is sincere, he will quietly resign himself to his fate. Repentance cheerfully recognizes that it deserves condemnation, not forgiveness. It only inquires whether the offended party can forgive the very one who, on his own spiritual admission, is altogether unworthy of forgiveness.

Therefore, since we are out of fellowship with God, and since fellowship cannot be restored by offering a word of apology, we have no other moral alternative than to repent. If we postpone repentance, we merely prove that we still look for some legally satisfying way out.

9. THE PROBLEM OF REPENTING BEFORE GOD

Even this does not end the matter, however, for in our very effort to repent we contradict ourselves. We have already shown why humility cannot be made an object of conscious striving. Humility does not exist until we yield to the claims of the moral and spiritual environment. We cannot *strive* to repent, therefore. If we were truly sorry for our lack of fellowship with God, we would be so moved by this knowledge that moral fear would immediately engulf us. "Woe is me! For I am lost; for I am a man of unclean lips, and I dwell in the midst of a people of unclean lips; for my eyes have seen the King, the Lord of hosts!" (Isaiah 6:5).

This seems to be the root of the difficulty: although we have successfully sketched the anatomy of repentance we are not yet convinced that it is necessary for us to repent. Unless one has an accurate knowledge of what he has done wrong, he cannot even apologize, let alone repent. But as yet we do not have this knowledge. What law have we transgressed? And how do we measure our guilt? Until questions such as these are answered, it is sheer affectation to repent.

Thus far we have only been confronted with the moral predicament. Although we contemplate God's daily works of goodness, a knowledge of this beneficence does not stir up spontaneous sentiments of gratitude. But reasons have already been cited to suggest that the moral predicament need not *necessarily* be the result of any spiritual delinquency on our part. And as long as this theoretical possibility exists, there is little practical point in trying to stir up sentiments of repentance.

There certainly is no legal way out of our predicament, for the more we strive to be holy, the more enmeshed in law we become. The only question is whether the moral predicament is a sufficient ground for repentance. We seem to be held in this predicament from creation itself; or at least from our birth into the human family. "That which is born of the flesh, is flesh . . ." (John 3:6). We have no memory of having once loved God with spontaneous affections—as if our present condition can be traced back to either mismanagement or incaution on our part. We may be sorry for our predicament, as indeed we are. But this is a sorrow of the world. We are also sorry that we are going to die. Until worldly sorrow yields to godly sorrow, a rational contemplation of our task will never convert to spiritual fulfillment.

Chapter Eight

DEFINING THE LAW OF LIFE

1. THE PITH AND MARROW OF THE IMPERATIVE ESSENCE

It has been my claim, from the very beginning, that the nature of man can be comprehended under two interpermeating essences: the descriptive (height, weight, color of eyes, and so on), and the imperative (rectitude, compunction, sense of decency, and so on). The one tells what man is, while the other tells what man ought to be. The scientific method deals with the descriptive essence, while the third method of knowing deals with the imperative essence.

Although critical use of the third method of knowing has given us a number of provocative insights into the imperative essence, the pith and marrow of this essence, despite all, remains a mystery. But until we spell out the content of the imperative essence, we cannot name the content of rectitude; and, apart from a knowledge of rectitude, we cannot evaluate our moral standing before God. Whether or not we ought to repent depends entirely on the moral quality of our own souls; but this quality cannot be judged without a standard.

Each insight supports the next. The third type of truth (rectitude) does not come into being until moral decision closes the gap between what we are and what we ought to be. But unless we have a cognitive grasp of what we ought to be (the imperative essence), our moral life is left without a guiding criterion. We cannot resolve the problem of repentance until the quality of our lives is judged by this criterion.

It now ought to be clear that the term "imperative essence" is nothing but a name for that phase of the moral and spiritual environment which defines a truly upright life. The third method of knowing is a special way of gaining access to this norm.

2. THE LAW BY WHICH WE JUDGE OTHERS

As I reviewed the argument up to this point, however, I uncovered a very significant omission. The following has been repeatedly asserted: When others enter the circle of nearness, our participation in the moral and spiritual environment authorizes us to pass judgment on their moral standing. If they accept us, and so fulfill the terms of rectitude, we extend fellowship; but if they fail to accept us they arouse the judicial sentiment and we judge them guilty. Or better, God judges them through us. Now, here is the omission: Although we are custodians of the law, we have never given a precise name to this law. This is significant, for if such a law measures rectitude in others, should it not likewise measure rectitude in ourselves? The possibility, at least, must be seriously investigated.

So we now inquire, "By what law do we judge others?" When others refuse to accept our dignity, they are guilty; but what law have they transgressed? Of what are they guilty?

3. THE LAW OF JUSTICE

Hardly had I set my mind to the question but what, like a flash, I decided that *we judge others by the law of justice*. I grounded my confidence in what I felt was a self-evident element in the most routine affairs of life.

For example, at an earlier point in the discussion I referred to the time when I went to a nursery to purchase a small quantity

Defining the Law of Life

of grass seed. Since the young clerk failed to wait on me in my rightful turn, he aroused the judicial sentiment and I judged him guilty. If we may argue from the elements in this illustration—and from all others like it—it is obvious that we judge by the law of justice. Since we express our dignity through a free pursuit of human rights, whoever violates these rights is guilty of violating our person.

Whenever we wait in line for something, a defrauding of our privileges immediately excites the judicial sentiment. Suppose we are anxious to have a window seat in a cross-country airliner. We make our way to the gate well in advance of departure. When the time comes to board the plane, however, a number of airline officials are escorted to their seats ahead of us. Sensing favoritism, a surge of indignation floods our hearts. Those who granted this privilege are guilty; they had no right to show preference. "Men seem to resent injustice more than violence; the former is regarded as unfair advantage taken by an equal, the latter is compulsion applied by a superior."*

Whatever else may make up the pith and marrow of the imperative essence, therefore, justice seems to be an important ingredient. We are entitled to such things as a just share of the highway or sidewalk, the privilege of walking through the city park, and a fair slice of the benefits and securities of citizenship. We demand justice because we live and move and are in God. We are held by a sense of our own dignity from existence itself. Our claims on justice, therefore, are moral, not aesthetic. If we pay for goods, we demand a just return for our money; if we sign a contract we expect to have its terms honored. Justice pertains to the administration of the right, and God's image in man is the fixed point for defining this administration. If a professor gives exceptionally high grades to students he happens to like, he violates justice. A knowledge of his act arouses the judicial sentiment. God judges him through us.

This means that if a person enters the circle of nearness, he

---

* Thucydides, *The Peloponnesian War* (Oxford), p. 63.

meets rectitude, and thus brings the third type of truth into being, whenever he sees to justice.

4. DIFFICULTIES WITH JUSTICE

We cannot consider the case closed, however, until we subject it to close rational scrutiny. Truth must answer to all the important facts.

If justice is the pith and marrow of rectitude, why can we meet flagrant instances of injustice without having the judicial sentiment aroused? This is the first difficulty. Perhaps we read of distant, exploited people. The account is interesting as news, but it does not excite moral indignation in us. We soon turn to the comics, quite indifferent to the matter.

But we may classify this first objection as trivial, for we have shown, over and again, that the judicial sentiment is *never* aroused —whatever the pith and marrow of the imperative essence may be—until others enter the circle of nearness and penetrate our interests. The third method of knowing is valid only under very special conditions. It is without force unless others actually appear before us. Distant, exploited people are not in the circle of nearness; therefore, they cannot occasion a conscious awareness of the moral and spiritual environment.

If the first difficulty is trivial, however, the second is not. We are all familiar with the fact that justice and injustice cannot accurately be measured unless optimum conditions prevail. Whenever evidences are buried in ambiguous or confused contexts, it is difficult to render a decision. Juries sincerely hope their verdict harmonizes with absolute justice, but they rarely have such a control of the facts that the threat of error is altogether eliminated.

This would not be a problem, except for the fact that it runs counter to one of the clearest aspects of our moral experience. Suppose a person enters the circle of nearness. It make no difference how complex or involved the context may be. If he gives the least sign of disregarding the dignity of our person, we immediately judge him guilty. Even though a third party may see nothing wrong with our neighbor's attitude, we detect deviation from rectitude with instantaneous precision. A glance or a word can betray such deviation. We experience no grades of uncertainty; there are no times when we must postpone decision because of ambiguous evidences. We enjoy spiritual clairvoyance. No other datum is needed than the sheer presence of another person before us. Either he receives our dignity or he does not. There is no third possibility.

If we are so skilled in deciding matters of justice, however, why does this ability vanish whenever we act as judges in civil trials? We are no more efficient in jury duty than others are. Does this not suggest that we really do not judge others by the law of justice?

Suppose the family next door owns a hound dog. And suppose the dog enjoys barking on moonlit nights, greatly disturbing our sleep. As we lie in bed listening to the hound, the judicial sentiment is aroused and we judge the neighbor guilty. But do we judge by the law of justice? City laws permit the ownership of dogs, and dogs, with few exceptions, like to bark. On what ground, then, do we complain? How loud may a dog bark? And how often may he bark at night? No precise answers can be given. Justice, it seems, is a limiting concept; it is seldom applied with exactness.

But this is at variance with our experience. Whether the disregard of our life is trivial or serious, the judicial sentiment is instantly aroused. We are no less certain of the evil in an oblique glance than we are of the evil in a misrepresentation of merchandise. A sneering remark is as clearly a violation of rectitude as the quartering of troops against our will. But if we judge by the law of justice, how can we be so sure of our ground? That is the problem.

There is yet another angle to consider. What if a person *does* see to justice? Does this end the matter? Not at all. Unless he acts with a good will, he merely provokes the judicial sentiment. Suppose a politician relieves a tax injustice, in order that he might poll more votes at election time. Although we are happy for the relief, we are morally repelled by the motive; and the more we reflect on the motive, the more rigidly the judicial sentiment is aroused. The politician is not moved by a regard for our person. To the contrary, he is guilty of using our person as a means to his own interested ends.

Furthermore, one becomes evil if he sees to justice out of a grudging sense of necessity. Suppose a drugstore clerk does not want to serve us, but is forced to do so by the manager. Although he sees to justice, he falls short of rectitude. His act is shorn of moral value because it is not carried away by the law of the spirit of life. The clerk is motivated by the law of legal necessity.

This is enough to show that the pith and marrow of rectitude is *not* the mere formal fact of justice. Although rectitude may never exist apart from justice, justice is not necessarily the same thing as rectitude. Justice has no moral worth unless it is a fruit of the moral and spiritual environment. Work is the result of conscious striving; fruit is a natural growth. Thus, the Apostle Paul speaks of "works of the flesh," but the "fruit of the Spirit" (Galatians 5:19-22). An act has no moral value unless it flows from the unfree necessities of the moral and spiritual environment. God releases right affections into our heart whenever we are spiritually willing to be transformed by the truth. As we dwell in God, our interest in justice is inspired by the law of the spirit of life.

5. JUSTICE AND REPENTANCE

This tie-in between justice and affections is a severe blow to pride, of course, for pride would be delighted if rectitude could be measured by works of righteousness rather than by fruits of the Spirit. Since we seldom perpetrate gross acts of injustice, a rather convincing case for our goodness could be made out. We drive on the proper side of the street; we never dump ashes in our neighbor's yard; and we unfailingly honor contractual obligations. Who could possibly challenge our righteousness?

Defining the Law of Life

Furthermore, since every social situation is ambiguous, pride could always interpret the data in its own favor. Instead of repenting, pride would hire more lawyers; for the lawyers would certainly hold things up on a technicality in either the definition or the detection of justice.

But once we realize that rectitude is formed of affections which flow from the person of God, pride is left without defense. "For the word of God is living and active, sharper than any two-edged sword, piercing to the division of soul and spirit, of joints and marrow, and discerning the thoughts and intentions of the heart. And before him no creature is hidden, but all are open and laid bare to the eyes of him with whom we have to do" (Hebrews 4:12-13). We may deceive one another, but we cannot deceive God, for God knows our hearts better than we ourselves do.

6. EXCEPTIONS TO JUSTICE

In an effort to clarify the matter still further, I decided to raise the following question: "Is the judicial sentiment ever aroused when issues of justice cannot meaningfully be entertained?" If we can successfully name such instances, we may conclude that rectitude is more delicate in its texture than justice.

When we are altogether honest with ourselves, we discover that we *frequently* judge people with other interests in mind than justice. Suppose we are going to work, only to be delayed by a very slow driver. If he would bear to the right, we could pass and be on our way. Yet, he will not oblige us. We sound our horn, but to no avail. The firmness of his stand arouses the judicial sentiment and we judge him guilty. But we certainly are not morally excited by interests of justice, for the other driver has the law on his side. Not only is he moving within the proper speed limit, but he is taking no more of the highway than he is justly entitled to. We may fuss and fume, but the fact remains that he is under no legal obligation to bear to the right and let us go by. Still, we entertain an aroused judicial sentiment. We intuitively feel that if he were held by affections that flow from the moral and spiritual environment, he would gladly let us pass. But by what law do we judge? In what way has rectitude been violated?

Again, suppose we want to make a very important telephone call. Lifting the receiver, we find that the line is being used at the time. So, we wait. After two or three minutes we try again, only to be frustrated once more. We then kindly ask the other parties to hang up, but with no success. By this time the judicial sentiment is aroused and we judge the offenders guilty. But we certainly do not judge by the law of justice, for there is no contract which defines the length of time that a phone may be used. If there is guilt, it is because some other rule has been violated. But what, precisely, is this rule?

Illustrations such as these could be multiplied indefinitely. Perhaps we are in a serve-yourself grocery store, buying a quart of milk. Anxious to return home, we take the milk and head for the cashier. As we near the register, however, a woman with a full cart of groceries goes ahead of us. Since she saw that we had nothing but a quart of milk, and yet deliberately went first, the judicial sentiment is aroused and we judge her guilty. But by what law do we judge? Certainly the woman did not violate justice, for customers are entitled to be served in the order of their appearance at the cashier. Since the woman was there first, she had a right to go ahead. And yet, since she did not relinquish this right, we judge her guilty.*

Nothing will be gained by reviewing further instances of this sort. If a person will live by the realities that already hold him, the illustrations from the highway, the telephone, and the grocery store will suffice. And if he refuses to be honest with himself, no volume of evidence will unseat his prejudice.

Now that we have cited instances where the judicial sentiment is aroused by issues other than justice, we have convincingly shown that rectitude is formed of a more delicate stuff than justice. But what is this stuff? And how can it be distinguished from justice?

---

* If these illustrations do not happen to fit the experiences of the reader, let him simply substitute others of his own. All of us are judicially irked in one way or another. It makes no difference how, for the issue remains quite the same.

7. THE PROBLEM OF EVIDENCES

One of the most interesting features in the above illustrations is the rather consistent refusal of the offended party to see matters through. Regardless of how judicially peeved one may be in his heart, he shrinks from the prospect of making a public issue of things. A driver may shout angry words at another, but his outburst betrays an effort to take vengeance. It is not a lawful investigation of the right.

Revenge always deteriorates the life. No upright individual can look back on a burst of temper without being shamed by the moral and spiritual environment. Shame is nothing but a negative witness to the imperative essence. Whereas rectitude makes one feel clean inside, evil makes one feel soiled. Whenever the heart is separated from the Spirit of God, demonic spirits control our affections; and the more we strive to reform ourselves in our own strength, the more firmly our affections are held by alien powers.

But back to our problem: Why is it so painful to go to another person and charge him with guilt? Why will we defend ourselves before a large insurance company, but not before a woman in a grocery store? Our fear does not arise out of an uncertainty that evil has been done. On the contrary, if a woman with a full cart of groceries will not let us pass, we can reflect on our displeasure with the consent of our nobler faculties and the praise of men of character. Furthermore, it is not because we think the matter is not worth litigating. Nothing immoral is trivial to an upright person. Nor is it because we fear we will appear conceited or overweening. Rectitude fears nothing.

Here, I am convinced, is the profound reason we shrink from the prospect of confronting others with a charge of guilt: *We cannot convince them of guilt unless we exhibit the very moral perfection that we suspect them of violating.* This is so important that it must be developed with considerable care.

Let us begin by returning to the civil courts. All normal adults are subject to jury duty, for the evidences which they are called upon to judge are public and measurable. If the terms of a contract are violated, or if property rights are removed, any honest individual can render a reasonable verdict. Freedom to plant the grass of one's choosing is an indefeasible right. A challenge of such a right can be litigated in any court of justice.

But when we go to another individual and confront him with guilt, we are dealing with evidences that are not public and open. Our purpose in going consists, we may say, in the delicate task of acquainting him with the evidences on which a decision must turn. But we cannot convincingly present these evidences unless we exhibit the very moral perfection that we suspect him of violating.

Suppose we go to the library to study for a final examination in chemistry. Since it is extremely important that we pass the course, every minute must count. But as we settle down to concentrate, we find that a student near us is making notes with a hard lead pencil. He is not using a second sheet, and the rhythm of his pencil can be heard against the surface of the library table. Our powers of concentration are frustrated. The more we try to put the noise out of our mind, the more conscious we become of it. Distressed by the fact that valuable time is slipping away, the judicial sentiment is aroused and we judge the student guilty.*

But by what canon do we judge? Although library rules prohibit whispering and other unnecessary noise, they do not make one use a second sheet when making notes with a hard lead pencil. The student is legally within his rights; he does not transgress a known precept in the university.

* The reader must not fasten on the circumstantials in this illustration, and thus miss the main point. We are piqued by things that offend the uniqueness and mystery of our person. If one is not troubled by noise in a library, let him simply shift to the theater, opera, or church. Let him then reflect on typical annoyances in such situations: undertones of whispering, loud yawns, the crinkling of cellophane bags, munching of popcorn, disagreeable body odors, periodic pressures on the back of the chair, or passing individuals who step on his feet or muss his hair. *How* people arouse the judicial sentiment is beside the point; *that* they do is what matters. Every conclusion established by a study of the problem in the library will apply to all other valid instances of judicial annoyance.

Defining the Law of Life

But here is the most interesting element in such an illustration: although we are swift to decide the guilt of the student, we hesitate to announce the verdict. And why do we hesitate? The answer, once again, is that we cannot convince others of guilt unless we show the very moral perfection that we suspect them of violating. Shrinking from this, we pick up our books and leave.

It must be observed that the problem in this particular illustration grew out of a conflict in personal dispositions. On the one hand, there happens to be a student whose hard lead pencil makes rhythmic noises against the library table. He is of such a temperament that the noise does not bother him. In fact, he rather enjoys it, for it gives him a feeling of industry. On the other hand, we are of such a temperament that the noise frustrates our powers of concentration. Try though we may, we cannot disengage ourselves from the distraction. But if it were not for this mysterious conflict in dispositions, the problem would not exist. There is no rational explanation for why we cannot concentrate, while he can; but we cannot, and that is all there is to it. Each person is a spiritual mystery.

Because of the unusual circumstances, the evidences on which our judgment rests are not open for public inspection. A disinterested observer might even chide us for being irked. It follows, therefore, that the one making the noise is unaware that he is frustrating our powers of concentration. Or at least this is what we must believe. Since *he* is not troubled by the sound of his pencil against the library table, why should others be troubled? His error, of course, is that he approaches the problem by way of his own life, and not by way of others about him. He universalizes from his particular experience.

Before the student will sense a moral responsibility to change his habits, he must be confronted with the evidences. We must get out of our library chair, walk around the table, and in a friendly tone of voice review the problem. "I beg your pardon," we might say, "but I am having a difficult time concentrating on this chemistry lesson. I find that the noise of your pencil distracts me. Would you greatly mind using a second sheet when you write?" No charge of guilt can be made until a known rule has been violated.

Hence, when we go to the student and acquaint him with our problem, we do nothing but create an occasion for the claims of the moral and spiritual environment to touch his life. We have no power to arouse a sense of duty in him. We are simply a channel through which the Spirit of God works.

This means that unless we are spiritually artistic in our approach, the student will fail to hear the voice of God. All we can do is maneuver him into a position where his affections are touched by the moral and spiritual environment. Conviction comes from God; it cannot be aroused by human ingenuity.

Let me illustrate this. Suppose a little boy rudely talks back to his mother. The sobbing mother turns to her son and asks if he is not ashamed of what he has done. Smitten by the sight of his mother's tears, the child chokes out a confession: "Yes, Mommy, I'm sorry." Pleased though the mother may be, she cannot claim credit for this confession. Her overtures are only an occasion for the boy to be convicted by God. If he should chance to feel no conviction, the mother would be at wit's end. She has no direct control over his heart.*

This leads us to our first significant conclusion: *Before we can confront the student with a sense of guilt, we must sincerely believe in his innocence.* He will not recognize his duty until we acquaint him with the evidences; but in providing these evidences we must witness to his moral innocence. This is why it is extremely difficult to go to him and hold court vis-à-vis. In our haste to involve him in guilt, we inadvertently involve ourselves.

Before developing this point, however, a difficulty must be faced. Why must we *explain* ourselves to the other student? Have

---

* This opens the way for an acceptable philosophy of prayer. Suppose a mother fervently prays for her children to be pure. God, on the occasion of her faith, releases the claims of the moral and spiritual environment into their hearts. Conviction results. "The prayer of a righteous man has great power in its effects" (James 5:16). The mother looks to causal connections that are unknown to science and philosophy.

Defining the Law of Life

we not already shown that the sheer presence of our person places others under responsibility?

There is no conflict. In going to the student and telling him about our inability to concentrate, we still believe that the sheer presence of our person places him under moral obligation. Our review is simply an effort to acquaint him with elements in our dignity that cannot be detected by public observation. Our dignity includes many mysteries and particularities—not the least of which is our inability to concentrate when we hear the rhythmic noise of a pencil against the library table. If we did not believe that the sheer presence of our person placed the student under conviction, we would never have courage to appear before him in the first place; or better, we would have no moral right to do so. Our courage is a fruit of the moral and spiritual environment. We are custodians of a law which proceeds from the divine tribunal.

This is why we cannot acquaint a person with guilt unless we approach him with a sincere eye to his innocence. We must create an atmosphere for the moral and spiritual environment to release its own sense of duty. If a person is charged with violating a duty he has never felt, he will experience moral indignation, not conviction. He will sense no obligation to accept the mysteries of our life until we reveal the nature of these mysteries.

In properly balancing these two truths—the first, that the sheer presence of our person morally obliges others; the second, that others cannot meaningfully be judged until they are acquainted with the evidences—I decided that this was the resolution: *In asking a student to use a second sheet when he writes, we merely provide an occasion for him to reveal whether or not he is already morally related to us.* His response, once the new evidences are before him, tells the tale. If he hears us out, cheerfully saying he is sorry for having bothered us, he proves that his life is good. But if he arrogantly ignores our plea, he proves that he was not rightly related to us in the first place. Sensing no necessity to respect our life in general, he senses no necessity to respect it in particular. His affections are not held by the moral and spiritual environment. God says we must never knowingly frustrate one another's powers of concentration; but he says that since the noise does not bother him he will continue to make it. If others do not like it, they can move; for he violates no college rule. Comforted by the law of legal necessity, he remains blinded to the law of the spirit of life. He cannot see because he will not see.

This leads to further complications, however. *Not only must we assume the innocence of the student before we can confront him with guilt, but we must submit to the grievous fact of our own guilt—the guilt of having judged him on the testimony of insufficient evidence.* We entertained an aroused judicial sentiment before we made any critical effort to learn whether he was in possession of the information needed to clarify his obligation toward us. Whenever a civil magistrate condemns the innocent, he desecrates his office. Yet this is precisely what we do each time we judge those who do not as yet know the mysteries and particularities of our life. If a student is not bothered by pencil noises, he will hardly be concerned to learn whether others are. It is our duty to correct his error by revealing ourselves. But our hesitation to do this proves that sin lies at the door. We are ashamed of having prematurely judged him.

A spirit of vindictiveness renders it impossible to approach another person with an eye to his innocence and to our guilt. If we express a wrong attitude—that is, if we angrily accuse him of doing wrong—we arouse the judicial sentiment and he judges us guilty. Vindictiveness not only proves that we judge in advance of the evidences, but it drains away moral courage to see and accept our own guilt. Anger blinds the heart to righteousness.

If we inwardly judge another, though outwardly we pretend we do not, we add new guilt. It is sheer hypocrisy to feign fellowship. God knows this, whether we do or not. "Nothing is covered up that will not be revealed, or hidden that will not be known. Whatever you have said in the dark shall be heard in the light, and what you have whispered in private rooms shall be proclaimed upon the housetops" (Luke 12:2-3).

8. A FURTHER WORD ABOUT THE COUNSEL OF CHRIST

This progression in the argument gives us a vantage point from which to rethink the counsel of Christ. Jesus says, "Judge not, that you be not judged" (Matthew 7:1). But the judicial sentiment replies, "Judge, and judge again. Otherwise the moral cycle is incomplete." Is there any way of harmonizing these words of counsel?

Jesus seems to be saying this: No man should judge another unless he himself is willing to be judged by the same standard. We are prone to tattle, and neither God nor man likes a tattler. We must never use the law of God to bolster up our own security.

Notice how Christ continues (verses 3-5): "Why do you see the speck that is in your brother's eye [the speck of his acts of inconsideration], but do not notice the log that is in your own eye [the log of not only judging him in advance of the evidences, but of stubbornly refusing to admit guilt for having done so]? Or how can you say to your brother, 'Let me take the speck out of your eye,' when there is the log in your own eye? [Since we are prone to take vengeance against those who judicially annoy us, passion and interest becloud our vision.] You hypocrite, first take the log out of your own eye, and then you will see clearly to take the speck out of your brother's eye." (We must recognize that he acts in ignorance, for he does not realize that he is offending us; while we sin against knowledge—the knowledge that he is not aware of the mysteries and particularities that make up the substance of our dignity.)

Therefore, it should not be supposed that Christ is forbidding judgment per se. If we were unable to tell the difference between good and bad people, we could not distinguish Christ from Beelzebul. The counsel of Jesus is this: When judging others, we make ourselves liable to the same judgment. We cannot judge in good conscience until our affections are in conformity with the moral and spiritual environment. "Beloved, if our hearts do not condemn us, we have confidence before God" (I John 3:21). If we use the law of God to mortar up our own egoistic security, we simply implicate ourselves in further guilt. The Apostle Paul puts it this way: "Therefore you have no excuse, O man, whoever you are, when you judge another; for in passing judgment upon him you condemn yourself, because you, the judge, are doing the very same things" (Romans 2:1).

Our zeal to judge others is a revelation of at least two things: first, that we know the law of God; second, that our difficulty is not lack of knowledge, but lack of moral courage to act on the knowledge we already have. Whether or not men realize what they are doing is beside the point. They *know* the implications of their conduct because they are morally *responsible* for knowing. No normal man can escape the third condition of knowing. A refusal to exercise moral and rational self-transcendence is simply further evidence of a culpable heart.

9. WHY WE MUST HUMBLY ASK A FAVOR

If others are morally obliged to respect the mysteries and particularities of our person, however, why must we approach them in a spirit of meekness? Rather than asking a favor, should we not come in the name of law and order? A police officer does not softly urge people to do the right; he forthrightly demands compliance.

The answer, once again, is that this is the only way we have of acquainting others with a knowledge of their duty toward us. Duty is never experienced until one stands in the center of duty; and one can only do this by cordially submitting to the claims of the moral and spiritual environment. When we appear before others and reveal the mysteries and particularities of our person, we simply provide an occasion for the Spirit of God to work. We come in the name of law and order, to be sure, but the force of law does not break through until one is confronted by the moral

Defining the Law of Life

and spiritual environment. There is no straight-line way of acquainting others with duty.

Here is the proof that law is on our side: If we ask a favor in the spirit of humility, only to have it rejected in the spirit of pride, the judicial sentiment is aroused.* Suppose we graciously ask a neighbor to move his automobile. If he refuses, he shows that he is not morally held by a sense of our dignity. Asking a favor, therefore, is really a form of revelation. It is a revelation of those phases of our life that could never be discovered by a scientific study of the race.

Let me illustrate this further. A visiting guest may be allergic to cat's hair; but since the hostess does not realize this, he must speak up. He must reveal himself. And when he does, an upright hostess will say with sincerity and conviction, "Oh, my dear, I'm dreadfully sorry! I didn't know you suffered this way." Since the hostess is willing to limit her interests by the interests of her guest, out goes the cat. *She knows that the duty to respect a person in particular is analytically included in the duty to respect him in general.*

If the guest were to *demand* that the cat be put out, not only would he betray poor breeding, but he would arouse the judicial sentiment in the hostess. She is not obliged to accept the mysteries and particularities of his person until he reveals himself. This simply reinforces our oft-repeated dictum: We cannot convince others of guilt unless we show the very moral perfection that we suspect them of violating.

In sum, a person in the circle of nearness will never become acquainted with the mysteries and particularities of our person until we walk up and reveal ourselves. This act of revelation, in turn, provides an occasion for the other person to make his own revelation; a revelation of whether or not, in the light of this new evidence, he feels morally obliged to accept the dignity of

---

* We refer to *lawful* conduct, of course. If we ask a person to help us steal a car, no amount of humility on our part can excite a sense of duty in him. Our evil designs are at variance with the claims of the moral and spiritual environment.

our person. The clarity of his revelation will depend, in part, on the clarity of our own revelation. This means that an adjudication of wrongs through personal confrontation is a very perilous task. If our demand is not savored by meekness, our overtures may be misunderstood and new evil will result. This is why we hire lawyers, or why we prefer to write anonymous letters. Such strategies spare us the hazards of personal encounter. We know that if we fail to approach others in the right spirit, we do nothing but excite the judicial sentiment in them.

This is the major reason why it is difficult to confront others. We cannot communicate a sense of conviction until we ourselves have been convicted. Our lives must mirror the very rule that we expect others to meet. But we cannot make this revelation unless we are in the Holy Spirit. Right affections are never a product of our own striving; they are a fruit of the moral and spiritual environment.

10. THE LAW OF CONSIDERATION

With this background before us, we can now advance the argument by a new use of an old criterion. If we apply this criterion with critical skill, we may find ourselves in possession of the pith and marrow of the imperative essence.

Here is the old criterion: *Types of being are revealed by grades of personal enthusiasm.* Routine conduct reveals one's belief in general being; excited conduct reveals one's belief in values; and judicially inspired conduct reveals one's belief in the content of the moral and spiritual environment.

And having stated the old criterion, let us now state its new use: *At no point in the discussion have we found a clearer instance of judicially inspired conduct than when we rally courage to ask another person a favor.* The instance is clear because a consciousness of obligation makes us hesitant to go through with the act. Our very caution is proof that we are sensitive to the claims of the moral and spiritual environment. We know we shall not excite moral conviction in others unless we ourselves are moral.

Defining the Law of Life

Therefore, rather than asking, "By what law do we judge others?" it is much more pointed to ask, "To what law are we committed when we go to another person and ask a favor of him?" This is more pointed because our contact with the moral and spiritual environment is more precise. Let us establish this by setting down a series of interconnected evidences.

First, we are natively held by a sense of our own dignity. "Then God said, 'Let us make man in our image, after our likeness . . .'" (Genesis 1:26). If a small girl is asked to do the dishes out of turn, she has no hesitation to put her own parents under judgment. "But I did the dishes last night!" she firmly protests, "It's Mary's turn tonight." The girl lives and moves and is in God; she knows her parents have no right to violate her dignity.

Second, included in human dignity are many elements of mystery and particularity that could never be discovered by an external study of the race. Each person is unique. He prefers things which seem strange to those about him.

Third, when others enter the circle of nearness, they are obliged to accept all of us, particularities and mysteries included. The reason for this is obvious. We are the sum of such mysteries and particularities. Whoever offends them offends us.

Fourth, the cycle of evidences is incomplete unless we go to others and tell them in a friendly voice that such and such *are* the mysteries and particularities of our person. Since these features cannot be detected by an external study of our lives, we must reveal ourselves. Others may be quite willing to accept our dignity, but until we reveal the depth and width and height of our lives they will not know what they are being called upon to accept. We must speak up. "Do you mind preparing me a plain tossed salad? You see, nut meats make me ill."

Fifth, if we judge others before we make an effort to reveal ourselves, we arouse the judicial sentiment in them. We are guilty of failing to consider the problem from their point of view. How can others accept elements in us that remain hidden? If a man does not know that his neighbor is drowning, is he culpable for not going next door to save him? Certainly not. Culpability is without meaning unless one is confronted by known responsibilities.

Sixth, when we finally rally courage to reveal ourselves, we must communicate two separate things: (*a*) we must review the mysteries and particularities of our person; (*b*) we must give cordial signs that we have not prejudged the motives of others. We cannot convince others of guilt until we sincerely believe in their innocence. This second element is as important as the first, for without it others will sense no moral necessity to accept the mysteries and particularities of our person. We must come with the right attitude. If we accuse others before we introduce them to the evidences, we are guilty of failing to look at the matter from their perspective.

When we approach others in the right spirit, we become channels through which the claims of God flow. "Let your light so shine before men, that they may see your good works and give glory to your Father who is in heaven" (Matthew 5:16). Unless others were in contact with the moral and spiritual environment, it would be pointless to try to bring them under conviction by an example of rectitude. We could be as thoughtful and kind as we wanted, but without the image of God as a point of contact the gesture would have no effect. We might as well recite poems to a turtle.

We are now in a position to answer our question. We have asked, "To what law are we committed when we go to another person and ask a favor of him?" The answer is, *We are committed to the law of consideration.* Unless we meet this law, we will never excite a sense of obligation in him. We suspect him of being inconsiderate of us; but we will never prove it until we are considerate of him. The student who makes noise in the library; the slow driver on the highway; and the woman who would not let us precede her to the cashier—all were judged by the law of consideration. But because we judged them before we made an effort to reveal the mysteries and particularities of our person, we betrayed our own guilt: the guilt of inconsideration. To be considerate means to take in the feelings and the point of view of

Defining the Law of Life

others. It means to stand in their place. It means to believe in their innocence until they reveal convincing evidences to the contrary.

Suppose we are watching a travelogue on Germany, only to be distracted by a person who periodically cracks his knuckles or draws small jets of air through his front teeth. The more we try to put the noise out of our mind, the more we are distracted. But if we entertain an aroused judicial sentiment, we violate the law of consideration; for we are guilty of judging him before he has been confronted by the evidences. We have not been considerate of him; we have not viewed the problem from his point of view. Possibly his enjoyment is increased by doing the very thing that decreases ours. We must go to him and negotiate the matter.

In so doing, however, we must submit our own affections to the moral and spiritual environment. Otherwise, we will not be loosed from the desire to take revenge. Rather than charging him with guilt, we must sincerely believe in his innocence. He will sense no necessity to be considerate of us until we are considerate of him. We must confront him with an ocular demonstration of rectitude. He does not knowingly disturb us—or at least this is what we must believe. He is innocent until he reveals convincing evidences to the contrary.

But if he deliberately cracks his knuckles or draws jets of air through his front teeth, despite our humble plea, we then may entertain an aroused judicial sentiment. Since we are willing to be judged by the same law by which we judge him, we do not violate the counsels of Christ.

If his stubborn ways excite feelings of revenge in us, however, we become culpable in a new way. By taking the law into our own hands, we usurp prerogatives that belong to God alone. Since we are sinners, we cannot administer the law in personal relations. The law is too easily used as an engine in the defense of pride. Children continually judge each other by standards that they refuse to live by. While they expect others to be considerate of them, they are not natively considerate in return. They hold the truth in unrighteousness. They would rather save face than be moral. And when they grow up, they merely learn how to save face with greater dexterity.

This is why education cannot save the world. Since the real defect in man is moral, not rational, education simply makes it possible for a wicked person to become more efficient in his wickedness. "So convenient a thing it is to be a *reasonable creature*, since it enables one to find or make a reason for every thing one has a mind to do."* God entrusts us with custody of the law, but he never entrusts us with power to enforce the law. And the moment we try, we are betrayed into sentiments of revenge.†

11. IMPLICATIONS AND INFERENCES

It may seem strange that others must have the law of life called to their attention. But this is not as strange as it seems. Because others are able to decide whether or not we are considerate of them, they prove that they, like ourselves, are in contact with the law of life. But pride drives this knowledge into the subconscious. Men know the truth, but they hold it in unrighteousness. While they are solicitous to exact signs of consideration from others, they have little native desire to be considerate in return. Their very solicitude is an evidence of self-sufficiency, for if they were *really* concerned with the things of God, they would be humbled by the fact that they do the very evil that they detect in a neighbor.

This is why we must be careful how we approach others. We can only arouse conviction by letting the claims of God flow through us. Our thoughtful manners remind others of a moral

---

* Benjamin Franklin, *Autobiography* (Pocket Books, Inc.), p. 45.

† It must be observed that we speak only of *personal* relations. A distinction must be made between "personal" and "official" conduct. God has entrusted the state with power to "bear the sword" (capital punishment), Romans 13:4. The ruler is a "servant of God to execute his wrath on the wrongdoer." An officer may shoot a fleeing felon, but he acts in an official, not a personal, capacity. As individuals, we have authority to judge the moral standing of those who enter the circle of nearness; but we have no authority to administer the law. If we have a case against a neighbor, we must either proceed through the civil courts or wait for the final judgment.

Defining the Law of Life

content which they already know, but which is seldom brought to the attention of mind.

Since we are prone to judge others in advance of the evidences, and since others are equally prone to judge us for having done so, each proves by his judicial response that he knows the law of life. This is only another way of enforcing our claim that man's problem is not lack of knowledge, but lack of moral courage to act on the knowledge he already has.

Whether in ourselves or in others, a tendency to premature judgment can only be checked as we measure ourselves by the same standard by which we measure others. Suppose we are peeved because a person near us is very fidgety. Are we justified in condemning him? Would *we* want to be judged by such ambiguous evidence? Perhaps he is ill or nervous; perhaps he has just passed through some tragedy; perhaps he is under conviction of sin. Judgment should be postponed until the facts are known.

And once we make a sincere effort to see things from his point of view, arrogance will give way to humility; for we cannot confront him with guilt until we have dealt with our own guilt. He will sense no obligation to stop fidgeting unless we meet the very law that we suspect him of violating. Furthermore, we will discover that human relations are too complex to justify final judgment. Only God can explore the human heart. Others need sympathy, not scorn, for they act out of suasions which are just as mysterious as the suasions that control us.

We tend to view each situation from the perspective of our own interests. When others delay us, we are irked by their carelessness; but when we delay others we are irked by their impatience. Our difficulty is that we are sinners; we hold the law in unrighteousness. We ask others to live by a higher standard than we natively meet. Observe the wisdom of Thomas à Kempis: "Be not angry that you cannot make others as you wish them to be, since you cannot make yourself as you wish to be." Though we know God's law, we refuse to be transformed by this knowledge. We expect others to be considerate of us, but we are not considerate in return.

Society is held together by inconsiderate people who are willing to give and seek forgiveness. The law of consideration places one under an infinite, progressive obligation to a neighbor. A truly moral individual is no less willing to forgive than he is to judge. If he finds it difficult to forgive, he reveals the degree to which he uses God's law in the defense of pride. He is guilty of passing final judgment on a neighbor. All final judgment belongs to the Searcher of Hearts.

So, we conclude: Consideration is more nearly the pith and marrow of the imperative essence than justice. "So whatever you wish that men would do to you, do so to them; for this is the law and the prophets" (Matthew 7:12). Consideration includes the Ten Commandments by going beyond them. If a friend gets a headache from tobacco smoke, a considerate individual will not smoke in his friend's society. His response will be cheerful, for right affections are carried along by the law of the spirit of life.

Our lives literally bristle with habits and preferences which seem foolish when divorced from the sweet mystery of human personality. Personality is unique; it baffles all rational expectation. Take the celebrated idiosyncrasy in Samuel Johnson, for example: "He had another peculiarity, of which none of his friends ever ventured to ask an explanation. It appeared to me some superstitious habit, which he had contracted early, and from which he had never called upon his reason to disentangle him. This was his anxious care to go out or in at a door or passage by a certain number of steps from a certain point, or at least so as that either his right or his left foot, (I am not certain which,) should constantly make the first actual movement when he came close to the door or passage. Thus I conjecture: for I have, upon innumerable occasions, observed him suddenly stop, and then seem to count his steps with a deep earnestness; and when he had neglected or gone wrong in this sort of magical movement, I have seen him go back again, put himself in a proper posture to begin

Defining the Law of Life

the ceremony, and, having gone through it, break from his abstraction, walk briskly on, and join his companion."* Boswell wisely observes that the friends of Johnson never pressed him for an explanation. Rather than being offended by what seemed to be a deviation from the habits of the race, they were so anxious to learn all they could about the inimitable Doctor that they joyfully submitted to every trait and mannerism. If they had been inconsiderate of Johnson's idiosyncrasies, they would have been inconsiderate of his person; for the person is made up of just such features. Friendship rejoices in all that belongs to the beloved. "Love bears all things" (I Corinthians 13:7).

12. A NEW DIMENSION TO THE MORAL PREDICAMENT

We not only judge others before we make an effort to acquaint them with the evidences, but we are morally impotent to deliver ourselves from such a habit. This is further proof that we are held by power as well as thought. If we expect to solve our problem, therefore, we must look to moral resources beyond ourselves.

In this one stroke we challenge the optimistic expectations of all forms of this-worldly humanism and rationalism. Once we submit to the moral limits of our own lives, we shall nurse no illusions about the moral limits of the race; for virtue, like water, can rise no higher than its source.

For example, we are able to explain why other nations look with such suspicion on American prosperity. Diplomats are shocked that our billion-dollar gifts have evoked resentment rather than gratitude. But they would not be shocked if they comprehended the elements of resentment in their own lives. The prosperity of a neighbor works for our insecurity, not our security. The higher he rises and the more goods he accumulates, the lower we fall and the more we feel we are missing. The same is true between nations.

* Boswell, *Life of Samuel Johnson LL.D.* (Britannica), p. 138.

The very prosperity of America arouses insecurity in nations that are less fortunate. While we may like to think that our prosperity is a proof of our virtue, other nations know that it is a proof of our arrogance; for our prosperity results more from the natural resources of the land than from the virtue of the people. Think of what American prosperity would be like if the industry and shrewdness of the Japanese were to control its development! In Japan, every inch of land is carefully cultivated, while we think nothing of wasting hundreds of square miles. No wonder undeveloped nations conclude that our prosperity was gained by exploitation and injustice. This is the same kind of response we entertain when we learn that a friend has just purchased a new boat or a complete set of power tools. We murmur inside, "How *does* he do it?" We relieve our own insecurity by putting a morally inferior interpretation on his prosperity. And this is how other nations respond to prosperous, but not virtuous, America. If diplomats would realize this, their opinion of resentful nations would not be so adolescent.

This construction also helps explain why university students are easy prey for revolutionary ideologies. Being ignorant of the moral limits of their own lives, they are ignorant of the moral limits of history. They imagine that injustice and tyranny can easily be overturned. Visionaries always see things in black and white. The students would temper their optimism if they understood that their own position in the university is maintained by a prudential balance of interests that is out of harmony with an equalitarian ideal.

Christian theology speaks of man's congenital pride as "original sin." The more we seek to be good, the more we confront our own moral limitations. We have insufficient virtue to close the gap between what we are and what we ought to be. There is a defect in our will and in our affections, a defect which thought cannot mend. If we were moral by nature, we would do the right out of a necessity that is unconscious of law. We would be borne away by the law of the spirit of life. But because we must

Defining the Law of Life

be confronted by a code of duty, we show that we are somewhat inspired by the law of legal necessity. Whoever must be *reminded* of duty is deficient in natural affections. God never urges himself to be good.

Since this is a book on Christian apologetics, let me point out that moral self-acceptance has now verified one of the cardinal presuppositions of the Christian faith. "I do not understand my own actions. For I do not do what I want, but I do the very thing I hate. Now if I do what I do not want, I agree that the law is good. So then it is no longer I that do it, but sin which dwells within me. For I know that nothing good dwells within me, that is, in my flesh" (Romans 7:15-18). I do not want to make more out of this than the facts will warrant, but I do believe this buttresses a claim I have made from the beginning: namely, that if one will proceed to reality with a humble attitude, he will discover that the presuppositions of Christianity are friendly to the highest tests of reason.

Since this may shock those who are charmed by traditional platitudes, let me point out that it in no way contradicts Paul's assertion: "The unspiritual man does not receive the gifts of the Spirit of God, for they are folly to him, and he is not able to understand them because they are spiritually discerned" (I Corinthians 2:14). If it is necessary to repeat it, I will repeat it: Man's trouble is not lack of knowledge, but lack of moral courage to act on the knowledge he already has. The warfare is in the will and in the affections.* *The intellect is corrupt only to the extent that it is a servant of evil affections.* For example: suppose a college alumnus confesses to a friend that he cheated in a chemistry quiz some twenty years earlier. "Then you ought to write back to the college and make things right," his friend counsels. "Oh, but that's *foolish!*" the alumnus curtly replies. "Why, who would care about the incident at this late date?" The counsel is not foolish because the law of contradiction is violated; nor is it foolish because it

---

* As the lady who said: "My mind is already made up. Please don't confuse me with the facts."

is out of harmony with the claims of the moral and spiritual environment. Rather, it is foolish because the alumnus morally despises the conclusion. The will disqualifies the verdict of the intellect because the conclusion is refractory to personal interests. It would take humility to write back to the chemistry professor and make things right. But pride wars against humility. When Savonarola said to Florence, "Be free," Florence applauded him; but when he said to Florence, "Be pure," Florence slew him. This means that man's rational difficulties stem from his moral difficulties. Whenever he hates a conclusion, he finds relief by denying the premise. But his denial does not change the truth: ". . . for as ten millions of circles can never make a square, so the united voice of myriads cannot lend the smallest foundation to falsehood."*

Hence, it is the *unspiritual* man who thinks that Christianity is foolish. And why not? If an alumnus refuses to humble himself before a distant chemistry professor, is it likely that he will humble himself before a being who knows the very thoughts and intentions of the heart?

But the fact remains that man *can* be honest; he *has* powers of moral and rational self-transcendence. Whenever man wills to know the right, he assuredly will know it. "If any man's will is to do his will, he shall know whether the teaching is from God or whether I am speaking on my own authority" (John 7:17). But he must first win the battle of pride. He must submit to the realities that already hold him from existence itself.

I think we hear too many vague homilies on "the noetic effects of sin." Are theologians unconsciously trying to avoid the hard labor of thinking? The truly peccant part of man is his will, not his intellect. The intellect is not corrupt until it is made a servant of depraved affections. As long as I have breath, I shall argue that faith is a whole-souled response to critically tested evidences. To believe in defiance of such evidences would outrage the image of God in man. William Law expresses this very succinctly: "It is

* Oliver Goldsmith, *The Vicar of Wakefield* (Oxford), p. 186.

Defining the Law of Life

therefore an immutable law of God, that all rational beings should act *reasonably* in *all* their actions; not at this *time* or in that *place*, or upon this *occasion*, or in all the use of some particular thing, but at *all* times, in *all* places, on *all* occasions, and in the use of *all* things. This is a law that is as unchangeable as God, and can no more cease to be, than God can cease to be a God of wisdom and order."*

"Original sin," it appears, is nothing but theological language for what we have all along called the moral predicament. Even as we have no natural affections for God, so we have no natural affections for the multitudes about us. We judge our neighbor by a higher standard than we ourselves meet. Though we expect him to be considerate of us, we are not natively considerate in return. We are considerate only as our affections are converted by the moral and spiritual environment. We are, in short, "totally depraved."

To be totally depraved, however, does not mean that we are as bad as we might be; nor does it mean that we are incapable of social decency and goodness. It means, first, that our affections are under the control of pride; second, that we have no native resources to deliver ourselves. All we can do is express pride on new and higher levels. We may consent to the right; we may strive for it with all our might; but we negate the possibility of success by the very fact that we must strive. "In reality, there is, perhaps, no one of our natural passions so hard to subdue as *pride*. Disguise it, struggle with it, beat it down, stifle it, mortify it as much as one pleases, it is still alive, and will every now and then peep out and show itself; you will see it, perhaps, often in this history; for, even if I could conceive that I had compleatly overcome it, I should probably be proud of my humility."† Virtue is a fruit, not a work; it is a gift of God on the occasion of our becoming humble.

* *A Serious Call to a Devout and Holy Life* (Hazard and Binns, 1806), pp. 70-71.
† Benjamin Franklin, *Autobiography* (Pocket Books, Inc.), p. 114.

13. THE DIALECTIC OF STRIVING

We must carefully guard against a misunderstanding of total depravity. Human limitations should always be balanced by human possibilities.* We can meet law in one of two ways: either by being good, or by being sorry for our failure to be good. The one is direct fulfillment, the other is indirect fulfillment. One can be thoughtful of his wife at dinner, or he can express sincere sorrow for having been unthoughtful. In either case the moral nature of the wife is pacified.

Total depravity simply warns that we can never *directly* meet the terms of law. We are powerless to establish our own righteousness. We cannot convert our selfish affections into a spontaneous love for God and our neighbor. "Now it is evident that no man is justified before God by the law" (Galatians 3:11). Since we must deliberately strive for righteousness, we prove that we shall never be righteous.

But total depravity in no way invalidates our responsibility to be sincerely sorry for our self-centered affections. Although we cannot make ourselves righteous, we can be sorry for our want of rectitude. We *are* capable of humbling ourselves before God and our neighbor. We remain free to accept or reject the claims of the moral and spiritual environment.

Therefore, what we can do and what we cannot do must be kept in delicate balance. Otherwise we fall on Scylla in trying to

---

* Hamilton and Madison were shrewd enough to see this. "The sincere friends of liberty, who give themselves up to the extravagancies of this passion, are not aware of the injury they do their own cause. As there is a degree of depravity in mankind which requires a certain degree of circumspection and distrust, so there are other qualities in human nature which justify a certain portion of esteem and confidence. Republican government presupposes the existence of these qualities in a higher degree than any other form. Were the pictures which have been drawn by the political jealousy of some of us faithful likenesses of the human character, the inference would be that there is not sufficient virtue among men for self-government; and that nothing less than the chains of despotism can restrain them from destroying and devouring one another." *The Federalist*, 55.

Defining the Law of Life

avoid Charybdis. If we say we are *responsible* for original sin, we violate the law of justice. One is not culpable unless he is able to do what is right. But if we say we are *not* responsible for original sin, we violate the law of consideration. There is no time when we are incapable of being more considerate of a neighbor—even though by our very effort to be considerate we are betrayed into the law of legal necessity. We cannot incarnate perfection; neither can we withdraw from a moment-by-moment obligation to try. An upright man is sorry for his selfish ways; and his sorrow is proof that he could have acted differently.

Habits of inconsideration distress a moral man. He experiences a warfare between the self as it is and the self as it ought to be. Mutinous impulses in his life do not conform themselves to mind. The transcendent self makes contact with an absolute which the empirical self refuses to be conformed to. The result is moral uneasiness. And it is this very uneasiness which proves that in some mysterious way, and to some unnamed extent, man is inconsiderate of his neighbor because he wants to be.* If one were inconsiderate out of pathological necessity, he could not entertain feelings of guilt with the consent of his nobler faculties.

Thus, we leave the claims of the moral and spiritual environment unless we, like Paul, *hate* our inability to be perfect. A sincere hatred of moral weakness is an acceptable expression of rectitude. It is evidence of cordial affections. This is what little children prove when they climb on their father's knee and with words of sincerity say, "I love you very, very much; I love you very, very much." Their random cries mean, "Please do not judge us by our disobedience. Behind our rebellious habits are sweet reservoirs of love and devotion; *they* are the real self." The children sincerely

---

* "For it still seemed to me that it was not we that sin, but that I know not what other nature sinned in us. And it gratified my pride to be free from blame, and, after I had committed any fault, not to acknowledge that I had done any—that Thou mightest heal my soul because it had sinned against Thee; but I loved to excuse it, and to accuse something else (I wot not what) which was with me, but was not I. But assuredly it was wholly I, and my impiety had divided me against myself; and that sin was all the more incurable in that I did not deem myself a sinner." Augustine, *The Confessions*, V, 10.

hate the very thing they do, and this expression of sincerity is accepted by the father as moral perfection.

A hatred of our inability to be perfect is proof of at least two things: first, that we know the right and desire it; second, that "another law" is at work in our members, a law that is unsubject to our reigning affections. "So I find it to be a law that when I want to do right, evil lies close at hand. For I delight in the law of God, in my inmost self, but I see in my members another law at war with the law of my mind and making me captive to the law of sin which dwells in my members. Wretched man that I am! Who will deliver me from this body of death?" (Romans 7:21-24). A delight in the law of God, plus a regret that this law betrays us into unmeet conduct—these have the effect of transmuting decisions into tragic moral choices. A choice is tragic, and thus invites moral admiration, when one confronts a situation where he must consciously choose evil in order that a greater good may come. Paul *tried* to be perfect, but sin prevented him from realizing his desires.

This leads us back to the importance of what we have called the principle of double fulfillment. When a man confronts a tragic moral choice, the sincerity of his effort issues in judicial peace. His hatred of imperfection may be either a lingering overtone in his life—as it usually is—or a conscious outcry of spiritual dissatisfaction. But sorrow over evil, when judged by love, is always accepted as one fruit of love. If a husband sincerely hates his unworthy conduct, his wife views this as evidence that he is really a good husband. Love looks for nothing but love.

It is easy for one to *deny* the presence of evil affections—very easy, indeed. He may even become the head of the religion department in a state university. Man is capable of endless self-deception. Self-righteous people make one of two capital mistakes: either they misunderstand the height of God's law, or they misunderstand the depth of their own moral conduct. "Undoubtedly philosophers are in the right when they tell us that nothing is great or little otherwise than by comparison."* A low view of law

---
* Jonathan Swift, *Gulliver's Travels* (Oxford), p. 71.

Defining the Law of Life

reduces God to man, while a high view of conduct elevates man to God. In either event a false comparison is being made. Even as an ignorant man can think he is learned, and even as a poor man can think he is rich, so a wretched man can indulge the illusion that he is righteous. He can think so because he measures himself by the wrong standard. "I am not aware of anything against myself, but I am not thereby acquitted. It is the Lord who judges me" (I Corinthians 4:4).

Those who seek righteousness outside Christ are like little children who get egoistic satisfaction from tattling on one another. The more they scheme, the more they betray their own ignorance and pathos. "But when they measure themselves by one another, and compare themselves with one another, they are without understanding" (II Corinthians 10:12). Man-made righteousness is as spurious as it is dangerous. It is spurious because it is not in accord with the facts. And it is dangerous because it leaves the affections prey to demonic impulses. Whenever man divorces himself from the moral and spiritual environment, the most heinous acts can be perpetrated in the name of God. "They will put you out of the synagogues; indeed, the hour is coming when whoever kills you will think he is offering service to God" (John 16:2). Christ was crucified by religious enthusiasts who sought to preserve the law of Moses. Having more zeal than enlightenment, they could not see that righteousness incarnate was standing before their very eyes. "It is to fulfil the word that is written in their law, 'They hated me without a cause'" (John 15:25).

14. CONSIDERATION AND REPENTANCE

Now that we have shown that the law of consideration surpasses the law of justice, the time has come to inquire whether it is necessary to repent. So, let us get on with it.

A plausible case can be made out on either side. If one wants to show that repentance *is* necessary, he need only point out that his life is too morally ambiguous to support legal righteousness. He must repent. But if one wants to prove that repentance is *not* necessary, he need only point out that selfishness is simply another expression of the moral predicament. Why be sorry for what cannot be avoided?

Fortunately, we can spare ourselves this debate. The question need not be taken up until we are satisfied that the law of consideration actually forms the pith and marrow of the imperative essence. And hardly have we put the matter this way, but what it appears that we are searching for something richer and more comprehensive than even the law of consideration itself.

15. JUSTICE AND CONSIDERATION

Justice and consideration, it seems, are complementary moral tasks. Although justice is somewhat grosser than consideration, it is nonetheless as much a part of the law of life as consideration. Or rather, consideration overcomes justice by taking in more than justice. Let us develop this.

Although our life is never *materially* identical with the race, it is *formally* identical most of the time. And it is this formal identity which makes it meaningful to speak of our just rights in society. If we purchase a piece of property, we expect to receive it; and we judicially cry out if we do not. In every situation where nothing but the formal side of our life is revealed, the moral sense is satisfied with justice. But when our difference from the race is revealed, the judicial sentiment is aroused if those who enter the circle of nearness fail to pass from justice to consideration.

Let us illustrate this by another trip to the library. In entering the reading room, we make only those demands that are common to the race. We want a convenient place to study. But if we chance to sit near students who frustrate our powers of concentration, a unique element in our life, hitherto concealed, is revealed; and we immediately call on the students to regard this uniqueness. They must not view us with an eye to our formal inclusion in the race, but with a spiritual appreciation of our inability to concentrate when the movement of a hard lead pencil can be heard against the

Defining the Law of Life

library table. *Others* may be able to study, but we are not. If our plea is ignored, and we are viewed simply as members of the human race, the judicial sentiment is aroused. Our life is not accepted in general unless it is also accepted in particular.

Those who go as far as consideration have already seen to justice, for no one will be sensitive to the delicate elements in moral response unless he is also in the habit of regarding the elements that are gross. If men reject our similarity to the race, they will certainly reject the features that set us apart from the race.

16. BEYOND CONSIDERATION

But even this does not fully resolve things, for though consideration goes beyond justice it falls short of perfect moral response. Yet, how can this deficiency be measured? If justice takes in our formal identity with the race, while consideration takes in our material difference from the race, what is lacking? Add formal identity to material uniqueness, and the sum seems to be the whole of our person. But is this really the case? The answer is in the negative, and for a very good reason.

Here is the crux of the problem: *Justice and consideration only answer to as much of our person as we happen to reveal.* Justice answers to our similarity to the race, while consideration answers to our difference from the race. But what about the scores of mysteries that lie unrevealed? A moral acceptance of our person must include an acceptance of these mysteries. There are many things in our heart which we either cannot, or do not wish to, unbosom. Yet, they are as truly part of our person as the features we publicly reveal. They may, in fact, be even more intimately part of the real self; for the less we have in common with the race, the more we express the true particularities of selfhood. Conformity is the enemy of individuality. The precious things in children flow from the unique elements in their lives. Each child is different.

This is why there is good reason to believe that consideration, like justice, sums up part, but not all, of the law of life; and that lying beyond both justice and consideration is a virtue that takes in the total mysteries of the self. A just and considerate person may believe he has received the totality of our person, when he may, in reality, have received no more than what we happen to reveal at a given moment. Even as justice is not relevant until we express our formal identity with the race, so consideration is not relevant until we express our material difference from the race. In both cases, however, it is the *revelation* of ourselves, not the sheer presence of our person, that obliges others. Although consideration goes deeper into the self than justice, it makes no effort to address itself to elements in the heart which remain unknown because they are unrevealed.

A considerate individual may conceivably propose the following plan: "Please draw up a complete list of the unique elements in your life, in order that I may know precisely what is required when you are in my presence." The very fact that such a plan can meaningfully be proposed is a proof that the law of consideration, like the law of justice, is less than perfect rectitude; for it is impossible to compile a catalogue of all the unique elements that comprise our life. The core of the self is formed of such a conflict of affections, interests, fears, and volitions, that only God, the monitor of the judicial sentiment, can fully comprehend its essence. We are mysteries to ourselves; we do not know what makes up the stuff of our own lives. "I do not understand my own actions" (Romans 7:15). How, then, can an objective code of duty be drawn up?

The deficiencies that threaten justice are equally threats to consideration. A person can be considerate of us because it is to his interest; or he can be considerate because someone forces him. Both attempts arouse the judicial sentiment in us, for neither justice nor consideration has moral worth unless it is a fruit of the law of the spirit of life.

It ought to be perfectly clear, hence, that if we are ever going to name the pith and marrow of the imperative essence, and thus solve the problem of repentance, we must pass from *fruits* of rectitude (justice and consideration) to the center of rectitude itself

Defining the Law of Life

(the law of the spirit of life). Since nothing has moral value unless it is done in the right spirit, this "right spirit" must be the illusive stuff we are trying to isolate and name.

17. THE LAW OF LOVE

Here is the self: depth and width and height of vital personality, interests and affections compounded by rational mystery, and a fathomless spiritual unity within moral and rational self-transcendence. The core of selfhood has been conditioned and pitted by hereditary influences, cultural-ethnic ties, and the total impact of a complex physical, rational, aesthetic, and moral and spiritual environment. Life is more than freedom and involvement; it is vital uniqueness. Some like to play golf, while others prefer to walk through distant canyons. But no one can give a rational explanation for his preference. The reason for personal preference is as mysterious as the metaphysics of the soul itself.

When I was within an ace of giving up my search for the pith and marrow of the imperative essence, I again remembered that there are two ways of being good: by direct or indirect fulfillment. Justice and consideration may constitute a direct attempt to receive the dignity of our person. But the real mystery of selfhood can only be taken in as one abandons all rational and legal hope that the self is capable of full revelation. A truly moral individual accepts our lives for what they are, both in the way they are revealed and in the way they are hidden. *This is only to say, in other words, that a moral individual is one who loves.* Only love accepts another without forecast, interest, or calculation. Love fulfills the law without consciously trying. Love cheerfully limits itself by the mystery of the beloved; it banishes calculation by submitting to the complexity of life; it rejoices at the burgeoning particularities of personality; it never challenges or distrusts; it bears up under all phase changes, wishing nothing but good. Love fulfills the law, but it does it indirectly. "Owe no one anything, except to love one another; for he who loves his neighbor has fulfilled the law. The commandments, 'You shall not commit adultery, You shall not kill, You shall not steal, You shall not covet,' and any other commandment, are summed up in this sentence, 'You shall love your neighbor as yourself.' Love does no wrong to a neighbor; therefore love is the fulfilling of the law" (Romans 13:8-10).

When I realized that only love can take in life without forecast, interest, or calculation, I not only recognized that the pith and marrow of the imperative essence had been found, but I swiftly perceived that love is the only standard by which we judge those who enter the circle of nearness. The total effort of the third method of knowing has been directed to a clarification of this one truth. God and man share the same moral and spiritual environment, and the content of this environment is love. "God is love, and he who abides in love abides in God, and God abides in him" (I John 4:16). Since personal rectitude forms the stuff of the third species of truth, and since the third species of truth comes into existence the moment an individual closes the gap between what he is (the descriptive essence) and what he ought to be (the imperative essence), it follows that love comprises the stuff of rectitude, the third type of truth, the imperative essence, the law of life, the moral and spiritual environment, and the essence of God. Love is the univocal element which makes it possible to say, "God is good," and "An upright man is good," for good is but another name for love.

This unity must be stressed, lest it be supposed from previous discussion that justice, consideration, and love are three separate moral responses—as if at times we look only for justice; at other times for consideration; while under very special conditions we look for love. Quite to the contrary, we look for nothing but love. Love answers to the claims of the moral and spiritual environment, even as the want of love—whatever else may remain—arouses the judicial sentiment. When others enter the circle of nearness, we expect them to receive the whole of our person; which is only to say that we look for love. If we suspect that a person sees to justice and consideration, without being morally moved to regard the

Defining the Law of Life

whole of our person, the judicial sentiment is aroused and we judge him guilty. Love and calculation exhaust the possibilities. If we are not viewed through the eyes of love, we are being treated as a thing.

This discussion in no way contradicts our assertion that the judicial sentiment is the narrow point of contact between time and eternity. An aroused judicial sentiment is but the negative sign of love. Even as acts of kindness show that one is in harmony with the moral and spiritual environment, so acts of injustice and inconsideration show that one is not. By examining the aroused side of our moral nature (the judicial sentiment), we discover the essence of rectitude (love). This is why it is entirely acceptable to speak of the judicial sentiment as the narrow point of contact between God and man. Even as God blesses those who love, so he creates judicial unrest in those who hate. An offense against love is an offense against God.

This verifies the Christian teaching that justice and consideration, apart from love, profit nothing. "If I speak in the tongues of men and of angels, but have not love, I am a noisy gong or a clanging cymbal. And if I have prophetic powers, and understand all mysteries and all knowledge, and if I have all faith, so as to remove mountains, but have not love, I am nothing. If I give away all I have, and if I deliver my body to be burned, but have not love, I gain nothing" (I Corinthians 13:1-3). Love is the enemy of forecast, interest, and calculation. If a person is just or considerate because of a burdensome or lawful sense of necessity, or if he accepts us out of a zeal to advance his own interests, not only is his act shorn of moral worth, but a knowledge of it arouses the judicial sentiment in us. Whenever conduct is safely escorted past the moral sense, it is love, not justice or consideration, which prepares the way. Love is but another name for rectitude; it alone answers to the essential self. Whoever offends love is guilty of offending character. *"This is the last* Philosophy *that we must study upon* Earth; *let us therefore that yet remain here, as our days and friends waste, reinforce our love to each other; which of all vertues, both* spiritual *and* moral, *hath the highest privilege, because death it self cannot end it.*"*

Yet, one does not love unless he is both just and considerate, for whoever takes in the hidden phases of another's life must also take in all that is revealed. Shakespeare counsels well: they do not love who do not show their love. If a person affects a regard for our life, but senses no moral necessity to see to justice and consideration, he is a deceiver; for he cannot boast of the greater when he fails in the lesser.

Rather than teasing out the attributes of love by a prolonged application of the third method of knowing, let us appeal once again to the normative teaching of the Apostle Paul. Centuries of definition have not eclipsed the precision and luster of the Christian view of love. "Love is patient and kind; love is not jealous or boastful; it is not arrogant or rude. Love does not insist on its own way; it is not irritable or resentful; it does not rejoice at wrong, but rejoices in the right. Love bears all things, believes all things, hopes all things, endures all things" (I Corinthians 13:4-7).

Hitherto I have assumed, but not defined, the meaning of love. And the reason for this is plain. Since we look for others to love us, we already know what love is; and, knowing it, we should acknowledge it.

For those who crave a definition of love, however, I offer the following. Here and elsewhere I intend the term "love" to signify all that Paul includes in the above list of attributes. This is a denotative definition, for it denotes the ways that love expresses itself. Aristotle might chide us for not giving a connotative definition, but his attitude would only show how really little he understands about love. Since love has no existence apart from an act of love, it is impossible to give a rationally accurate account of its essence. It can be known only as one loves or is loved. Knowledge by inference must yield to knowledge by acquaintance.

Paul makes no effort to examine the shades of difference between *agape* and *eros* love, for he learned the essence of love in the same

* Izaak Walton, *Lives* (Oxford), pp. 134-135.

way that all Christians learn it: by a spiritual confrontation with Jesus Christ. "In this the love of God was made manifest among us, that God sent his only Son into the world, so that we might live through him" (I John 4:9). A mother who fondles her child knows more about love than all the savants; but the person who is confronted by the love of God in Christ knows more than the mother. "I have more understanding than all my teachers, for thy testimonies are my meditation" (Psalm 119:99).

Chapter Nine

THE LOGIC OF REPENTANCE

1. THE PARADOX OF MORAL STRIVING

Our search for the imperative essence has been motivated by one interest. We have sought a rule by which we might evaluate our moral standing before God. Until we apprehend the content of the imperative essence we shall be ignorant of rectitude; and until we apprehend the nature of rectitude we shall have no way of solving the problem of repentance. But our search is over. *Love* is the stuff both of the imperative essence and of rectitude. Or better, rectitude and the imperative essence are only facets of the same thing. Now that this has been successfully established, we may proceed with an evaluation of our moral standing before God.

If God judges us by the heights of the law of love, we are in a perilous moral position, for we simply do not have natural affections for the careless multitudes who crowd the highways, who compete with us for cafeteria tables, and who scatter beer cans and watermelon rinds around our favorite picnic areas. Merely getting along with others, let alone loving them, is a very taxing responsibility.

Deliberately *trying* to love people will not help, for love is a fruit, not a work. One cannot love until his affections receive their dye from the moral and spiritual environment. This is why a Christian prays for grace to love. Only by the help of God can he love those who are unlovely. Christianity and Kantianism, therefore, are incompatible approaches. Kant says, *We ought, therefore we can.*

The Logic of Repentance

Christianity says, *We ought, therefore we cannot*. The more we make rectitude a calculated object of striving, the further we recede from moral fulfillment; for moral fulfillment is spontaneous, affectionate fulfillment. Love carries its own sense of compulsion. It is borne on the wings of the law of the spirit of life. When we must be motivated by either rational or legal necessity, love gives way to forecast, interest, and calculation. Suppose a mother rushes to help her terrified child. She acts out of spontaneous love. She would be offended by even the suggestion that she must help her child from a legal sense of duty.

The more we probe, the more deeply we become involved in a paradox of moral striving. If we were upright by nature, we should not be concerned to discover the law of life; we should do the good from a sense of compulsion that is unconscious of law.

Moral striving is paradoxical because we shall never love God unless we make a conscious effort; and yet because we must strive for legal righteousness, we prove that we shall never be righteous. If our affections were a fruit of the moral and spiritual environment, we should fulfill the law with the same unconscious necessity with which we breathe.

The paradox can perhaps be illustrated by a painter who deliberately tries to become great. Unless he strives, he will never be an artist at all, let alone a great artist. But since he makes genius a deliberate goal of striving, he proves that he is not, and never will be, a genius. A master artist is great without trying to be great. His abilities unfold like the petals of a rose before the sun. Genius is a gift of God. It is a fruit, not a work.

But if this is the case, how can we take any steps toward God? Rectitude, we know, is met in one of two ways: either by a spontaneous expression of the good or by spontaneous sorrow for having failed. The one is direct fulfillment; the other is indirect fulfillment. This has been repeatedly pointed out. But hitherto we have not made it clear that indirect fulfillment, like direct fulfillment, has no moral value unless it takes its rise from the unfree moral necessities of the imperative essence. Indirect fulfillment is stripped of virtue whenever it is made a goal of conscious striving. Whoever deliberately tries to be sorry will never be sorry. Sorrow cannot be induced by human effort.

2. VENTURING A RADICAL HYPOTHESIS

Unless our effort is to collapse at the very door of heaven, therefore, the third method of knowing must come to grips with this question: "Ought we to repent for our selfish ways?" An academic admission of selfishness is morally insipid.

To stimulate discussion, therefore, let us venture a radical hypothesis. Either God judges us by the heights of the law of love, or he does not. And since no evidence has clinched the first alternative, let us search for evidences to clinch the second. Possibly others must show signs of spontaneous love for us, but we are under no moral obligation to return such signs to them. The direction of love is from them to us, not from us to them.

Radical though this hypothesis may appear, it at least has a modicum of plausibility to it. For example, can we not say that self-love is nothing but protective spiritual armor; and that just as the wolf guards itself by its sharp teeth and the rabbit by its swift legs, so we guard ourselves by the insistence that others accept our dignity? God devised the judicial sentiment as a means of preventing us from being spiritually indifferent to the image of God in us. Only total moral degeneration can deliver an individual from a circumambient assurance that his life is sacred. The obligation to respect life is written into the universe itself. "Whoever sheds the blood of man, by man shall his blood be shed; for God made man in his own image" (Genesis 9:6). It is no innocent thing to offend human dignity, for in striving against man one strives against God.

If we can bring ourselves to act on the truth of this radical hypothesis, we can shift our attitude toward the whole problem of repentance. Rather than chiding ourselves for judging others by a standard that we do not meet, let us reverently bow before

The Logic of Repentance

providence. The ways of God are past finding out. The moral and spiritual environment is only an *ad hoc* method by which God sees to it that men will not be cavalier about the image of God in them.

3. SELFISHNESS AND THE JUDICIAL SENTIMENT

It should not be difficult to put this hypothesis to a specific test. Let us stand in the center of any one of the many times during the day when we fail to regard others by the law of love. If God disapproves our conduct, and if his disapproval is registered in the claims of the moral and spiritual environment, a sincere participation in this environment ought to arouse culpable feelings in us.

Let us work our way into the problem by posing a guiding question. Even as we previously asked, "How are we affected when others fail to regard our dignity?" so we now ask, "How are we affected when we fail to regard the dignity of others?" If God is active in the one case, it would be presumptuous to think that he is inactive in the other.

Suppose we entertain evil thoughts toward those whose driving habits irk us. Does the Holy Spirit convict us? Are we culpable? Others are guilty if they fail to love us, but are we guilty if we fail to love them?

Before we shift from guilt in others to guilt in ourselves, however, it is necessary that we win a new victory over our tendency to see only those evidences which are congenial to self-love. "There is no fact better ascertained than the facility with which men are persuaded to believe what they wish."* As we have stressed from the beginning, one cannot perceive ultimates until his heart is right. Bad affections distort truth by inducing the mind to comply with personal preference. Pascal states the matter rather well: "There is a universal and essential difference between the actions of the will and all other actions. The will is one of the

---

* John Stuart Mill, Speech on "The Utility of Knowledge," in *Autobiography* (Oxford), p. 273.

chief factors in belief, not that it creates belief, but because things are true or false according to the aspect in which we look at them. The will, which prefers one aspect to another, turns away the mind from considering the qualities of all that it does not like to see; and thus the mind, moving in accord with the will, stops to consider the aspect which it likes, and so judges by what it sees."* Guilt has no speculative existence. It can be rationally known only as it is spiritually felt.

The basic ingredients of guilt are, first, a humble admission that law has been transgressed; second, a cordial willingness to be responsible for whatever judicial consequences flow from this act of transgression. If either element is negated, the essence of guilt is destroyed. Guilt is never known by science or philosophy. Reason may clarify our moral predicament, but it cannot excite culpable feelings. Moral insight is a fruit of affections that are touched by the Spirit of God.

Once we are willing to accept damaging as well as supporting evidences, we may proceed with our question: "How are we affected when we fail to regard the dignity of others?" Do we have a guilty conscience? Does God judge us?

If we may argue from the most ordinary experiences of life, God does *not* disapprove our selfishness. Even though we are habitually inconsiderate of others, we are able to jostle our way through the city crowds with a surprisingly easy conscience. The judicial sentiment is not aroused against us. This seems to prove that, though God judges unfriendly people through us, we are judged by some other standard, whatever that may be. And if this is not the case, why is the judicial sentiment dormant?

4. A CHECK AGAINST HASTE

But we have already shown that we cannot defend selfishness with the consent of our nobler faculties and the praise of men of character. Even as we conceal physical faults from others, so we

* *Pensées*, 99.

The Logic of Repentance

conceal selfish motives. We pretend that we are innocently in pursuit of universal values. We would not dare stand in the market and say to others, "Although you are morally obliged to be friendly to us, we are under no moral obligation to be friendly to you." We may *believe* this, even as we may act on it; but we will never let others know it.

This is no insignificant matter, for moral self-acceptance has already proved that a person is not in contact with the moral and spiritual environment, and thus does not know the content of the imperative essence, until his convictions can be defended with the consent of his nobler faculties and the praise of men of character. And since we are obliged to conceal selfishness, we prove that selfishness is *not* a fruit of the moral and spiritual environment.

Notice the counsel we give those we love, for such counsel is a sure way of proving what we really believe. Parents often urge higher standards on their children than they themselves will follow. They teach the little ones to be thoughtful of others in the school and on the playground. Their solicitude is a direct fruit of the moral and spiritual environment. They know that if their children form selfish habits, they will not only become anxious by losing friends, but they will progressively deteriorate their own character. The difference between a saint and a felon is the difference between affections that are, and affections that are not, regenerated by the Spirit of God. A felon uses others as a means to his own selfish ends, while a saint subordinates himself to others.

5. A FAULTY APPLICATION OF METHOD

If selfishness is not a fruit of the moral and spiritual environment, however, how did we succeed in defending it by what purported to be a valid application of the third method of knowing? When I traced back the connections in the argument, I discovered that, despite the assumed precision of our effort, we were really not applying moral self-acceptance at all. Let me show why.

When we established guilt in others, we did *not* appeal to their subjective feelings. Quite to the contrary; it made no difference whether they felt culpable or innocent. We did not walk up and down the street, notebook in hand, taking a moral census of how many people experience guilt when they are inconsiderate of us. God judges them through us, and that is the end of it. If others do not feel culpable for their thoughtless ways, it is their own fault. They stand under judgment the moment they refuse to be morally limited by the sheer presence of our person. An aroused judicial sentiment in us proves this. Therefore, to ask if we feel guilty for not being considerate of others is as pointless as asking if others feel guilty for not being considerate of us.

We have been unconsciously betrayed into a *non sequitur* argument. From the absence of a feeling of guilt we cannot argue to our own virtue. If we were to reason in this fashion, we would contradict good procedure. Just as God judges others through us, though they may be quite unaware of their guilt, so with an equal want of consciousness we may be culpable for being inconsiderate of others. If God completes the moral cycle in the one case, there is no reason to believe that he fails to do so in the other.

Pride might pertinaciously insist that we are not culpable until we experience guilt. But its stand is futile for at least two somewhat overlapping reasons. First, it does violence to the third condition of knowing. We already *know* the law of God, and thus can be judged by it, for we are morally *responsible* for knowing. Whether we entertain subjective guilt is beside the point. Second, we have already shown that those who enter the circle of nearness are culpable if they fail to give evidence of receiving the dignity of our person. How they *feel* about their conduct is irrelevant. And if this is true of others, it is likewise true of ourselves. Since God has created us in his own image—" 'For we are indeed his offspring' " (Acts 17:28)—the conditions that hold one individual equally hold all.

There is yet another point. We may fail to sense guilt because our hearts are evil. "Behold, the Lord's hand is not shortened, that it cannot save, or his ear dull, that it cannot hear; but your

The Logic of Repentance

iniquities have made a separation between you and your God, and your sins have hid his face from you so that he does not hear" (Isaiah 59:1-2). The mere assertion that we are evil does not, of course, establish the fact. But the assertion does at least buttress the possibility that the absence of a *feeling* of guilt need not imply the absence of *guilt*. Just as others are insensitive to transgression when they are inconsiderate of us, so we may be equally insensitive, though equally culpable, when we are inconsiderate of them.

6. A CORRECTION OF PROCEDURE

If we are going to use the third method of knowing in clarifying our own relation to the person of God, we must apply it to ourselves in the same way that we applied it to others. A shift in procedure, however small, would be unfair.

As we look back on how we used moral self-acceptance when approaching others, we note that one indispensable condition had to be met. *Others had to enter the circle of nearness.* Unless this condition prevailed, the third method of knowing was inapplicable. Distant people, or people in the abstract, are powerless to put our souls in touch with the claims of the moral and spiritual environment. Unless the wall of our interests is pierced, the judicial sentiment remains dormant. This means that if we hope to use moral self-acceptance when defining the place of our life in God, we must duplicate the conditions that others meet when God judges them through us. We must stand in the circle of nearness; we must look into their eyes and feel the warmth of their personality.

Now that this has been clarified, it is not difficult to decide which way to go. Having already inquired into the terms that must be met when others *reject* us, let us now reverse our procedure and inquire into the terms that must be met when others *accept* us. Suppose a large act of kindness has been done for us. When our benefactor enters the circle of nearness and his personality touches ours, does the sheer presence of his life acquaint us with any new elements in the moral and spiritual environment? The answer is patently clear to men of character. *Whenever another person limits his life by a loving regard for ours, his very presence obliges us to respond with like gestures of love. If we refuse, we become guilty.*

Let us return to the illustration used at an earlier point in the book. We asserted that if we recover a young mother's rowboat from a muddy river, only to have our clothing drenched and our plans for the day inconvenienced, we judge her guilty if she fails to express spontaneous words of thanks. Let us now reverse the illustration. Suppose *our* boat has been recovered. When our benefactor enters the circle of nearness, what is required of us? The answer is as clear as any yet discovered by the third method of knowing. Either we express spontaneous signs of love, or we become guilty. This is proved by our deliberate avoidance of an offended benefactor. A man of character cannot elude the debt of love. He cannot look into the eyes of an incensed friend without experiencing guilt. And this sense of guilt is just as surely a fruit of his participation in the moral and spiritual environment, and thus of his participation in the person of God, as his initial confidence that others are guilty if they fail to show signs of accepting his dignity.

This is quite sufficient to prove that God judges us by the same law by which we judge others. But to give added prestige to the demonstration, let us strengthen it by an appeal to secondary evidences.

7. THE BUTTRESSING FORCE OF CUMULATIVE EVIDENCES

Since it is spiritually impossible to draw near to a person without making contact with a kind of being which is different in quality from that of things, it follows that the *sheer presence* of another individual is an echo of the law of life. As long as we keep our distance, of course, the idea of ownership can be entertained with relative ease. But we are talking about nearness. Whenever we let another personality touch ours, we lose self-respect if we try to act as if we are touching a thing rather than a person. Signs of

The Logic of Repentance

friendship cannot be withheld—whether sincere or feigned. We must smile, say a kind word, or inquire if we can be of any assistance. Plato's arguments for slavery are attractive to those who sit by the fire and munch popcorn; but no man of character can entertain the thought of buying and selling his neighbor's children. Euthanasia as a problem of thought is easy to manage; but no morally upright doctor can take a knife and cut the throat of a feeble-minded child sitting in the waiting room.

Furthermore, acts of love always leave deposits of moral satisfaction on the heart. We are never more at peace with ourselves than when we have made a conscientious effort to be thoughtful of others. The best in the self is drawn out. It is impossible to be helpful without experiencing the kind of moral release that would follow if love *were* the law of life. Even as hatred disintegrates the life, so kindness integrates it. "But the fruit of the Spirit is love, joy, peace, patience, kindness, goodness, faithfulness, gentleness, self-control; against such there is no law" (Galatians 5:22-23). Whenever we are unkind to a person, we are morally uneasy in his presence. We are ashamed of any conduct that is out of harmony with the law of love. A lost temper outrages our nobler faculties. We try to hide what we have done; we cannot speak of it before men of character without tones of repentance; we teach our loved ones to avoid our folly. "For every one who does evil hates the light, and does not come to the light, lest his deeds should be exposed. But he who does what is true comes to the light, that it may be clearly seen that his deeds have been wrought in God" (John 3:20-21). Degrees of moral peace measure the degree to which our affections conform to the will of God. The peace we feel when we love, and the guilt we feel when we hate, are equally fruits of the moral and spiritual environment. Because we live and move and are in God, we have no more control over the one response than we have over the other. Moral release and moral bondage are divine judgments against the soul. The one is a verdict of satisfaction, the other a verdict of dissatisfaction; but the norm of judgment is always love.

I am not asserting that the Ten Commandments, and other laws in the Bible, are analytically included in the law of love. The law of love is the *greatest* of the laws, but it is certainly not the *only* law. I simply say that nothing has moral value unless it is done out of love. We prove our love by keeping God's commandments. And this is accomplished in one of two ways: either by a spontaneous fulfillment of the right or by spontaneous sorrow for having failed. The one is direct fulfillment, the other is indirect fulfillment. Our positional righteousness in Christ makes it possible for God to view us through the eyes of love rather than law. An oversight of the filial bond betrayed the Roman Catholic Church into its legalistic concept of "second justification" and too confident a distinction between "venial" and "mortal" sins.

Once we recognize that kindness lays deposits of moral relief on our heart, we at once confront the fact that a man of character is held by greater moral responsibilities than he has resources to meet. "For the desires of the flesh are against the Spirit, and the desires of the Spirit are against the flesh; for these are opposed to each other, to prevent you from doing what you would" (Galatians 5:17). Each time an upright man enters a social situation, he faces an infinite task. Perhaps he boards a bus. He can assist a mother with her groceries, offer his seat to an elderly gentleman, or give a sage word of counsel to a freckled lad beside him. But he experiences a warfare in him. "The spirit indeed is willing, but the flesh is weak" (Matthew 26:41). Since he is weary from a day's work at the office, he flies to his seat and begins reading the newspaper. This cheats him of spiritual satisfaction. And the more sensitive he becomes to his loss, the more uneasy he feels. The transcendent self makes contact with a rule that the empirical self does not find convenient to obey. This rule is the law of love, for no other rule can account for the infinite task that one confronts when he enters a social situation.

In sum, each time a person stands before us we are on trial before God. We can always do more good than we have in the past: more to relieve destitution and distress, more to guide, direct, and forgive. Being made in the image of God, we are already in contact

The Logic of Repentance

with the essence of rectitude; for God is love. Moral uneasiness over selfishness is the voice of God speaking to and against our heart. The more perfect a man becomes, the clearer this truth becomes. To a wretch, of course, such a construction would hold no appeal. But a wretch would see no evil in murder, either.

8. TRAGIC MORAL CHOICES

Tragic moral choices are a further proof that we are held by the law of love. A choice is tragic when one consciously chooses evil in order that a greater good may come. A serious recognition of such choices gave the Greek tragedians a profounder insight into the nature of man than that of the classical philosophers. Duty to the gods and duty to the state often conflict with filial duty. Which should yield to the other? Clytemnestra murders Agamemnon, her husband and king. The son, Orestes, is moved by filial piety to avenge his father; Apollo orders him to do so. But this sets the son against himself, for matricide is a sin against filial piety. The bond between mother and son is sacred; it must not be violated. What should Orestes do?

Again, Antigone learns that her brother, Polynices, has been slain in battle. Creon forbids the burial. Should Antigone obey Creon or the laws of family sanctity? Her duty to Polynices preponderates, and she inters his body by night. Creon orders her to be buried alive, but Antigone kills herself before the sentence is carried out.

We do not have to read Aeschylus and Sophocles to feel the force of tragic moral choices. The claims of the moral and spiritual environment are never easily harmonized. Notice these two laws, for example: (1) You shall love your neighbor as yourself; (2) You shall not bear false witness against your neighbor. I assert that most tragic moral choices stem from our inability to adjust the law of love to the other laws in the second table of the Ten Commandments. The Hippocratic Oath obliges a doctor to prolong life: "I will give no deadly medicine to any one if asked, nor suggest any such counsel." But in complying with this oath a doctor must prolong the lives of the incurable, thus adding to human misery. Whenever one deliberately causes people to suffer, does he not sin? Again, if a doctor forthrightly tells his patient how serious his illness is, he may hasten death; but if he conceals the truth he violates the trust which the patient has placed in him. The first struggle is between elements in the law of love itself, while the second struggle is between the law of love and the law of veracity.

And what is true of the doctor is equally true of all who are spiritually honest with their own hearts. Our participation in the moral and spiritual environment makes it impossible to escape the threat of tragic moral choices. Suppose we attend a neighborhood dinner. Although the meal was poorly prepared, we find it difficult, if not impossible, to be perfectly truthful when we leave. "My dear," we say, "I had a lovely evening; thank you for your kindness." We are not to bear false witness, and yet we are morally bound to do to her as we would that she should do to us. We know that if we prepared an elaborate dinner, we would be morally offended if our departing guests did not express their appreciation. How, then, can we morally *avoid* flattering the hostess? There may be a way out, but what is it? We end by telling her what she expects to hear, not what we really want to say.

Our difficulty is accentuated by the unreasonable demands which the hostess places on us. When she extends her hand and bids us good night, she wants us to confirm her pride. She is not unlike a wife who buys a very expensive dress and then bursts in on her husband with the excited question: "What do you think of it, honey? Isn't it just *lovely*?" She has no right to expect a completely candid answer until she releases him from his fear that he will violate the law of love. She must add, "Now, now—I want the truth!" Relieved of his fear, he replies, "Well, my dear, to be perfectly frank, I don't think it flatters you one bit." Apart from such relief he would not know how to state himself without offending either love or truth. He knows how important praise is

The Logic of Repentance

to a woman's security. And he knows it because he knows how important praise is to his own security. "I have ever had a wish to be liked by those around me,—a wish that during the first half of my life was never gratified. In my school-days no small part of my misery came from the envy with which I regarded the popularity of popular boys. They seemed to me to live in a social paradise, while the desolation of my pandemonium was complete."* The desire to be appreciated is perhaps the strongest social force in man. When employees are no longer appreciated, they will migrate to other, and often less lucrative, positions. It is only when we feel loved and admired that we have anything to live up to.

But because we give in to flattery so easily, we prove that we not only sense a conflict between love and truth, but we show that we are sinners; for we fear man more than God. Like small children, we would rather save face than be moral. Our own ego is bolstered up by the blandishments that others give us in return.

Since our vision is not always clear, we often add, "as God gives us to see the right." A father is bound to obey the state, yet he is also bound to provide for his family. Should he go to war, or should he see to the needs of his children? A minister must preach the gospel, yet he must honor his father and his mother. Should he care for his kin, or leave home and preach to the needy? On one remarkable occasion Christ counseled a disciple to violate the law of filial piety. "Another of the disciples said to him, 'Lord, let me first go and bury my father.' But Jesus said to him, 'Follow me, and leave the dead to bury their own dead'" (Matthew 8:21-22). Christ revealed his lordship by declaring the order in obedience that this particular disciple should follow. Preaching the gospel took precedence over filial piety.

Theologians have devised many casuistical schemes to harmonize truth and love. For example, rather than thanking the hostess for the dinner, we should only thank her for her effort: "Thank you, my dear, for all you have done." Smile sincerely, shake her hand,

* Anthony Trollope, *An Autobiography* (Oxford), p. 136.

and then depart. In this way one can be both truthful and loving. But the difficulty is that truth pertains to what we know others *think* we intend, rather than to the strict semantical limits of our words. And this is what we know the hostess thinks we mean: "Your dinner was a great success; my friends will soon learn of your triumph." She believes we are confirming the interpretation which she has already put on her efforts. The only way to disabuse her would be by coming out forthrightly and saying, "Although we did not care for your dinner, we thank you for your effort." But if we did this, we would instantly arouse the judicial sentiment in her. She would charge us with failing to approach the situation from her point of view. We are boors and ingrates.

But she is equally distant from rectitude, for she has not only made unreasonable demands on us, but she does not consider the problem from our point of view. She violates the law of love just as much as we do. Each must seek and give forgiveness.

This is why the insights of Samuel Johnson are often profounder than those of the classical theologians. Johnson had the good sense to look at the matter from within the truths that already held him. "There is a great difference between what is said without our being urged to it, and what is said from a kind of compulsion. If I praise a man's book without being asked my opinion of it, that is honest praise, to which one may trust. But if an author asks me if I like his book, and I give him something like praise, it must not be taken as my real opinion."*

Machiavelli illustrates the perversion that results when only one side of the problem is appreciated. Realizing that it is impossible to rid the court of flatterers, Machiavelli tells a prince that he ought not to expect truth from everybody. To do so would be foolish, for truth cannot always be told. "A prudent prince must therefore take a third course, by choosing for his council wise men, and giving these alone full liberty to speak the truth to him, but only of those things that he asks and of nothing else; . . ."†

---

* Boswell, *Life of Samuel Johnson LL.D.* (Britannica), p. 158.
† *The Prince*, XXIII.

The Logic of Repentance

Machiavelli is wise enough to see that tragic moral choices are inevitable. But for him they are not really tragic at all. Morality is only a name for political expediency. Whether it is good for a prince to say in word what he intends in meaning is decided by the calculus of power. If political hegemony is secured, the most villainous and nefarious means are morally justified. "Therefore, a prudent ruler ought not to keep faith when by so doing it would be against his interest, and when the reasons which made him bind himself no longer exist.... Nor have legitimate grounds ever failed a prince who wished to show colourable excuse for the non-fulfillment of his promise."* The prince can tell lies without having to hate the thing he does. The *inevitability* of flattery converts to the *necessity* of flattery. Once Machiavelli succeeded in destroying the metaphysical foundations of morals, he ended up with no morals at all. His counsel to the prince is not a fruit of the moral and spiritual environment. He is simply telling the prince to follow the canons of enlightened self-interest, for this is the chief passport to power.

The seventeenth century Jesuits were only a shade removed from Machiavelli. Whether it is right to say in word what one intends in meaning is decided by religious expedience, not by the inflexible claims of the moral and spiritual environment. Pascal wrote *The Provincial Letters* as a scathing attack on the maxim that "opinions probable in speculation may be followed with a safe conscience in practice." The *Letters* are not only a paragon of polemical writing; they remain a literary masterpiece in their own right. They prove that when a man deliberately prefers one law to another, he can use the canons of rectitude to shield his own wickedness.

Some may deny the inescapability of tragic moral choices, but they do so only by ignoring the realities that already hold them. They fail to appreciate the degree to which they themselves seek and give flattery. Flattery, as Edward Gibbon observes, is the prolific parent of falsehood. Whenever we do something which has

---

* *Ibid.*, XVIII. "And thus dishonesty begets dishonesty, till dishonesty seems to be beautiful." Trollope, *op. cit.*, p. 227.

called for effort, we want others to confirm our pride. Each Sunday a minister expects his family to comfort him with the warm assurance that he delivered a fine sermon. Although he preaches humility to others, he digests no small share of pride himself. He somehow manages to preach more effectively when the church is full. Again, an artist may crave neither money nor popularity, but he cannot throw off his craving for appreciation. Not to be understood and appreciated is too great a price for him to pay.

The Apostle Paul was very sensitive to the reality of tragic moral choices in his own life. Although he wanted to mediate the law of God with perfection, he found he had insufficient moral resources to do it. "For I delight in the law of God, in my inmost self, but I see in my members another law at war with the law of my mind and making me captive to the law of sin which dwells in my members" (Romans 7:22-23). Unlike Machiavelli, however, Paul took moral consolation from the fact that he *hated* the very thing he did. This was proof that he cordially submitted to the claims of the moral and spiritual environment. Because he did not excuse himself, he showed that his failure to be perfect was somehow of his own doing.

Paul was so sensitive to the heights of the law of love that he passed judgment on himself in a way that none but the children of light can appreciate. For example, he solemnly wrote that "love is not . . . boastful" (I Corinthians 13:4). Since a boastful person gains stature at the expense of others, it is sin to boast. Paul knew and accepted this. Boasting is a direct violation of the law of love. And yet, despite all his prayers and striving, Paul found he could not disaffiliate himself from a desire to boast. "I repeat, let no one think me foolish; but even if you do, accept me as a fool, so that I too may boast a little. (What I am saying I say not with the Lord's authority but as a fool, in this boastful confidence; since many boast of worldly things, I too will boast.)" (II Corinthians 11:16-18). Some may reply that Paul deliberately used this technique to quell the claims of the false prophets. No doubt. Paul *did* face a tragic moral choice. But because he was unable to resolve

The Logic of Repentance

the choice without boasting, he showed his distance from the perfection of Christ. Christ *never* defended his Messianic office by boasting.

Christians are sometimes troubled by the fact that God justified Rahab the harlot, even though she told a lie (Hebrews 11:31). They would not be troubled if they were not already confused about the reality of tragic moral choices. What, may I ask, *should* Rahab have done? If she had forthrightly told the king that she was concealing the spies, she would have abetted the murder of God's chosen people. Realizing that a choice between levels of good had to be made, she did what any moral person in her place would have done. "We must obey God rather than men" (Acts 5:29). God, who reads the heart, saw that she would have told the truth if she had been morally free to do so. She was a good woman because she hated the very thing she did.

This leads to an interesting question. Did Christ ever feel the insecurity of tragic moral choices? For example—and here we intend nothing but reverent conjecture—what would Christ have done if he had stood in the place of Rahab? He might have remained silent, or he might have simply disappeared from the scene. These are possibilities. But it is more in accord with the gospels to believe that his holiness would have so disarmed the messengers of the king that they would have departed of their own accord. As long as "his hour had not yet come," his enemies had no power over him.

Yet, Christ's holiness did not disarm Pilate. May we therefore conclude that the trial of our Lord constituted a tragic moral choice? Possibly it was better to submit to injustice than to disobey the state. Socrates had to make such a tragic choice. But this would violate the clear Scriptural teaching that Christ had power to lay down his life and power to take it up again. He yielded to Pilate because he had come into the world to save sinners. His submission, thus, was not a tragic moral choice, for death was not imposed on him against his will. He freely gave up his life.

Tragedians do not look to Christ for subject matter. Christ's power to confront the limits of history is solid evidence that he earned the title Son of Man. We have no right to such a title and thus we trust in the righteousness of Christ for our salvation, because we cannot escape the insecurity of tragic moral choices. There is a gap between what we are and what we ought to be.

9. THE CLAIMS OF LOVE ON THE HEART

Here is the crux of the argument: *Unless we love those who love us we deteriorate our own character, and judicial fear enters.* Selfishness sets the moral self against the empirical self. We cannot face an offended benefactor without provoking a dialogue between the self as it is and the self as it ought to be. Even as we edify our souls whenever we are kind to others, so we deteriorate our souls whenever we offend. Suppose a neighbor goes to a great deal of effort to help us change an automobile tire, while we do not even take time to thank him. What is the result? We are smitten by the claims of the moral and spiritual environment. We are guilty of not treating him as a person; we violate the law of love. This is proved by the way we deliberately avoid his society. We know we cannot look into his eyes without experiencing moral uneasiness. Having aroused the judicial sentiment in him, we feel his life is a judgment against us. He cannot receive us in fellowship until we apologize.

Echoes of this truth can be heard on all sides. If we are assisted to a platform, we show our participation in the law of love by giving a hearty word of thanks. And if we fail in this, though we are conscious that a favor has been done, the sheer presence of our benefactor makes us judicially uneasy. The greater the sacrifice is, the more conscious we become of love's duty. If a war buddy has given his life for us, while we have not even taken time to write a sincere note of thanks to his widow, our guilt is so strong that we will go to great lengths to avoid facing her.

Whenever we are able to relieve destitution, or whenever we have a chance to save life by an act of heroism, a neglect of duty

The Logic of Repentance

destroys our moral peace. We are afraid to mention what we have done, for our children would rise up and shame us. We dare not look into the eyes of the destitute; we dare not visit the bereaved. Unless there is confession and offers of restitution, the self continues to shrivel up inside. Dickens's *A Christmas Carol* immortalized this truth. The more we defy the law of love, in order to safeguard our own egoistic security, the more insecure we become. "Whoever seeks to gain his life will lose it, but whoever loses his life will preserve it" (Luke 17:33). The self cannot be released until it engages in the infinite task of love.

Offended people provide an occasion for God to judge us. Just as God judges others through us, so he judges us through others. In each case the moral cycle is completed: inconsideration arouses the judicial sentiment, and the verdict of this sentiment, when morally pure, is the voice of God speaking against transgressors.

I am aware of the ease with which this can be ridiculed by self-righteous pedants who refuse to bring the matter to the touchstone. But this possibility in no way disheartens me. No moral ultimates can be apprehended until one humbles himself. Whoever is spiritually unwilling to be transformed by truth will remain ignorant of the truth. Carlyle sagaciously observes that only sincere people can appreciate sincerity. Power to perceive one's place in God is itself a gift of God. A proud individual does not realize that he lives and moves and is in God. And the explanation of his ignorance is simple. Rather than being shattered by God's law, he consciously or unconsciously uses this law in his arsenal of self-security. He judges others by a standard that he himself refuses to be judged by. Although inconsiderate action is a sign of guilt, his own inconsiderate acts are never such a sign. He knows the truth, but he holds it in unrighteousness. "For the wrath of God is revealed from heaven against all ungodliness and wickedness of men who by their wickedness suppress the truth" (Romans 1:18). To "suppress the truth" is to prevent truth from morally transforming the self. Since an admission of God's law would be spiritually taxing, pride prefers to suppress the law.

For example, we cite the conduct of the Nazis at the end of the Nuremberg trial. During their years under Hitler they did not shrink from murdering millions of Jews and political nonconformists. But when the hour of their own execution drew near, they tearfully sought the comfort of the Christian religion. Once the veil of pride and will-to-power had been torn away by the imminence of death, they were no longer solaced by their habit of suppressing the truth. Realizing they would have no peace until they submitted to the law of God, they piously summoned the priest or minister.* "There are no atheists in foxholes."

Other evidence is drawn from court records of a different sort. Often a person will find moral relief by bringing past crimes to the light. He can no longer stand the oppression of a guilty conscience. He ends his habit of holding the truth in unrighteousness.

Now and then a case appears which illustrates the dictum "There is honor even among thieves." Although it is well known that rogues impose a very severe standard of ethics on one another, evidence to prove this is not always easy to come by. But a perfect illustration has emerged from the famous 1950 million-dollar Brink's robbery in Boston. One of the accomplices was a man named Joseph J. (Specs) O'Keefe. As a result of participating in the crime, he was promised a share in the loot. But when he was defrauded of this share, he turned against his confederates and became the principal witness for the prosecution. This is a most interesting case. Since O'Keefe was made in the image of God, a defrauding of his rights aroused the judicial sentiment in him. This proves that he already knew the law of God. Those who violate contracts are guilty. But he refused to let God complete the moral cycle by answering to the judicial sentiment. He took the law into his own hands by exposing his confederates. This

---

* This is an imperfect example, of course, for not all of those on trial showed outward signs of remorse. We draw our principle from Scripture, not from dying criminals. But the great weight of testimony lies on the side of the position we defend. Suppose a commercial airliner is about to crash. The survivors consistently testify that the plane was filled with prayers of contrition. The abundance of this kind of evidence cannot be ignored.

pacified his urge for revenge, but it did not pacify his unrighteous soul. And the reason for this, as Paul has shown, is that one cannot enjoy God until he is spiritually transformed by the terms of the moral and spiritual environment.

10. THE CONDITIONED ELEMENT IN CONSCIENCE

At an earlier point in the book we paused to examine Darwin's claim that the moral sense can be adequately explained without reference to the divine tribunal. We admitted that the problem did not lend itself to an easy solution, for it certainly *seems* that conscience is the monitor of nothing but provincial mores. But now that love is known to be the law of life, we have a perspective from which to re-evaluate the matter.

Since we cannot spurn an act of love without experiencing shame when we stand in the presence of our benefactor, it follows that there is at least *one* verdict of conscience which cannot be traced back to either social or cultural conditioning.* If a person saves another, the saved individual will experience no moral relief until he sincerely and affectionately expresses thanks. It makes no difference who the saved person is or when or where he happens to live—providing, of course, he still has a spark of moral decency in him. The alternative to love is degeneration. Degeneration always dulls one's sensitivity to the claims of the moral and spiritual environment.

But assuming that embers of decency and self-respect still glow in the heart, it remains universally true that one cannot spurn an act of love without experiencing the judgment of God. Love *must* be answered by love. The love can be either a spontaneous word of thanks, or a spontaneous word of sorrow for having been so calloused in the first place. The one meets law directly, the other indirectly. If an apology is offered in the right spirit, only to be

---

* In saying this, we are not contradicting our earlier assertion that conscience and the judicial sentiment are separate faculties. We only imply that the judicial sentiment sometimes works *through* conscience. There is a functional identity, though not an identity of being.

rejected in the wrong spirit, guilt passes from the one to the other; and the one apologizing goes away justified rather than the other.

The point will be missed unless it is remembered that the judicial sentiment constitutes man's most precise insight into the moral and spiritual environment. It is the narrow point of contact between God and man. An aroused judicial sentiment, when pure, is God's displeasure with those who violate the law of love. Others may arouse this sentiment in us, or we may arouse it in others; the elements remain quite the same. Judgment always proceeds from a heavenly tribunal, for we have no inherent authority to judge one another.

To my knowledge, this is the only instance where the judicial sentiment functions through conscience. *Judicial rebuke for our failure to honor love with love is as certainly the voice of God as God's judicial rebuke of those who outrage our dignity.* If others are guilty when they mistreat us, we are equally guilty when we mistreat them. The reason is quite the same. An aroused judicial sentiment witnesses against both us and them. Sociologists and moralists ought to come to terms with this. Otherwise, they will suppose, like Darwin, that conscience can be explained without any serious reference to the divine tribunal. But in this one instance, at least, conscience monitors an absolute which proceeds directly from God. An act of kindness is either answered by kindness, or the very presence of the offended party renders us judicially uneasy.

The conditioned elements in conscience in no way invalidate the elements that are unconditioned. Quite to the contrary. Since new duty is always an offspring of a duty that already exists, there could *be* no conditioned elements unless there were already unconditioned elements. Culture can extend and apply a sense of duty that already exists, but it cannot generate man's first sense of duty. Just as the reality of contingent being proves the reality of noncontingent being, so the reality of conditioned elements in conscience proves the reality of unconditioned elements. Parents could not condition the moral sense of their children unless the children were already held by a moral fear of their parents.

The Logic of Repentance

In asserting this, however, we are not implying that the conditioned elements in conscience take their rise outside the moral and spiritual environment. *All conviction is wrought by God.** A sense of moral compunction cannot be aroused by cultural or social forces. Conscience communicates guilt, and guilt is always a work of the Holy Spirit. Conscience demands that good be done and evil be avoided. The standards of good and bad may be twisted and warped by a depraved culture, but that makes no difference. Conscience is still a fruit of the moral and spiritual environment; it is still the Word of God speaking to man. Under no conditions may a person violate conscience. As another has observed, he that loses his conscience has nothing left that is worth keeping.

Some may stumble at the idea that conscience is the voice of God, for how can God command in one culture what he condemns in another? Darwin, for example, spoke of the Indian Thug who conscientiously regretted he had not robbed and strangled as many travelers as did his father before him. Since his sense of moral compulsion was in direct violation of the Ten Commandments, would it be meaningful to say that it came from God? Strange though it may sound, the answer is unequivocally in the affirmative.

But before one scoffs at the answer, let him first make sure he understands it. Although man has no right to offend conscience, he *is* morally responsible for bringing the conditioned elements of conscience into harmony with the unconditioned. Since the Indian Thug judges inconsiderate Indians guilty, he knows the law of life; and since he knows this law it is his moral responsibility to conform himself to it. This is but a pure application of the third condition of knowing. A gnarled conscience is the penalty man must pay for his refusal to be humble. Man's very effort to withdraw from the moral and spiritual environment winds the chains of depravity all the more tightly about him.

* We are not attempting to pass to the existence of God from the empirical witness of conscience. We have no intention of repeating Kant's error. We are simply saying that, having found God, we believe that sufficient evidence exists to show that the accusing power of conscience originates in the divine tribunal. We may not be able to argue from a given pair of shoes to the existence of a particular shoemaker; but once we *know* the shoemaker, we can identify the shoes he has made by his trade-mark.

God punishes sin by sin. All men are born with a knowledge of God. But when men refuse to hold God in their knowledge—that is, when they refuse to conform themselves to the truth that God is God—the Holy Spirit withdraws, and the claims of the moral and spiritual environment become less distinct. Demonic impulses take control of the affections and the will defends the lowest evil in the name of the highest good. The more stubbornly a man persists in his pride, the more difficult it is for him to see his error. "There is a way which seems right to a man, but its end is the way to death" (Proverbs 14:12). God hardened Pharaoh's heart as a punishment for Pharaoh's having hardened his own heart. And the harder Pharaoh's heart grew, the blinder it became to the reality and power of Jehovah God. "And since they did not see fit to acknowledge God, God gave them up to a base mind and to improper conduct" (Romans 1:28).

This is one reason that depraved cultures are such pitiful moral sights. The consciences of savages are bound by standards which outrage those of civilized people. "For this reason God gave them up to dishonorable passions. Their women exchanged natural relations for unnatural, and the men likewise gave up natural relations with women and were consumed with passion for one another, men committing shameless acts with men and receiving in their own persons the due penalty for their error" (Romans 1:26-27). Unless men walk humbly before God, their life in God becomes the very cause of their confusion and misery. "Your wickedness will chasten you, and your apostasy will reprove you" (Jeremiah 2:19). They cannot withdraw from the moral and spiritual environment, for they are committed to it from existence itself; yet they cannot conform to its claims because they refuse to hold God in their knowledge. The result is unremitting moral anxiety. "But the wicked are like the tossing sea; for it cannot rest, and its waters toss up mire and dirt. There is no peace, says my God, for the wicked" (Isaiah 57:20-21).

Whenever one's conscience has been conditioned to believe that the destruction of life is a good thing, it is his solemn moral

The Logic of Repentance

responsibility to unlearn himself by bringing this erroneous conditioning into conformity with the law of love. This means that the Indian Thug is in the anomalous paradox of being bound to obey the very law that he ought not to obey. To violate conscience is evil, but the evil worsens when one will not take steps to bring his conscience into harmony with rectitude. The Indian Thug must alter the voice of conscience by subjecting the whole self to new moral conditioning. In short, he must humble himself before God by acknowledging his guilt. God exalts the humble, but he abases the proud. The Indian Thug *knows* it is wrong to rob and strangle strangers because he is morally *responsible* for knowing.* It matters not how firmly he is held by error, or how difficult it may be for him to break from tribal mores. If he will trace things back far enough, he will find that God's withdrawal from him is simply a judicial punishment for his having withdrawn from God. Since sin is punished by sin, moral blindness is a witness to moral guilt.

If the Thug refuses to hold God in his knowledge, it is no more meaningful to exculpate him than it is to exculpate one who refuses to thank us when we save his life. The third condition of knowing binds all normal men equally; it admits no exceptions.

11. THE PROBLEM OF THE HEATHEN

With this information before us, it is possible to give a provisional answer to the difficult problem of the heathen. Here is the problem: How can God justly judge those who are fettered by superstition? How can men humble themselves, when they are part of a culture that is steeped in idolatry? The answer is that men could know God if they would only will to know him, for the divine tribunal reveals itself in both conscience and the judicial sentiment. Since men are made in the image of God, and since participation in the moral and spiritual environment fills

---

* This is not to be pressed to the place where we offend the juridical maxim *Ignorantia facti excusat*. We pointed this out at an earlier place.

this image with content, it follows, once again, that the heathen *know* God for they are morally *responsible* for knowing. We are only affirming what the Apostle Paul has taught from the beginning. "When Gentiles [heathen] who have not the law do by nature what the law requires, they are a law to themselves, even though they do not have the law. They show that what the law requires is written on their hearts, while their conscience also bears witness and their conflicting thoughts accuse or perhaps excuse them on that day when, according to my gospel, God judges the secrets of men by Christ Jesus" (Romans 2:14-16). All normal men are held by the third condition of knowing, heathen and philosopher alike.

We are not so foolish as to assert, of course, that all men have either an equal opportunity or an equal ability to clarify their relation to God. Fortunately for the common man, "Almighty God intends not to lead us to Heaven by hard Questions, but by meekness and charity, and a frequent practice of Devotion."* Jonathan Edwards sagaciously observes that the question at last will be not Had you such a demonstration that you could not resist? but Had you such evidence as you ought to have yielded to? not Was it made so plain that you could not misunderstand it? but Was it made plain enough that you might have understood it?

God only asks humility, and humility is within the reach of one who feels even the faintest stirring of guilt in his heart—even the guilt of the Indian Thug who is grieved over not having robbed and strangled as many strangers as did his father before him. *Whether or not one has right moral standards is irrelevant, for all men should be sorry for not doing the good as they know it.* It is very important that this be understood. Suppose an African society demands that three cows be exchanged for a wife; but a young man slyly deceives his father-in-law and exchanges only two. He tries to conceal his deception, thus betraying his guilt. He has not done the right as he knows it; he is smitten by the claims of the moral and spiritual environment. And being guilty, it is his

* Izaak Walton, *Lives* (Oxford), p. 394.

The Logic of Repentance

moral responsibility to humble himself. He should allow himself to be transformed by this guilt, for his uneasy conscience is as clearly the voice of God as the moral uneasiness of a criminal of the deepest dye. If the young man refuses to humble himself, he shows, once again, that man's trouble is not lack of knowledge, but lack of moral courage to act on the knowledge he already has. "Though they know God's decree that those who do such things deserve to die, they not only do them but approve those who practice them" (Romans 1:32).

It is wrong, therefore, to think that God's condemnation of a truculent savage is unjust. It is no more unjust than the condemnation of a proud philosopher, for each refuses to hold God in his knowledge. No man is rightly related to God unless he is humbly sorry for not doing the good as he knows it. There is honor even among thieves. We have argued from the beginning that the third condition of knowing answers to the complex station and place of each individual. "Every one to whom much is given, of him will much be required; and of him to whom men commit much they will demand the more" (Luke 12:48). A child knows more than a savage because he is morally responsible for more; and a philosopher knows more than a child because he is morally responsible for more. But savage, child, or philosopher —all know that it is wrong to violate conscience. God commands that good be done and evil be avoided. All men are made in the image of God, and this image is the faculty of receptivity for the claims of the moral and spiritual environment. Unless one is altogether beyond moral remedy (this is only a hypothetical possibility), each man is held by the moral necessity of doing the good and avoiding the evil. It makes no difference how twisted or contorted his standards may be. Man must do the right and avoid the wrong, otherwise he is guilty before God. And since no one is ever fully free from the pricks of an accusing conscience, all men must humble themselves. ". . . all have sinned and fall short of the glory of God" (Romans 3:23). If a man will not humble himself, the guilt is his own. He may be justly judged by God.

12. A FINAL REVIEW OF THE MORAL PREDICAMENT

The elements in our moral experience are so complex that it is not easy to arrange them into a single, harmonious pattern. And it is this very complexity which makes it convenient for rationalists to evade the necessity of repentance. As long as responsibility and obligation are kept in dialectical balance, we recognize that we are held by a standard of perfection more demanding than we have powers to meet. But if we make a straight-line rationalistic interpretation of our moral life, the balance is broken and the claims of the moral and spiritual environment are corrupted from one side or another.

One can argue, for example, that it is as rationally repugnant to repent of one's inability to love others as it is to repent of one's want of natural affection for God. ". . . he is no more to be blamed for his errors, than the governor of a city without walls for the shelter he is obliged to afford an invading enemy."* No other evidence need be adduced than the strange fact that the law of love is *law*. The very fact that we must legally remind ourselves to love is proof that we neither do nor can love. Love is a fruit, not a work; it is unconscious of any lawful sense of obligation. "For the whole law is fulfilled in one word, 'You shall love your neighbor as yourself'" (Galatians 5:14). Since it is repugnant to repent for what we cannot avoid, it would seem that our failure to love our neighbor no more justifies repentance than our failure to love God; and for precisely the same reason. This is one side of the picture.

On the other side, it can be argued with equal plausibility that not only are we obliged by the law of love, but that in a very meaningful sense we are natively capable of meeting it. Even as those who enter the circle of nearness are morally free to receive our dignity (they are guilty if they fail), so we are morally free

---

* Oliver Goldsmith, *The Vicar of Wakefield* (Oxford), p. 38.

The Logic of Repentance

to receive their dignity. Spiritual uneasiness in the presence of those we have offended is proof that our failure is somehow due to our own refusal to be moral. We do not feel guilty for not being able to fly, but we do feel guilty when we are in the society of those whose kindness we have spurned.

Moralists may reply that we are offending logic by asserting and denying the same thing at the same time. The truth, however, is that we are merely being honest with the whole of our moral experience. A cautious application of the third method of knowing has proved that in a very meaningful sense we can and cannot fulfill the law of love. Both parts belong to the real. We are always more perfectly able to limit our interests in favor of the interests of others, thus showing that we judge our conduct by the law of love. We counsel our children to shun the subordination of life to life. But since we must conceive of this ideal as *law*, we prove that we are morally incapable of perfect love, for jural necessity and love are incompatible. Love has no existence until our affections are divorced from legal and rational interests. But we have no native resources to accomplish this conversion. The power must come from God.

13. WHY IT IS NECESSARY TO REPENT

We have come a great distance in the examination of our relation to God. Our conclusion is that we must repent. One cannot legally thread his way through the labyrinth of human relations. Everything we do is morally ambiguous. Self-love taints all but the rarest expressions of sacrifice and courage.

Since the necessity of repentance cannot be legally established, however, some might sigh with relief; their expectation being that this lack of necessity is the same thing as an affirmation of virtue, which is far from the case. In order that this might be appreciated, let us forthrightly state the axiom that undergirds all upright conduct. Since the truth of this axiom holds us from existence itself, it is our moral and spiritual duty to act on it. *In any situ-*

ation where the fact of guilt is certain, though no legal proof can be devised to show how much guilt is one's own, it is a mark of moral firmness and spiritual rectitude for one cheerfully to own all the guilt that can be included in a charitable interpretation of the situation. This is the axiom. Let us now illustrate it.

Suppose a person bumps another while entering an elevator. He knocks several packages out of the other person's arms. For a moment he is morally suspended between pride and humility. Pride argues that it was solely the other person's fault. And there is enough plausibility in the suggestion to make it sound attractive. After all, the other person was not watching where he was going. But humility counters that this cannot be legally proved, for the self was not very careful about the direction of its own conduct, either. The evidences are too equivocal to justify final judgment. Humility wins out, and the individual submits to the claims of the moral and spiritual environment. At this point God spiritually fortifies the life with power to act against egoistic interests. Rather than proudly defending himself, he manfully apologizes. "I beg your pardon, sir! How clumsy of me. . . . May I help you with these packages?"

His humility immediately releases the other person from the necessity of arbitrating the issue on the table of legal give and take. Since he has been treated in a kindly way, he finds it difficult not to respond with equal kindness. "Oh, thank you! . . . But I assure you, the fault was *entirely* mine." If he should fail to be kind in return, he would only excite the judicial sentiment in the one who has apologized.

Both parties knew what was morally required of them. Each had to show a sincere willingness to accept all the guilt that could be included in a charitable interpretation of the situation. One proves his respect for the law of life by his spiritual humility in the face of moral ambiguity.

Whenever a person humbles himself, therefore, he announces that he is subjectively willing to submit to the judgment of God. "Search me, O God, and know my heart! Try me and know my thoughts! And see if there be any wicked way in me, and lead me in the way everlasting!" (Psalm 139:23-24.) Only God can separate the shades of better and worse in moral ambiguity; only God can pronounce final judgment against the life. This is why moral equivocation confronts one with the alternative of either searching for a legal proof of righteousness or of humbly submitting to the righteousness of God.

Were we to postpone repentance, therefore, we would simply prove that our affections are dominated by pride, rather than humility. A refusal to repent betrays one of two things: either one disbelieves that his life is morally ambiguous, and thus nurses the false expectation that he conforms to rectitude; or he senses his distance from rectitude, but clings to the undefined hope that some legally satisfying way out can be found. In either case he flies in the face of truth. He may be able to plot the course of single stones, but when he confronts the landslide of a totally self-centered life, no escape by rational calculation is possible. Emergency action is the order of the day; and this action, as proved by the third method of knowing, is *repentance*.

> "Who by repentance is not satisfied
> Is nor of heaven nor earth, for these are pleased.
> By penitence the Eternal's wrath's appeased."*

* Shakespeare, *The Two Gentlemen of Verona*, Act V, Scene 4.

Part Four

CONCLUDING INFERENCES AND PROBLEMS

Chapter Ten

CHRIST THE POWER AND THE WISDOM OF GOD

1. THE POSSIBILITIES AND LIMITS OF HUMAN WISDOM

From the start we have said that the law of contradiction forms the rational environment of man, for all other laws of inference are analytically included in it. Whenever our terms are consistent with one another and with reality, we enjoy possession of the second kind of truth. A logical contradiction is never valid; there are no limits to reason as a test for truth.

But this does not imply that reason knows no limits as a *source* of truth. Although the law of contradiction is an indispensable tool in the construing of consistent judgments, it cannot furnish the data with which the judgment works—it cannot, that is, except in the single instance of formal validity (geometry, mathematics, logic, and so on). If we seek material truth, we must critically yield to the claims of the fourfold environment—physical, rational, aesthetic, and moral and spiritual.

By faithfully submitting to the realities that already hold us, we have been able to establish some very important truths. We know (*a*) that God is a person; (*b*) that man is made in God's image; and (*c*) that God and man share the same moral and spiritual environment.

In reviewing such truths, however, we are also reviewing the limits of reason as a source of truth. We cannot develop a world view by our own wisdom because we have insufficient information.

We are able to name the moral predicament, but we do not have a perspective sufficiently high or wide to resolve it.

At this point a critic may possibly make the following charge: "Whenever an enthusiast runs into a problem, or whenever he wearies of the hard labor of thinking, he pretends to have some religious shortcut to truth. This is the end of science and philosophy." The critic is supremely right in believing that this is the end of science and philosophy, for man by wisdom knows not God. But before he settles back in his complacency, let him candidly review the realities that already hold him as a human being. He is offended when we say that reason has limits; yet fellowship is never enjoyed until one sees and accepts such limits. A person, let us remember, is "freedom expressed through moral self-consciousness." Unlike machines that solve problems out of electronic necessity, a person is motivated by values and interests. He wants what he wants because he wants it. If someone tries to press him for a more transcendent explanation, the judicial sentiment is aroused and he judges his critic guilty. "I am going hunting at four in the morning—and that is that!" There is no abstract justification for personal choices. Therefore, unless we are going to violate one of the truths that already hold us, we *must* acknowledge the limits of reason as a source of truth. Freely inspired choices flow from the heart; they are not under the control of an abstract system of logic.

And if this is true on the finite level, we would nullify the analogy between God and man if we failed to believe that it is also true on the divine level; for God and man are both persons. Why God made the world, and how he plans to dispose of it, cannot be discovered by a scientific or philosophic analysis of the world itself. The universe is ordered by personal interest, not logic. God created as many stars as he did because he wanted to. A housewife arranges the furniture to please herself, and God arranges the universe to please himself. One would offend God if he were to press for a reason beyond the desires and preferences of God himself.

Since God is a person, and since the judicial sentiment is

aroused whenever personal dignity is offended, it follows that man is not rightly related to God until he *trusts* God. "And without faith it is impossible to please him. For whoever would draw near to God must believe that he exists and that he rewards those who seek him" (Hebrews 11:6). To subject God to abstract standards is a proof that God is not man's highest ultimate.

2. THE JUDICIAL SENTIMENT IN GOD

Moral self-acceptance has shown that God cannot receive sinners until right moral conditions prevail. But it has not succeeded in naming these conditions. It cannot answer the question, "How can a sinner be just before God?" We know (*a*) that humility is the moral precondition of fellowship; (*b*) that whenever fellowship is rejected, the judicial sentiment is aroused; and (*c*) that the judicial sentiment stays aroused until right moral conditions prevail. These are far-reaching truths, but they do not reach far enough to solve the problem of how a sinner can be just before God. This is established by two salient facts.

First, there is the "anatomy of repentance." Since we must repent, rather than apologize, we have no recourse except to throw ourselves on the mercy of the court. Repentance, let us remember, is the direct offspring of two convictions: (*a*) that there is no legal way back into fellowship; (*b*) that if the offended party finds the crime too heinous to forgive, the guilty party, if sincere, will acknowledge that he receives nothing but what he deserves. Therefore, if God is morally free to forgive sinners, it it because some way has been found to propitiate the aroused judicial sentiment in his character. Forgiveness always comes by pity and mercy, never by lawful necessity. This is why we cannot solve the moral predicament unless God reveals himself. He must tell us whether or not he is morally free to forgive.

Second, though somewhat overlapping, is the finite limitation of our perspective. Because we are men and not God, we have no final way of knowing how sin affects the divine life. The moral and spiritual environment names the conditions that others must meet when they propitiate the judicial sentiment in us, but it does not name the conditions that we must meet when the judicial sentiment in God is propitiated. If others offend us, they humble themselves before us. But is this sufficient when we approach God? As debtors we forgive our debtors. But God owes no moral debt, for he is unconditionally holy. This means that, though we must be humble before God, we cannot be certain whether such a moral overture will fully satisfy the divine character. Once again, we are frustrated unless God reveals himself.

3. THE CROSS OF CHRIST

Here is the question: "How can a sinner be just before God?" But before we try to answer it, let us clarify the nature of justification.* To be just means to be free from legal condemnation; it means to stand in a right relation to law. The work of justification is declaratory, not constitutive. When members of a jury announce their verdict, they forensically declare the relation of the accused to law. They do not constitute him guilty or innocent by their word. This should be understood, lest it be supposed that men must be inherently righteous to enter the kingdom of God. God can extend pardon the moment the judicial sentiment in his character is propitiated. If inherent righteousness were the passport to heaven, none but the Lord would gain this estate.

Here is the mystery that is concealed from the wise and the prudent, but is revealed to men of faith: *God propitiated his own judicial sentiment by sending Christ to die in the stead of sinners.* From Genesis to Revelation the reconciliation of man by a sub-

* At this point the reader will detect a radical shift in method. Rather than proceeding to reality by way of the third method of knowing, we are dogmatically reviewing the Christian doctrine of salvation. This must be accepted as a literary convention. In the final chapter an effort will be made to show the relation between moral self-acceptance and our present appeal to Scripture. In the meantime we simply ask, how *can* one decide whether Christianity answers to reality, unless he acquaints himself with the essence of Christianity? Even if a man rejects the way of the cross, he at least ought to have an accurate understanding of what he is rejecting.

stitute sacrifice is taught. But perhaps it is expressed no more beautifully and succinctly than in the prophecy of Isaiah. "Surely he has borne our griefs and carried our sorrows; yet we esteemed him stricken, smitten by God, and afflicted. But he was wounded for our transgressions, he was bruised for our iniquities; upon him was the chastisement that made us whole, and with his stripes we are healed. All we like sheep have gone astray; we have turned every one to his own way; and the Lord has laid on him the iniquity of us all" (53:4-6). Since human beings are sinners, and since a holy God cannot look on sin, God created a race of righteous men through his incarnate Son. Those who share in the ignominy of Christ's death will also share in the glory of his resurrection. Christ is the vine, and men of faith are the branches. They draw new life from him.

Christ propitiated the judicial sentiment in God by his "active and passive obedience." His active obedience consisted in a perfect fulfillment of righteousness, for there was no gap between what he was and what he ought to be. "He committed no sin; no guile was found on his lips. When he was reviled, he did not revile in return; when he suffered, he did not threaten; but he trusted to him who judges justly" (I Peter 2:22-23). The third type of truth—truth as personal rectitude—was flawlessly actuated. Jesus did not say, "I *have* the truth," but, "I *am* the truth" (John 14:6). The full claims of the moral and spiritual environment were verified in him. He loved God with all his heart and his neighbor as himself. Since love is the law of life, and since Christ met the outside terms of this law, he is the incarnation of rectitude. If one wants to know how to regulate himself among men, he should bring his life to the touchstone.

Christ's passive obedience consisted in his substitutionary death on the cross. Its merit rests on four complementary virtues: who Christ was (the Son of God); the manner of his life (made perfect through suffering); the mode of his offering (the cursed death of the cross); and the attitude of his soul (voluntary obedience). Thus, it was not simply that the Son of God became incarnate, but that he lived a sinless life; not simply that he lived a sinless life, but that he died a cursed death on the cross; not simply that he died a cursed death on the cross, but that he freely offered himself to the Father as a supreme act of obedience.

Since many awesome mysteries cluster about the cross, one may miss its essence by focusing too attentively on its details. The cross moves us to piety as an example of love and sacrifice; it verifies God's solicitude for law and government; it humbles us by revealing the limits of human virtue. But these are subordinate features. The cross of Christ is the locus of a solemn juridical transaction. Christ propitiated the judicial sentiment in God, thus making it possible for God to offer pardon to sinners. *This* is the essence of the atonement. The divine person expired in the human nature as a substitute for sinners.

Although the first announcement of God's blessings through Christ appears at the fall of man (Genesis 3:15), it was not until God entered into covenant relations with Abraham that a systematic account of these blessings is mentioned (Genesis 12:1-3). And *how* will God bless man through Abraham? In two ways: first, God promises to receive sinners into fellowship; second, he promises to give them the land of Canaan (heaven). But the difficulty with such promises is that they cannot, in justice, be made. How can God be a friend of sinners, when the sheer presence of sinners arouses the judicial sentiment in him? God is of holier eyes than to look on sin. If upright men cannot have fellowship with ingrates, is it meaningful to say that God can?

Further investigation shows that Abraham can be a blessing, and God can have fellowship with sinners, because the offspring of Abraham is Jesus Christ (Galatians 3:16). God cannot impute righteousness to sinners unless there is actual righteousness to impute. Finding no righteousness in man, God put forth his own righteousness in the person of his Son. By his active obedience, Christ conformed human nature to the imperative essence; and by his passive obedience he offered up the fruits of this righteousness, thus propitiating the judicial sentiment in God. This made it possible for God to fulfill the promises made to Abraham and to the generations of faithful men after him. "Christ redeemed us from the curse of the law, having become a curse for us—for it is written, 'Cursed be every one who hangs on a tree'—that in Christ Jesus the blessing of Abraham might come upon the Gentiles, that we might receive the promise of the Spirit through faith" (Galatians 3:13-14).

When Christ cried, "My God, my God, why hast thou forsaken me?" (Mark 15:34), he was in the throes of judicial suffering. The divine person convulsed in the human nature as a vicarious victim. God withdrew fellowship from the Son, in order that he might be judicially free to have fellowship with sinners. Christ learned by experience what it meant for human nature to be penally afflicted because of sin—though not because of his own sin, but because of the sins of the world. It was a fear of judicial suffering, not merely the dread of physical agony, which provoked such inward distress as Jesus faced the ignominy and shame of the cross. "Now is my soul troubled. And what shall I say, 'Father save me from this hour'? No, for this purpose I have come to this hour" (John 12:27).

All who put their trust in Christ are delivered from the threat of judicial suffering and death. They will never face God as judge, for their sins were judged with Christ on the cross. "Truly, truly, I say to you, he who hears my word and believes him who sent me, has eternal life; he does not come into judgment, but has passed from death to life" (John 5:24). Christ is the judicial surety for us, even as he was for Abraham. As we despair of our own righteousness, we are clothed with the righteousness of Christ.

> "Not the labors of my hands
>   Can fulfill Thy law's demands;
> Could my zeal no respite know,
>   Could my tears forever flow,
> All for sin could not atone;
>   Thou must save, and Thou alone.

> "Nothing in my hand I bring,
> Simply to Thy cross I cling;
> Naked, come to Thee for dress,
> Helpless, look to Thee for grace;
> Foul, I to the fountain fly,
> Wash me, Saviour, or I die!"*

The Father bore witness to the acceptability of Christ's final sacrifice by raising him from the dead (Romans 1:4). All true children of Abraham will partake of his resurrection, for they are members of a new and holy race.

This *is* Christianity; let no one be deceived. "For no human being will be justified in his sight by works of the law since through the law comes knowledge of sin. But now the righteousness of God has been manifested apart from law, although the law and the prophets bear witness to it, the righteousness of God through faith in Jesus Christ for all who believe. For there is no distinction; since all have sinned and fall short of the glory of God, they are justified by his grace as a gift, through the redemption which is in Christ Jesus, whom God put forward as an expiation by his blood, to be received by faith . . . it was to prove at the present time that he himself is righteous and that he justifies him who has faith in Jesus" (Romans 3:20-26). The judicial order in redemption should be carefully noted. First, God is reconciled to man through the active and passive obedience of Jesus Christ; then, man is invited to become reconciled to God through the preaching of the gospel. God does not pardon sinners until he is able, in justice, to do it.

Because of his active obedience, Christ is the norm of human nature. If one seeks a final definition of the imperative essence, therefore, he must look to Jesus Christ. Nothing was left undone by him. When Christians are admonished to forgive one another, the reason is grounded in Christ rather than in the moral and spiritual environment. "And be kind to one another, tenderhearted, forgiving one another, as God in Christ forgave you"

---

* Augustus M. Toplady, "Rock of Ages, Cleft for Me."

(Ephesians 4:32). It is not that the moral and spiritual environment is defective in itself. The defect is in man. If we were not sinners, we should not have to be commanded to forgive. We should forgive with the same spontaneity with which we breathe. Jesus Christ must correct, as well as fulfill, our own finite standards of rectitude. Men *ought* to forgive those who seek forgiveness—even penitent enemies—but sinners are not easily motivated to such high acts of virtue. They prefer resentment and revenge. Motivation comes from our union with Jesus Christ. Even as Christ loved us while we were yet enemies, so we are to love one another. We must keep the doors of negotiation open for all men. Though we can forgive no one until he shows signs of repentance, we must always be *willing* to forgive.

The inability of sinners to forget what they forgive is background for the comfort that God removes our sins as far as the east is from the west. Unlike man, God harbors no revenge against those whose sins sent Christ to the cross. God can entertain an aroused judicial sentiment without mingling it with passion. This is why he, and he alone, can complete the moral cycle by answering to the judicial sentiment.

4. THE CROSS AND PERSONAL REPENTANCE

The necessity of coming to God through the righteousness of Christ in no way invalidates the truth that fellowship between God and sinners does not and cannot exist until sinners repent. Those who continue in their proud and self-sufficient ways will never see the kingdom of God.

Christ propitiated the judicial sentiment in God, thus making it possible for God to pardon those who deserve condemnation; but the cycle of pardon is not completed until sinners humble themselves and repent. Whether in God or man, a person is powerless to extend forgiveness until the offending party meets the right moral conditions. A wife may be propitious toward her husband, and thus be morally free to pardon him for his wicked ways; but her offer of pardon in no way relieves him of the necessity of grieving over his evil. He must appear before her as a suppliant.

Christ atoned for everything that prevented a just God from offering pardon to sinners; but he did not atone for the sin of rejecting this offer of pardon. *The reason for this is that an offer of pardon does not include a pardon of the rejection of pardon.* The cycle of pardon must be completed by the guilty party, not by the innocent.

All men are invited to become reconciled with God, for Christ "is the expiation for our sins, and not for ours only but also for the sins of the whole world" (I John 2:2). World brotherhood is the limiting ideal of Christianity. God will pardon the human race as soon as the human race completes the cycle of pardon. But the cycle *must* be completed. There is no redemption apart from repentance. "The times of ignorance God overlooked, but now he commands all men everywhere to repent, because he has fixed a day on which he will judge the world in righteousness by a man whom he has appointed, and of this he has given assurance to all men by raising him from the dead" (Acts 17:30-31).

5. THE FILIAL BOND

The moment a person submits to the righteousness of Christ, not only is he justified before the law, but God adopts him into the family of God. "Beloved, we are God's children now" (I John 3:2). The filial bond replaces the bond of law. Though God disciplines us for our good (Hebrews 12:5-11), he never treats us as criminals; for the criminality of our sins was put on Christ. "And you, who were dead in trespasses and the uncircumcision of your flesh, God made alive together with him, having forgiven us all our trespasses, having canceled the bond which stood against us with its legal demands; this he set aside, nailing it to the cross" (Colossians 2:13-14). God is our Father; we have a filial right to approach him. We have no fear, for perfect love casts out fear.

"Therefore, since we are justified by faith, we have peace with God through our Lord Jesus Christ. Through him we have obtained access to this grace in which we stand, and we rejoice in our hope of sharing the glory of God" (Romans 5:1-2).

Being positionally righteous in Christ does not mean, however, that we are natively righteous in ourselves. Although we love God in our reigning affections, another law wars against the law of the mind. This is the law of sin. It defeats our intentions. We *will* to do the right, but our conduct is betrayed into pride and self-sufficiency. The result is that we hate the very thing we do. We pledge our love to God; we strive to be righteous; yet, we end each day conscious of the gap between what we are and what we ought to be. But because we are spiritually grieved by our want of perfection, we prove that our reigning affections are regenerated. We are mystically joined to Christ; the perfection of his life flows through us. Hence, God views us through the eyes of paternal love; the moral predicament is powerless to challenge our judicial peace. "There is therefore now no condemnation for those who are in Christ Jesus. For the law of the Spirit of life in Christ Jesus has set me free from the law of sin and death. For God has done what the law, weakened by the flesh, could not do: sending his own Son in the likeness of sinful flesh and for sin, he condemned sin in the flesh, in order that the just requirement of the law might be fulfilled in us, who walk not according to the flesh but according to the Spirit" (Romans 8:1-4).

Critics of Christianity may be offended by our contention that man can be simultaneously righteous and sinful. They would not be offended if they paid closer attention to the true elements in the problem. The law of contradiction is not violated, for two different criteria are in purview. When we say that repentant sinners are *righteous*, we mean that God beholds them in Jesus Christ. They are viewed through the eyes of love. Christ fulfilled righteousness in their stead. But when we say that repentant sinners are *sinners*, we mean that their conduct does not measure up to the just requirements of law. This is not a novel insight, for the principle is somewhat at work wherever love reigns. A wife has an imperfect husband when judged by the law of ideal husbands, but a perfect husband when judged by love. Children are imperfect in themselves, but perfect as children. And so it is with sinners: when they repent they are judged by love, not law. God delivers them from the law of sin and death by justifying them in Christ and adopting them into the family of God. "Love bears all things, believes all things, hopes all things, endures all things" (I Corinthians 13:7).

Why God so loved us that he offered his Son as a vicarious sacrifice, we cannot fathom; for there is no saving virtue in man which attracts the divine being. We can only bow before the mystery itself: "It was not because you were more in number than any other people that the Lord set his love upon you and chose you, for you were the fewest of all peoples; but it is because the Lord loves you, and is keeping the oath which he swore to your fathers" (Deuteronomy 7:7-8).

Since God and a penitent sinner are joined by love and not law, we may now believe that the principle of double fulfillment rests on a theological foundation. Love meets the terms of rectitude by either spontaneously doing the good or by spontaneously expressing sorrow for having failed. "For if the readiness is there, it is acceptable according to what a man has, not according to what he has not" (II Corinthians 8:12). The filial bond gives Biblical justification to a principle that was long ago discovered by the third method of knowing.

6. OBJECTIONS TO POSITIONAL RIGHTEOUSNESS

Some may rebut that the doctrine of imputed righteousness is out of harmony with the claims of the moral and spiritual environment. How can God call us righteous when we are not, in fact, righteous? The answer is that we *are* righteous—right now, in history. But it is the righteousness of Christ in us, and not a righteousness that we have of ourselves. "I have been crucified with Christ; it is no longer I who live, but Christ who lives in me; and the life I now live in the flesh I live by faith in the Son of God, who loved me and gave himself for me" (Galatians 2:20). Hence, when God declares a sinner just, he is addressing reality as it is; he is not falsifying the facts. A repentant sinner is in a right relation to law, and thus is just before God; but his right relation to law is made possible by his right relation to the cross. He is righteous by virtue of his mystical union with Christ. Because the Reformers did not always succeed in making this clear, they needlessly exposed themselves to attack from Roman Catholic divines.

Some fear that the doctrine of imputed righteousness will lead to moral abuse. If Christ paid the debt of sin, let us eat, drink, and be merry. This objection overlooks the fact that whom Christ justifies, he also sanctifies. Love carries its own compulsion. Since we share in the divine nature, the love of Christ constrains us to righteousness: "No one born of God commits sin; for God's nature abides in him, and he cannot sin because he is born of God" (I John 3:9).

It must be pointed out, however, that this verse does not mean what it seems to say. Our mystical union with Christ does not eradicate the possibility of committing sin. Quite to the contrary, we sin daily in thought and word and deed, for pride and self-love corrupt all but the rarest expressions of spiritual striving. Though we have been redeemed from the curse of sin, we have not been redeemed from the presence of sin. The whole temporal order awaits a work of God, and we are part of this order. "We know that the whole creation has been groaning in travail together until now; and not only the creation, but we ourselves, who have the first fruits of the Spirit, groan inwardly as we wait for adoption as sons, the redemption of our bodies" (Romans 8:22-23). Regeneration is an instantaneous act; sanctification is a lifelong process.

But this verse does teach that justified sinners cannot *deliberately* sin. Sin takes occasion in us. We cannot look on sin with an af-

Christ the Power and the Wisdom of God 259

fectionate desire to possess it; we cannot yield to it with the consent of our better faculties. We strive to be more like Christ, and we inwardly grieve when we fail. This is only another way of expressing the principle of double fulfillment. Love either spontaneously does the right or it spontaneously expresses sorrow for having failed.

Our relation to God is like that of children to their parents. Children may hurt their parents by acts of waywardness, but they never deliberately hurt them. Waywardness takes occasion within them. They are betrayed into action that is at variance with their reigning impulses. Although they really want to do what is right, they are forthwith delivered into the counsels of pride and self-sufficiency. But this does not destroy their judicial peace, for the little ones are held by love, not law. Jesus asked Peter one question: "Peter, do you *love* me?" Since love looks for nothing but evidence of love, no other question was important. Peter denied his Lord; but he also went out and wept bitterly. And the Lord received his tears as an acceptable proof of love. Peter's conduct followed the typical pattern of human love. If love fails in direct fulfillment, it triumphs in the long run by indirect fulfillment.

We add the qualification "in the long run" because secondary obstacles may hinder the self from obeying its higher impulses. Love is always spontaneous, but it is not always instantaneous. Suppose a person offends his neighbor by an unkind act. He may sincerely want to apologize, but pride hinders him. In due time, however, he defeats his mutinous impulses and expresses spontaneous sorrow. This is why love never puts a time limit on the obligations of love. "Love bears all things, believes all things, hopes all things, endures all things" (I Corinthians 13:7).

But it is not merely the critic of Christ who has difficulty understanding how imperfect people can be perfect. The misunderstanding is frequently shared by friends of the cross. Enthusiasts are sometimes heard saying, "Believe on the Lord Jesus Christ and all your sins will be taken away." This is not in accord with Biblical truth. What they should say is, "Believe on the Lord Jesus

Christ and you will be saved." The church is a fellowship of *forgiven* sinners, not a fellowship of *former* sinners. Christ removes the judicial condemnation of pride and self-sufficiency, but he does not remove pride and self-sufficiency. Paul spoke normatively for the church when he declared that sin still dwells in our members.

Christ offered himself in order that the judicial sentiment in God might be propitiated. When this specific purpose is diluted by religious zeal, not only will the text be falsified, but those who come to Christ will either be disappointed with what they find or they will exaggerate what they receive. Their disappointment will come from a discovery that pride and self-sufficiency still tincture their affections; and their exaggeration will come from thinking that righteousness in Christ is equivalent to righteousness in themselves. The first leads to a new fear of the law, while the second leads to new self-righteousness. Neither would be possible if the specific purposes in Christ's death were not distorted by either ignorance or zeal.

Roman Catholic theology fails to harmonize sin and grace because it fails to see that love is an affection which carries its own compulsion. "For if we are beside ourselves, it is for God; . . . For the love of Christ controls us" (II Corinthians 5:13-14). Romanism is patterned after the ethos of the monastery. Even as monks render up obedience to their superiors by acts of reason and will, so by similar acts of reason and will do sinners render up obedience to God. But this analogy is Biblically deficient, for it illustrates law rather than love. It offends the Pauline teaching that by works of law—*any law*—shall no flesh be justified in God's sight.

Romanism accurately understands that pagans cannot be justified by keeping the laws of Moses. To the extent of this insight, Romanism is *not* tinctured by Pelagianism. Protestant critics seldom see and appreciate this. But when the doctrine of second justification is developed, Rome surrenders Biblical truth. A Roman Catholic believes he can merit heaven by performing

Christ the Power and the Wisdom of God

good works done in grace. But this optimism overlooks the limits that law places on human virtue. Whenever the good must be contemplated as law, one proves that his affections are defective; and this defect, in turn, sullies the purity of the act. If one's affections were really good, he would do righteousness with the same unconsciousness of law with which Christ did the will of the Father.

Here is the law that governs Roman Catholic striving: *Baptized Christians must either improve the grace of God in them or be lost.* This is as surely a law as any law of Moses, and for this reason it is just as impotent to effect justification. Law can be either an objective legal precept or a legal attitude in the heart. It makes no difference; love rejects both.

Because of its affiliation with legal motives, Rome appeals to hell as an incentive for doing good works. This appeal would never be made if the perfection of the filial bond were comprehended, for perfect love casts out fear. Just as lovers have no dread of divorce, so Christians have no dread of hell. Christians do not dread hell because Christ has delivered them from the second death. "For you did not receive the spirit of slavery to fall back into fear, but you have received the spirit of sonship. When we cry 'Abba! Father!' it is the Spirit himself bearing witness with our spirit that we are children of God" (Romans 8:15-16). Rome fears that if people knew they were safe before God, they would be lax in their moral improvement. But this anxiety is needless, for love is an affection that carries its own compulsion.

> "I'll say that he is wise who loveth well
> And that the soul most free is that most bound
> In thraldom to the ancient tyrant Love."*

Love either spontaneously does the will of the beloved or it spontaneously expresses sorrow for having failed. And in either event, love is satisfied.

---

* From "The Lay of Chrysostom" (Cervantes).

Thus, since God is a person, only fruits of love can satisfy his nature. But this is the one virtue that duty does not have. And this includes the duty of trying to merit heaven by good works done in grace. This is why the Reformers rejected second justification as a construction that is contrary to both Scripture and life.

7. THE PRINCIPLE OF FEDERAL HEADSHIP

We do not need special revelation to discover that our affections are depraved. Whoever is honest with his own life will recognize that he judges others by a more perfect standard than he himself lives by. Our problem is to explain why God allowed the human race to become depraved in the first place. Why did he not confirm us in righteousness from the beginning?

Since this is a question which cannot be answered by human wisdom, we are once again closed up to the hope that God, in grace and mercy, has revealed himself. And Christianity is satisfied that such a revelation *has* taken place. The God who entered into a covenant relation with Abraham is the very God who explains the means by which the blessings of this covenant are brought to men.

God has been pleased to deal with mankind under two federal heads: the first Adam and the last Adam (I Corinthians 15:45). A federal head is one who stands in a public capacity on behalf of those he represents. Two men acted in the stead of the human race. They lived under the terms of two covenants—works and grace. The one covenant was a failure, the other was a success. The first Adam brought the human race into moral ruin, while the last Adam brought the human race under God's offer of pardon and life. The Apostle Paul sums up this doctrine in one of the really crucial theological passages in the Bible. "For if many died through one man's trespass, much more have the grace of God and the free gift in the grace of that one man Jesus Christ abounded for many. And the free gift is not like the effect of that one man's sin. For the judgment following one trespass brought condemnation, but the free gift following many trespasses brings justification. If, because of one man's trespass, death reigned through that one man, much more will those who receive the abundance of grace and the free gift of righteousness reign in life through the one man Jesus Christ. Then as one man's trespass led to condemnation for all men, so one man's act of righteousness leads to acquittal and life for all men. For as by one man's disobedience many were made sinners, so by one man's obedience many will be made righteous" (Romans 5:15-19).

This passage contains a compendious review of the Christian philosophy of history. There are none before the first Adam; none after the last Adam; and none in between. All who quest for personal righteousness are of the family of the first Adam; whereas all who humbly repent are of the family of the last Adam. Just as we federally share in the bitter consequences of first Adam's disobedience, so we federally share in the pleasant fruits of last Adam's obedience.

8. OBJECTIONS TO FEDERAL HEADSHIP

Before a critic dismisses the principle of federal headship on the ground of inequity, let him review the realities that already hold him as a member of society. If he sees things rightly, and if he has the spiritual honesty to be transformed by what he sees, he will have to admit that society is *founded* on the principle of federal solidarity. We know, for example, that a head of government officially represents the citizens. If he blunders at the table of arbitration, and thus plunges the country into war, the young men in the land are called to fight. They fight because they are federally involved in his error, not because they made the error. Citizens cannot enjoy the privileges of society without sharing its responsibilities. Samuel Johnson points this out with his usual realism and candor: "The objection, in which is urged the injustice of making the innocent suffer with the guilty, is an objection not only against society, but against the possibility of society. All societies, great and small, subsist upon this condition; that as the individuals derive advantages from union, they may likewise suffer inconveniences; that as those who do nothing, and sometimes those who do ill, will have the honours and emoluments of general virtue and general prosperity, so those likewise who do nothing, or perhaps do well, must be involved in the consequences of predominant corruption."* It would be strange if men were to impugn God's use of federal representation, when a proper society is regulated by the very same principle. Families are taxed equally for municipal services, though it is known in advance that they do not use them equally.

The Apostle Paul does not debate the matter. He assumes that there is a gap between what we are and what we ought to be; and that the reason for this gap is that we suffer from depraved affections. If we repudiate our connection with the first Adam on the ground of injustice, we must also repudiate our connection with the last Adam; for we have no more to do with our judicial restoration than we had to do with our moral ruination. God only privileges us to declare the family of our allegiance: either we continue in pride, and thus remain in the family of the first Adam; or we humble ourselves, and thus enjoy adoption into the family of the last Adam.

9. OBJECTIONS TO TOTAL DEPRAVITY

Others might say that if God obliges us by a law greater than we can keep, he violates justice from another side; for how can man be condemned for failing in what he cannot perform? The charge betrays an inaccurate knowledge of man's relation to the divine requirements. It is true that we are held by a law greater than we can keep. But it is not true that God asks us to do what we cannot do. Since Christ fulfilled righteousness by his active and passive obedience, we are able to fulfill the law in him. Christ met the law directly, while we meet the law indirectly. A knowl-

* Boswell, *Life of Samuel Johnson LL.D.* (Britannica), p. 261.

edge of what we *cannot* do should excite us to a knowledge of what we *can* do. While we have no resident power to love God, we do have power to be sorry that we prefer ourselves to God.

Theologians often claim that men cannot repent until they are regenerated by the Spirit of God. The supposition is that repentance is invariably a fruit of love. A failure to see the fallacy in this argument is one reason for the judicial excesses in classical Calvinism. Calvin tried to harmonize the sincerity of God's offer of pardon with the reality of man's responsibility to receive it, but he failed. And he failed because he overlooked the truths to which he was already committed as a theologian in Geneva. If he had been obedient to such truths, he would have perceived that sincere expressions of sorrow are not necessarily a fruit of love. They may or may not be, depending on the situation. When one apologizes to an enemy, he responds out of a sincere regard for the moral and spiritual environment. He does *not* respond out of love. He apologizes because it is the right thing to do. And if this is true when sinners apologize to one another, it is equally true when sinners repent before God. They repent because of the claims of the moral and spiritual environment. Sinners cannot love God until they are regenerated; but this lack of love destroys neither their duty nor their ability to repent. Whenever theologians view repentance as a fruit of regeneration, they end up with a harsh view of predestination. The universal offer of the gospel becomes nothing but an empty form. Christ wept over Jerusalem, but his tears are robbed of their sincerity.

Arminians make the mistake of thinking that man can resist saving grace. Though pre-soteric synergism is within our power, soteric synergism is not. Just as we are passive in our physical birth, so we are passive in our spiritual birth. When one repents of his sins, God regenerates his nature; and this nature binds one to righteousness in the same way that an unregenerate nature binds one to sin. Affections carry their own compulsion. "No one who abides in him sins; no one who sins has either seen him or known him" (I John 3:6).

Total depravity does not invalidate human responsibility. Sin is sufficiently a fruit of our own choosing that we cannot assign it to pathological necessity. Depraved affections make sin attractive, but they do not destroy either our power to flee temptation or our power to be sorry after we yield. We sin by choice as well as by nature. The desire traces to depravity, but the act traces to a moment-by-moment refusal to be good. We simply enjoy being evil. Children tease one another because they like to.

God consigned the world to sin, in order that he might save men by the election of grace. The less sufficient we are in ourselves, the more sufficient God is toward us. "God chose what is low and despised in the world, even things that are not, to bring to nothing things that are, so that no human being might boast in the presence of God" (I Corinthians 1:28-29). If men had a legal claim on heaven, they would never know what it means to be saved by grace. Human weakness became the occasion for God to display the majesty of his justice through the beauty of his love. God's power is made perfect through weakness. "For what is more consistent with faith than to acknowledge ourselves naked of all virtue, that we may be clothed by God; empty of all good, that we may be filled by him; slaves to sin, that we may be liberated by him; blind, that we may be enlightened by him; lame, that we may be guided; weak, that we may be supported by him; to divest ourselves of all ground of glorying, that he alone may be eminently glorious, and that we may glory in him?"*

This principle is aptly illustrated in the struggles of the Apostle Paul with his "thorn in the flesh." "Three times I besought the Lord about this, that it should leave me" (II Corinthians 12:8). Certainly it was not unreasonable of Paul to believe that God would comply with his prayer. Yet, God knew that pride and self-love threatened to tincture the purity of Paul's sense of filial reliance. "But he said to me, 'My grace is sufficient for you, for my power is made perfect in weakness'" (verse 9). When Paul realized that his own frailty provided an occasion for God to

---

* Calvin, *Institutes of the Christian Religion*, Dedication.

display the consummate perfection of paternal love, he not only accepted the thorn in the flesh, but he thanked God for sending it. "For the sake of Christ, then, I am content with weaknesses, insults, hardships, persecutions, and calamities; for when I am weak, then I am strong" (verse 10).

10. SAVING FAITH

We have defined generic faith as a "resting of the mind in the sufficiency of the evidences." And by "resting" we do not mean bare mental apprehension. We mean a whole-souled satisfaction with critically tested judgments. But now that we have confronted God's judicial provision in Christ, our conception of faith must be refined somewhat. Hitherto we have only spoken of *generic* faith; we now pass to *saving* faith.

If generic faith is a "resting of the mind in the sufficiency of the evidences," saving faith is a "cordial trust in the person and work of Christ." When we sit in a chair, we demonstrate our faith in the chair; we yield to the sufficiency of the evidences; we act on the truth that this is a chair. But when we enter the society of a friend, we must do more than express a satisfaction with objective evidences; otherwise, we arouse the judicial sentiment in him. We are not rightly related to him unless we spiritually accept him. This is why saving faith is defined in terms of cordial trust rather than mere rational satisfaction. We leap into the heart of another person through fellowship.

But saving faith is built on the foundation of generic faith, for we could never yield ourselves in cordial trust unless the whole man rested in the sufficiency of the evidences. We must distinguish our friend from a tree; and not only from a tree, but from other people milling about him.

Saving faith is formed of three distinct, but complementary, elements: *knowledge* (the evidences of Christ's active and passive obedience are objectively sufficient); *assent* (I need what Christ has done, for I am a sinner); and *cordial trust* (I commit myself to Christ, firmly assured that he will deliver me from judicial suffering and death). Whereas only knowledge and assent belong to generic faith, saving faith is formed of knowledge, assent, and cordial trust.

If men *say* they trust Christ for salvation, when they merely give intellectual assent to the evidences, they deceive themselves; for one does not trust Christ until he loves him. "Not every one who says to me, 'Lord, Lord,' shall enter the kingdom of heaven, but he who does the will of my Father who is in heaven" (Matthew 7:21).

Roman Catholic divines adopt Augustine's view that faith is "reason with assent." They are entirely correct in this. But they are incorrect in thinking that this is the kind of faith that satisfies the sacred heart of Christ. If Romanism approached the problem of faith through the third method of knowing, rather than through medieval scholasticism, it would at once perceive that saving faith is far richer than intellectual assent. Whenever a person stands in the presence of another—whether God or man—he either mingles cordial trust with intellectual assent or he arouses the judicial sentiment in the other person. An oversight of this truth explains Rome's cultivated indifference to evangelical confrontation. A Catholic says, "Come, see my priest," not, "Come, meet my Savior." Intellectual assent to church tradition is elevated above spiritual encounter with Christ. The Reformers were banished from the church because they failed to give intellectual assent to tradition; not because they failed to give evidences of their mystical union with Jesus Christ.

Neo-orthodoxy cannot correct Rome's error because it does not build on Rome's truth. Common sense recognizes no such distinction as "thou-truth" and "it-truth." This is an *ad hoc* invention of theologians. Whenever a person enters the circle of nearness, he blends intellectual assent and spiritual commitment without any consciousness that he is leaving one realm of evidences for another. The individual before him is just as much a fact "out there" as a bottle or a tree. The essence of personality is hidden from the eyes of science and philosophy, of course, but that is quite beside the point. Science and philosophy have no access to the essence of pain either. *Many* facts are known only as they are felt. But this does not change matters. Facts are facts, whether they are persons, pains, or planets. Methods of knowing must simply answer to the kind of data under investigation. We have already pointed this out. In the instance of personality, knowledge by inference must yield to knowledge by acquaintance. But such an admission in no way supports the assumption that evangelical confrontation is a passionate leap in the face of objective paradox. Unless saving faith is grounded in generic faith, it is really not faith at all. It is blind trust. Evangelical encounter is man's whole-souled response to rationally objective evidences. Unless the whole man can be brought into the act of worship, one does not wholly worship. He must hold back some part, usually his intellect. But God never asks a man to bifurcate himself. Man does not encounter "thou-truth" on Sunday and "it-truth" the rest of the week. Any contact with truth is tantamount to contact with God, for God *is* truth. God illuminates the mind to perceive truth, and it makes no difference whether this perception takes place in the physics laboratory or in the Christian church. God has known all possible truth from eternity. We know truth because God graciously allows us to participate in the divine Logos. Christ is the Word of God; he is the everlasting repository of all wisdom.

11. GOD'S SOVEREIGNTY AND THE PROBLEM OF EVIL

At an earlier point in the book we had occasion to speak of the problem of evil: a tornado knifes through a sleeping village; a brilliant diplomat is killed by lightning; a mother is told that her newborn son is deformed; and crops fail where destitution is the greatest. At this point we forthrightly admitted that the problem of evil *was* a problem. And the reason for our candor was that we had insufficient information to give a rounded answer to the question, *Can we trust God?* But now that we have confronted the love of God in Christ, we have this missing information. Before turning to a solution to the problem, however, let us review the issue that separates the Biblical approach from all others.

God's sovereignty is the metaphysical foundation of the Christian world view. At no place is sovereignty compromised. "Who has directed the Spirit of the Lord, or as his counselor has instructed him? Whom did he consult for his enlightenment, and who taught him the path of justice, and taught him knowledge, and showed him the way of understanding? Behold, the nations are like a drop from a bucket, and are accounted as the dust on the scales; behold, he takes up the isles like fine dust" (Isaiah 40:13-15). God gives a critical account of himself to no one; there is no supreme court above him. Hence, the Scriptures entertain proportionately little discussion about the problem of evil. Any prolonged or morbid inquiry into the ways of God would show that those who question God do not really trust him. God is the final criterion of goodness; what he does is good because he does it.

This is why one does not have to examine nature to encounter the problem of evil, for the problem is in the Bible itself. As Butler observed long ago, the difficulties in general revelation have their counterpart in special revelation; for God is the author of both. When Moses protests that he cannot speak eloquently, God assures him that the deaf and the blind are of his own creation (Exodus 4:11); when Saul prepares to fight the Amalekites, he is commanded to slay even helpless infants (I Samuel 15:2-3); and when the disciples inquire about a man born blind, Jesus replies that the works of God are being made manifest in him (John 9:3). God keeps one question before man: Do you *trust* me? Since God is a person, his moral nature responds to nothing but cordial trust. To trust is to love, for love is the law of life.

All non-Biblical approaches lean on an abstract rule of teleology or justice. Leibnitz, for example, went to great lengths to develop

Christ the Power and the Wisdom of God   271

a "Christian theodicy." He thought it was perfectly decorous to judge the divine decrees by canons of thought which are accessible to all men. Whereas the Scriptures say that this is the best of all possible worlds because God made it, Leibnitz says that God created this world because he foresaw that it was the best of all possible worlds.

Men no longer read the arguments for theodicy, but they do continue to read the Bible. And this is not surprising, for the efforts of philosophy have come to naught. One does not have to examine Voltaire's *Candide* to see that the Leibnitzian argument is a tissue of fallacies. Even a child knows that the world would be more perfect if it were free of flies, mosquitoes, and poison ivy. To say that the Lisbon earthquake is an empirical proof of justice, or to assert that without such a catastrophe the quantity of moral values in the world would diminish, what is this but to utter a classic fatuity? The earthquake was an unspeakable tragedy to all who passed through it, and a memory of it is of no moral value to future generations.

Non-Biblical approaches fail to come at the problem by way of moral self-acceptance. If a philosopher would heed the realities that already hold him when he moves among people, he would realize that it is indecorous to approach God by way of an abstract system of justice or teleology. Since an analogy between God and man holds at all its pivotal points—for God and man are both persons—we must gauge our approach to God within limits that already hold us; for what could be less in accord with good procedure than to accost God with an attitude that we ourselves would not tolerate?

Here is what moral self-acceptance teaches: *If another person arouses the judicial sentiment in us by his want of appreciation for our favors, we will not let him probe into our life at other points until he faces his sin and apologizes.* This is not a speculative option; it is a reality that already holds us as creatures made in the image of God. A husband may want to know how his wife spends her time in the afternoon, and why she does not turn out more tasty meals; but if he has aroused the judicial sentiment by talking back to her, she will not let him interrogate her on these matters until he comes to her and apologizes.

Were we to admit that this is the universal order among upright men, but deny that it is the order when men approach God, we would turn our back on the truth that God and man are both persons. We have no right to inquire into God's general providence until we come to our senses and repent. Having aroused the judicial sentiment in God by our proud and self-sufficient ways, we have no right to speak to the problem of evil until we face the heinousness of sin.

God is propitious toward the human race—that is, he is morally willing to engage in friendly discussion about the problem of evil. But propitiation does not exempt man from the necessity of repenting. God is willing to prove the equity of his dealings, provided we address ourselves to the problem in the only way that the character of God permits. Before God will give an account of himself to man, man must give an account of himself to God; for the *worst* evil, the one that is first in the order of God's concern, is man's sin of pride and ingratitude. Man is not held by spontaneous sentiments of thankfulness for all God has done. Ingratitude arouses the judicial sentiment in any person, whether God or man.

As long as man insists that a discussion of "mud, hair, and filth" takes precedence over a discussion of sin, he proves how great is his sin. There is nothing new about such a truth. When a husband refuses to apologize to his wife, on the ground that his mean words should not be taken seriously, he does nothing but betray his distance from rectitude. He asks her to do what he would not do; namely, to ignore acts of cruelty.

If men of character demand an accounting from those who offend, should we not throw consistency to the wind to say that God, whose character is perfect, fails to make a like demand?

12. THE FILIAL BOND AND THE PROBLEM OF EVIL

The moment an individual comes to himself and repents, his relation to God at once changes. God justifies him before the law, adopts him into the divine family, and releases him to strive for goodness out of a spontaneity that is unconscious of law. These benefits are possible because Christ propitiated the judicial sentiment in God by his active and passive obedience. Even as the death of Christ changed God's relation to man, so God's acts of justification, adoption, and sanctification change man's relation to God. The filial bond replaces the bond of law: God is now our Father.

This creates an atmosphere within which the problem of evil can be faced and solved; for not only will a son approach his father in love, but the father will answer in pity and mercy. "As a father pities his children, so the Lord pities those who fear him. For he knows our frame; he remembers that we are dust" (Psalm 103:13-14). The bond between parents and children is so intimate that when the little ones innocently raise questions that suggest a lack of perfect trust, even in this the parents take delight. They are pleased by the filial boldness of their children, for perfect love casts out fear.

This is the context in which God entertains discussion about the problem of evil. God is not morally free to parley with sinners until they give sincere moral signs of repentance. If a king will not answer his subjects until they address him as king, is it meaningful to say that God will discuss the details of his providence with those who refuse to acknowledge him as God?

13. THE DIALOGUE OF HABAKKUK

Although God speaks to the problem of evil at several points in the Bible, perhaps the most majestic instance of the divine condescension is found in the minor prophet Habakkuk. The very plan and brevity of the book make it ideal for study. Let us review the matter under four convenient headings.

First, the dialogue takes place within the filial bond. Habakkuk complains that God is not paying enough attention to domestic oppressions. Why is *man* more solicitous about justice than God? "So the law is slacked and justice never goes forth. For the wicked surround the righteous, so justice goes forth perverted" (1:4). The Lord swiftly assures the prophet that injustices will be redressed. "For lo, I am rousing the Chaldeans, that bitter and hasty nation, who march through the breadth of the earth, to seize habitations not their own" (1:6). But rather than satisfying the prophet, this new information leaves him even more distressed. Since God is holy, how can he hire the wicked Chaldeans as agents in justice? Can sinners be judged by greater sinners? "Thou who art of purer eyes than to behold evil and canst not look on wrong, why dost thou look on faithless men, and art silent when the wicked swallows up the man more righteous than he?" (1:13). The confidence of the prophet is now at its zenith, for he finds a comfortable seat and, like Job, waits to hear what God will say. "I will take my stand to watch, and station myself on the tower, and look forth to see what he will say to me" (2:1).

Habakkuk's filial boldness is only surpassed by God's paternal love. Not only does the prophet sense no moral impropriety in petitioning God to give an account of himself, but God graciously complies with the prophet's attempt. God is willing to help a very confused, but very precious, child. If one were to judge the book apart from the filial bond, he would have to give up in despair; for not only would it be a pointless review of human arrogance, but it would leave us baffled to explain why a holy God would even descend to such parley.

Second, the prophet is assured that God is perfectly held by the standards that hold an upright man imperfectly. Rather than correcting Habakkuk's impression that God and man share the

Christ the Power and the Wisdom of God 275

same moral and spiritual environment, God dignifies his conviction by urging that it be held in patience. "For still the vision awaits its time; it hastens to the end—it will not lie. If it seem slow, wait for it; it will surely come, it will not delay" (2:3). God tells the prophet that justice *will* be done; and when it is done, it will fully pacify man's moral sense. But God's providence must not be hurried. There is a time and a place for everything. "It is appointed for men to die once, and after that comes judgment" (Hebrews 9:27).

The prophet is told to view things from the divine point of view, for the ways of God cannot be condensed into the ways of man. Impatience is always a by-product of time. Time is sequence, while eternity is simultaneity. "With the Lord one day is as a thousand years, and a thousand years as one day" (II Peter 3:8). Hence, a delay in justice does not imply the absence of justice. God gives his word for it. "Because you have plundered many nations, all the remnant of the peoples shall plunder you" (Habakkuk 2:8).

Third, faith, not inherent merit, is the true test of human righteousness. If the prophecy begins with holy boldness, it ends with holy meekness. This is exceedingly remarkable, but what accounts for it? Why does the prophet shift from filial doubt to filial trust? The answer is that God turns the discussion from the Chaldeans to Habakkuk. "Behold, he whose soul is not upright in him shall fail, but the righteous shall live by his faith" (2:4). Rather than allowing the prophet to continue his arrogant probe into how God deals with others, God launches an inquiry into how God deals with Habakkuk. How can God have fellowship with a sinner? Habakkuk had tacitly assumed that his right to come to God was due to inherent moral superiority. God shows him how wide of the mark his judgment is.

The mystery of God's justice does not begin with the Chaldeans; it begins with God's willingness to tolerate the complaints of Habakkuk. The prophet has no legal right to come to God; yet God assures him that he *does* have such a right. But on what ground does such a right exist? The answer is, Habakkuk must *believe* that such a right exists, for the just shall live by faith. Man must take God at his word.

Awed by the fact that he, a sinner, is allowed to have fellowship with the God of heaven and earth, Habakkuk now sees the problem of evil in a different light. If God were to execute justice in the way that Habakkuk first demanded it, Habakkuk himself would be condemned. Although there is a difference between the wickedness of the prophet and the wickedness of the Chaldeans—a difference that God respects—the difference is not absolute. Sin assumes various forms. The Chaldeans are guilty of idolatry, murder, and theft, while Habakkuk is guilty of pride, jealousy, and too eager a desire to question the integrity of God. The zeal with which Habakkuk is concerned to judge others, but not Habakkuk, is a proof that he, like the Chaldeans, is a sinner. Hence, *all* must remember, and the prophet in particular, that "the Lord is in his holy temple; let all the earth keep silence before him" (2:20).

Fourth, the proof of faith is love. When the prophet realizes that even his right to speak to God is grounded in judicial mystery, trust replaces inquiry. And since trust has no reality until one is in a state of trust, the prophet witnesses to the sincerity of his faith by spiritually conforming himself to the divine wisdom. To love God for his blessings, but not to love him as God, is not to love at all; for love takes in the whole person.

Habakkuk's soul is so overwhelmed with filial peace that he utters a majestic prayer of rejoicing to God. Subdued by the love of God, he joyfully submits to the mystery of God's justice—even the mystery of why God would ravage the land by the hand of the wicked Chaldeans. "Though the fig tree do not blossom, nor fruit be on the vines, the produce of the olive fail and the fields yield no food, the flock be cut off from the fold and there be no herd in the stalls, yet I will rejoice in the Lord, I will joy in the God of my salvation" (3:17-18). One may search the libraries of the world, but he will not find a more touching expression of man's faith in God.

Bear in mind that Habakkuk was not won by a detailed review of God's providence. He did not examine a cosmic handbook on how a just deity conducts himself. Rather than being broken on the wheel of justice, he was melted by the rays of love. If God can justly receive sinners, his justice is perfect; and his justice is perfect because his love is perfect. Men of faith are happy to take God at his word.

14. THE FAITH OF ABRAHAM

Purity of heart, says Kierkegaard, is to will one thing. Since God is absolute, mortals are given no other option than to trust or distrust God with their whole heart. Each new moment should be filled with spiritual commitment.

It is not without reason that Kierkegaard looked to Abraham as a perfect illustration of the perils and triumphs of faith, for on at least two separate occasions the Scriptures laud the purity of Abraham's filial piety. First, he defied the limits of human science by believing that he, though past age, would have a son. Since God had spoken, it was true; and being true, Abraham rested in it. "No distrust made him waver concerning the promise of God, but he grew strong in his faith as he gave glory to God, fully convinced that God was able to do what he had promised" (Romans 4:20-21). The fruits of empirical procedure and the counsels of worldly wisdom witnessed against the possibility of fatherhood. Yet, Abraham believed God; he took him at his word.

Second, when God told him to offer up his son, the son whom he loved, Abraham subordinated his own interpretation of rectitude to that of God. He could not see the ethical connection between God's promise in Isaac and the command to offer Isaac up; but he knew there was a connection, for God wills only good things for those who trust him (Romans 8:28). "He considered that God was able to raise men even from the dead; hence, figuratively speaking, he did receive him back" (Hebrews 11:19). This is why the Scriptures honor Abraham, rather than Habakkuk, as the father of the faithful (Romans 4:11). Instead of curiously inquiring into the causes of divine providence, Abraham submitted to the will of God itself. Habakkuk was a child of God, to be sure, but he did not always suppress his eagerness to question the wisdom of parental decision. Abraham believed that what God does is good because he does it—and for no other reason.

God makes one demand: *Trust me; take my word for it*. If God allowed men to compare him to an abstract standard, then such a standard, not God, would become the object of human confidence. Calvin summarizes this truth with unusual precision: "If such thoughts ever enter the minds of pious men, they will be sufficiently enabled to break their violence by this one consideration, how exceedingly presumptuous it is to inquire into the causes of the Divine will; which is in fact, and is justly entitled to be, the cause of every thing that exists. For if it has any cause, then there must be something antecedent, on which it depends; which it is impious to suppose. For the will of God is the highest rule of justice; so that what he wills must be considered just, for this very reason, because he wills it. When it is inquired, therefore, why the Lord did so, the answer must be, Because he would. But if you go further, and ask why he so determined, you are in search of something greater and higher than the will of God, which can never be found."* The Scriptures solve the problem of evil in the only way it *can* be solved: by showing a sinner how to trust God. God's justice is perfect because his love is perfect.

15. MAN'S SEARCH FOR ULTIMATE MEANING

God does not pacify man by a detailed review of how providence meshes with ideal justice, for man is rationally incapable of peering into the mysteries of the divine Logos. Man would faint at the very sight. Just as time and eternity are two orders of being, so the mind of man and the mind of God are two orders of thought. "For as the heavens are higher than the earth, so are my ways higher than your ways and my thoughts than

---

* *Institutes of the Christian Religion*, III, 23, 2.

your thoughts" (Isaiah 55:9). The *telos* of the universe is too complex for human faculties to grasp. Plato tried, but all who have read the trifling details of the *Timaeus* realize how sadly he failed. And he failed because man is nearsighted. He is too close to nature to know what nature means. He is like an ant on the side of a building. The ant sees nothing but an uneventful series of rough surfaces; it does not, and cannot, perceive the science and beauty of architecture.

Mystery is everywhere—just everywhere. And modern man should never forget it. Rational self-sufficiency is a sign of ignorance, not learning, for the totality of being is one massive miracle. A contemplation of it should elicit the deepest feelings of rational poverty. "It is not by our superior insight that we escape the difficulty; it is by our superior levity, our inattention, our *want* of insight. It is by *not* thinking that we cease to wonder at it. Hardened round us, encasing wholly every notion we form, is a wrappage of traditions, hearsays, mere *words*. We call that fire of the black thunder-cloud 'electricity,' and lecture learnedly about it, and grind the like of it out of glass and silk: but, *what is it?* What made it? Whence comes it? Whither goes it? Science has done much for us; but it is a poor science that would hide from us the great deep sacred infinitude of Nescience, whither we can never penetrate, on which all science swims as a mere superficial film. This world, after all our science and sciences, is still a miracle; wonderful, inscrutable, *magical* and more, to whosoever will *think* of it."*

Since it would take omniscience to understand and appreciate the connections in creation, God never wins us by a technical review of his decrees. God treats us as children. When a child says he does not believe that pictures can fly through the air and be seen on television, the father does not lead the child through the mathematics of electronics. He knows that the little one cannot understand such things. So, he turns to the answer of

---

* Thomas Carlyle, *On Heroes, Hero-Worship, and the Heroic in History* (Oxford), p. 10.

love: "I can't explain it just now, Bobby. You'll just have to take my word for it. When you grow up, you'll understand."

If a child cannot grasp the complexity of television, can we hope to grasp the complexity of providence? God dwells in unapproachable light, both in holiness and in knowledge. The order in being and becoming, the cycle of life and death, and the balance and distribution of attributes—all are so intricately interwoven that we cannot understand the *telos* of the universe at one point without understanding it at every point. But this would make us God.

Either we must learn to trust God or we must despair. God had to force Job into this disjunction before Job realized that the connectives in the universe are too mysterious for the human mind to fathom. God addresses Job in a way that he never addressed Habakkuk. Whereas Habakkuk quickly saw his error, Job prolonged the parley beyond its time. When God's children are stubborn, God answers them with paternal candor. "Then the Lord answered Job out of the whirlwind: 'Who is this that darkens counsel by words without knowledge? Gird up your loins like a man, I will question you, and you shall declare to me. Where were you when I laid the foundation of the earth? Tell me, if you have understanding. Who determined its measurements—surely you know! Or who stretched the line upon it?'" (Job 38:1-5). When Job came to his senses and reflected on the fact that he, a mere man, was trying to discover the counsels of eternity, he joined his faith with that of Habakkuk. "I know that thou canst do all things, and that no purpose of thine can be thwarted.... Therefore I have uttered what I did not understand, things too wonderful for me, which I did not know" (42:2-3).

With this, the wheel has come full turn. If one will leaf back to the first part of the book, he will find that the reality of human dependence was the first truth to be established by moral self-acceptance. Since then we have learned that we are limited in knowledge as well as strength; for we are not only helpless to sustain life, but we are not even sure what life is. All we have and are is from God.

16. THE PROBLEM OF EVIL AND THE CROSS OF CHRIST

The cross of Christ is God's final answer to the problem of evil because the problem of evil is in the cross itself. Judged by abstract standards of jurisprudence, the cross seems to be a miscarriage of justice. When a neighbor's child breaks a window, we do not punish our own children; and we do not because we cannot. Vicarious punishment offends our sense of fair play. And yet, God defied the judicial expectations of man by penally afflicting his own Son in the sinner's stead. "For our sake he made him to be sin who knew no sin, so that in him we might become the righteousness of God" (II Corinthians 5:21). We *believe* that Christ's death satisfied the judicial sentiment in God, but we believe on no other evidence than God's word. God assures us of his pleasure in Christ, and we trust him. We take his word for it.

Pride thinks that the cross is foolish, but the foolishness is in pride itself. When one is judicially offended by the principle of vicarious suffering, he is committed to the hopeless work of creating his own righteousness. But his very effort catapults him into the moral predicament, for the more he tries to exculpate himself by lawful righteousness, the more involved in guilt he becomes. "Some of the Pharisees near him heard this, and they said to him, 'Are we also blind?' Jesus said to them, 'If you were blind, you would have no guilt; but now that you say, "We see," your guilt remains' " (John 9:40-41).

This is why the cross is, was, and ever will be the focal point of moral decision for the human race. We cannot come to God unless we are righteous. Yet, we have insufficient righteousness unless we are mystically joined to Jesus Christ; for he alone, of all humanity, loved God with his whole heart and his neighbor as himself. But before we can enjoy positional righteousness, and thus be saved, we must reverently acknowledge that the details of God's justice cannot be anticipated by human criteria. We must subordinate our own interpretation of justice to that of God, for what God does is good because he does it.

God overturned the wisdom of men by providing a substitute for sinners. "For the foolishness of God is wiser than men, and the weakness of God is stronger than men" (I Corinthians 1:25). This is why the cross is the final solution to the problem of evil; for the *greatest* judicial mystery, the one that baffles all expectations, is that God can declare sinners righteous in his sight. Whereas we ought to suffer for our own guilt, God transferred this guilt to his Son.

If we can believe God for our justification, we can also believe that this is the best of all possible worlds; for just as it is good that Christ died for our sins, so it is also good that God decreed a world which is defiled by sin, sickness, and death. What God does is good because he does it. God proves the majesty of his justice by the consummate beauty of his love. Being good enough to receive sinners through the righteousness of Jesus Christ, he is good enough to be trusted for everything.

The cross is also an answer to the charge that God subdues men by an overpowering display of his sovereignty. God never violates the sanctity of human personality; he never asks men to commit themselves on the strength of insufficient evidences. God wins men by love. Rather than proportioning his benefits to our worthiness, he showers undeserved blessings on all. "He did not leave himself without witness, for he did good and gave you from heaven rains and fruitful seasons, satisfying your hearts with food and gladness" (Acts 14:17).

And if God's goodness in nature fails to move one to thankfulness, the Scriptures appeal to the death of Jesus Christ on the cross. "In this is love, not that we loved God but that he loved us and sent his Son to be the expiation for our sins" (I John 4:10). God not only promises to bring many sons into glory by way of a justice that does not inhere in them, but he graciously decrees the means by which this reconciliation is made possible. If we marvel at the bleeding heart of Abraham, what is the measure of our marvel when we contemplate the price of our redemption? God withdrew fellowship from his dying Son, in order that he might be judicially free to pardon sinners. Only the poet can limn the grief and majesty of such a holy scene:

> "O sacred Head, now wounded,
>   With grief and shame weighed down,
> Now scornfully surrounded
>   With thorns, Thine only crown;
> O sacred Head, what glory,
>   What bliss, till now was Thine!
> Yet, though despised and gory,
>   I joy to call Thee mine.
>
> "What language shall I borrow
>   To thank Thee, dearest Friend,
> For this, Thy dying sorrow,
>   Thy pity without end?
> Oh! make me Thine, forever;
>   And should I fainting be,
> Lord, let me never, never,
>   Out-live my love to Thee."*

* "O Sacred Head, Now Wounded" (ascribed to Bernard of Clairvaux).

Chapter Eleven

THE FINALITY OF JESUS CHRIST

1. THE VERIFICATION OF THE CHRISTIAN WORLD VIEW

Having reviewed the cardinal elements in the Christian plan of salvation, let us now show how these elements harmonize with the third method of knowing; and in particular how they can be rationally verified.

Let it be said at the outset that the plan of salvation *cannot* be established by a straight-line application of moral self-acceptance. Soteriology stands or falls according to the validity of the system of which it is a part. The rough elements of this system have already been established—the existence and personality of God, God's image in man, the moral and spiritual environment, love as the law of life, the spiritual defect in man's will and affections, and the necessity of repentance. But by no scheme of human inventiveness could one discover the doctrine of substitutionary atonement. God's provision of righteousness in Jesus Christ is a "mystery hidden for ages and generations but now made manifest to his saints" (Colossians 1:26). The third method of knowing acquaints us with the justice and love of God, but it does not tell us how these attributes harmonize in the one divine essence.

This is only another way of saying that the Christian system is chosen, not forced. Its claims are not part of a world system

The Finality of Jesus Christ

of reason and will. It is even inaccurate, though quite necessary, to use the term "Christian system." Revelation is fragmentary. "The secret things belong to the Lord our God; but the things that are revealed belong to us and to our children for ever" (Deuteronomy 29:29). Whenever a systematic theologian becomes too systematic, he ends up falsifying some aspect of revelation. It is extremely difficult, if not impossible, to coax all the data of Scripture into neat harmony. One must preserve a penumbral zone in his theology; new exegetical possibilities should be welcomed. "Now I know in part; then I shall understand fully, even as I have been fully understood" (I Corinthians 13:12).

But lest it be supposed that verification is uniquely a Christian problem, let it immediately be said that *all* systems, of whatever stripe, are chosen rather than forced. And more than this, a man cannot escape the necessity of choosing. The choice of a given system is optional, of course, but the choice of *some* system is not. This is the main point in Pascal's famous "wager." Since we are already embarked, life itself commits us to convictions which connect us with a particular system of thought. A man may not consciously spell out his convictions, but that is neither here nor there. Since he lives *as if* this or that is true about the ultimate nature of things, his conduct is a revelation of what he really believes. For example, condoned self-sufficiency is evidence that one does not filially rest in the righteousness of Christ.

Therefore, the problem of verifying a system, like the problem of justice and injustice, belongs to man qua man. Students end up Platonists, Aristotelians, or Christians because they choose to; and the difficulties that accompany one choice are not different in kind from the difficulties that accompany any other choice.

But what norm should one apply, in order that he might decide for the best system? Here is the answer, and the answer applies to both theology and philosophy: *Systems are chosen or rejected by reason of their power to explain areas of reality that a particular individual finds important.* Plato wanted to solve the problem of the one within the many, while Marx wanted to solve the problem of class injustice; and each chose his ultimates, and thus his system, with these interests in view. A Christian wants to solve the moral predicament.

But how are systems verified? How can one decide whether one system is better than another? Here is the answer, and the answer once again applies to both theology and philosophy: *Systems are verified by the degree to which their major elements are consistent with one another and with the broad facts of history and nature.* In short, a consistent system is a true system. Were a person to demand a higher or a more perfect test than this, he would only show his want of education.

This is about all that can be said. Christianity is true because its major elements are consistent with one another and with the broad facts of history and nature. The third method of knowing has shown that the human race is held in a moral predicament; and only Christianity can resolve this predicament without offending the larger features in man's fourfold environment—physical, rational, aesthetic, and moral and spiritual. Existence itself raises a question to which the righteousness of Christ is the only critically acceptable answer. Hence, Christianity is true.

I confess that no real effort has been made to show that Christianity *is* consistent with the broad facts of history and nature. My excuse is twofold: first, the really crucial elements in the system have been established, and this is the main thing; second, books on Christian evidences are in great abundance. The findings of archaeology have been conveniently catalogued. If the reader is interested in discovering whether Christianity vertically fits the facts, the sources are available.

2. A TERMINAL DIFFICULTY

Before considering the matter settled, however, a worthy objection must be faced. At an earlier point we asserted, first, that God completes the moral cycle by answering to the judicial sentiment; second, that the judicial sentiment is often aroused when

The Finality of Jesus Christ

the evidences do not warrant it. These assertions seem to contradict one another. Hence, the objection.

Let me say, by way of background, that the judicial sentiment cannot be considered our own act of judgment, for we have no power to arouse it and no power to pacify it once it has been aroused. Like all moral transactions, it is a fruit of our participation in the moral and spiritual environment. Hence, the judicial sentiment is a work of God.

If a man will be altogether honest with himself when he is squirted by a neighbor's garden hose or sneered at by a passing motorist, he will recognize that the judicial sentiment is provoked by the force of circumstances, and not by the force of either mind or will. Inconsideration arouses the judicial sentiment, and the sentiment stays aroused until right moral conditions prevail.

This disposes of the first half of the objection. To say that God completes the moral cycle by answering to the judicial sentiment, what is this but to describe reality as it actually is?

The second half of the objection is met by a new appreciation of the counsel of Christ. "Judge not, that you be not judged. For with the judgment you pronounce you will be judged, and the measure you give will be the measure you get" (Matthew 7:1-2). There is nothing in this counsel which embarrasses our contention that God completes the moral cycle by answering to the judicial sentiment. Rather, there is much that supports it. Christ says that if we abuse the work of God in us, God will judicially afflict us by turning the abuse back on us.*

But does this not violate our assertion that we have no direct control over the judicial sentiment? If God is the agent in judgment, what meaning is there in warning us not to judge others by a standard lower than that by which we would want to be judged? Here is the resolution: *Although we have no power to arouse or pacify the judicial sentiment, we do have power to purify or corrupt the conditions that give rise to this mysterious*

---

* When God does this—whether in this life or in the life to come—is not important. That he does is all that matters.

moral transaction. If we yield to churlish affections, we so corrupt the conditions of our life that the judicial sentiment is aroused by the least provocation. But if we yield to charitable affections, we so purify the conditions of our life that the judicial sentiment is seldom aroused. A frustrated person is easily frustrated. This is why the second greatest of the laws—that we must love our neighbor as ourself—is premised on the self's love for the self. Unless a man properly loves himself, he cannot properly love his neighbor; for love integrates the life. A child may try the patience of his parents, but he rarely arouses the judicial sentiment in them.

In sum: the judicial sentiment is always the work of God. We have no power to arouse or pacify it. But we are able to *direct* the divine activity. And this is decided by the extent to which our affections are captured by the law of love. A kindly life channels the work of God into righteous ends, whereas a surly life perverts this work by including it in the arsenal of pride. And the more one persists in such perversion, the more he comes to judicial grief; for God turns the corrupted standard back on him. The measure one gives is the measure one gets.

The critic's objection reinforces our assertion that existence itself raises a question to which Christ is the only critically acceptable answer. The moral predicament is ubiquitous and insoluble. This ensures the ambiguity of the entire human enterprise. God consigned the world to sin, in order that he might begin a race of righteous men through the resurrection of Jesus Christ. When man is weak toward God, God is strong toward man. Sin brings the weakness, and the law shows sin to be sin. "Now we know that whatever the law says it speaks to those who are under the law, so that every mouth may be stopped, and the whole world may be held accountable to God" (Romans 3:19). Law tells man what he cannot do, not what he can do; for if there were no sin, there would be no law. This is the essence of the moral predicament. Man's nobler faculties assent to a law which the self-in-act cannot meet. Whenever the good must be conceived as law, one confronts the very reason why he neither is nor can be good.

The Finality of Jesus Christ

If this structure offends the reader, I can only say that my effort to explain the nature of rectitude, despite all, has failed. From the very beginning I have asserted that an act has no moral worth unless it is a spontaneous fruit of the moral and spiritual environment. I do not retreat an inch from this assertion. But let me quickly point out that an inability to be moral does not imply an inability to be law-abiding. This *must* be appreciated. Otherwise serious misunderstanding will result. A self-righteous person need not be a liar or a thief. Quite to the contrary, he may be a very decent member of society. God rejects self-righteousness on one ground: it is not inspired by holy affections. When a person is motivated by law, he is not motivated by love. He offends God with each new effort to be righteous.

But how do we explain the fact that the Psalmist loved the law of God? The answer is, he loved the law of God because it was the will of God. Since his affections were united with God, he was motivated by a compulsion that inheres in love itself. A rational regard for law is pure calculation. This is why we confidently say that law tells us what we *cannot* do, not what we *can* do. As we humble ourselves before God, God gives us holy affections; and these holy affections make it possible for us to be good. We either spontaneously do the right, or we express spontaneous sorrow for having failed. In either case, God is satisfied. Love looks for nothing but evidences of love.

But what law have all men transgressed, in order that pride and self-sufficiency might be challenged before the divine tribunal? Many men have not committed fornication, and fewer still are murderers. The answer is, all men have transgressed the law of love. If we sincerely loved God with our whole heart and our neighbor as ourself, our life would be so perfectly integrated that we would never pervert God's judgment. But the manner of our life proves that we sin daily in thought and word and deed. Despite the protest of our nobler faculties, the empirical self continues to judge others by a higher standard than it can mediate. But this very habit is the cause of our moral undoing. Since God will judge us by the perverted standard by which we judge others, we are in a perilous state; for we judge more by interest and prejudice than by equity and truth. Only love can take in the mystery and particularity of selfhood.

We continue to judge inconsiderate people. This shows that we know the law of life. But we use this law in the defense of pride. This shows that we hold the law in unrighteousness. Hence, the inescapable disjunction: either we despair of judicial relief, or we throw ourselves on the mercy of the court. And the Christian confidently elects the latter, for he has met the goodness of God in Jesus Christ. "Law came in, to increase the trespass; but where sin increased, grace abounded all the more" (Romans 5:20). Since this is a final statement of the moral predicament, it is also a statement of the finality of Jesus Christ.

3. THE PROTESTANT REFORMATION

Once we recognize the moral ambiguity of all human conduct, we not only understand why Christians look to Christ for hope, but we also understand why Western Christianity is tragically divided into two separate efforts.

Classical Protestantism ends with a high view of imputed righteousness because it defends a low view of man's creative possibilities. Roman Catholicism ends with a low view of imputed righteousness because it defends a high view of man's creative possibilities. "If any one saith, that men are justified, either by the sole imputation of the justice of Christ, or by the sole remission of sins, to the exclusion of the grace and the charity which is poured forth in their hearts by the Holy Ghost, and is inherent in them; or even that the grace, whereby we are justified, is only the favor of God: let him be anathema."* This is very clear language. Its intention cannot be missed. But how can a Catholic learn whether the grace in him is sufficient to serve as the formal cause of second justification?

The answer is, he must discover what kind of sin he has com-

* Council of Trent, Sixth Session, Canon XI.

The Finality of Jesus Christ

mitted. Although there are three levels of sin, only two are relevant. The peccadilloes (slight faults) are too trivial to be processed by the confessional. Venial sins tincture grace, but they do not cause the loss of the soul. Mortal sins are crimes. They destroy the merit of grace by driving out the theological virtue of charity. This is a mortal loss because faith and hope, without charity, profit nothing.

It is obvious, therefore, that a Roman Catholic's peace before God is no more secure than the peace which he has in himself. He must be certain that he is free from mortal sins; otherwise he is lost. Venial sins need not be feared, for they can easily be forgiven. Even the saints, who earned merit beyond their own needs, were tinctured by venial sins.

But where can a Roman Catholic turn, in order that he might come by an official list of mortal sins? The answer is, there can be no such list, for the same act is rendered venial or mortal by the quality of the motive that inspires it. This is extremely important, for it means that Roman Catholicism, despite everything, is a subjective religion.

Since the spiritual well-being of a Catholic depends on his ability to measure the quality of his own motives, it is imperative that he have a clear rule to guide him. And the Angelic Doctor assures that such a rule is in hand. "Therefore, when the soul is so disordered by sin as to turn away from its last end, viz., God, to Whom it is united by charity, there is mortal sin; but when it is disordered without turning away from God, there is venial sin."* Again, "I answer that, Mortal sin . . . consists in turning away from our last end, which is God; which aversion pertains to the deliberating reason, whose function it is also to direct towards the end. Therefore, that which is contrary to the last end can happen not to be a mortal sin only when the deliberating reason is unable to come to the rescue, which is the case in sudden movements."†

* Aquinas, *Summa Theologica*, First Part of the Second Part, Q. 72, Art. 5.
† *Ibid.*, Q. 77, Art. 8.

There is only one trouble with this Thomistic rule: it is extremely difficult, if not impossible, to apply. When *is* a sin committed knowingly and willingly, rather than otherwise? And what does it mean to be *rationally conscious* of God as the end of the soul? The sins of pride can be indulged without any awareness of the law of God, for they are not preceded by any conscious temptation. The deliberating reason is inoperative. Pride is an immediate fruit of evil affections. Proud individuals violate the first and second greatest of the laws without any counsel from the deliberating reason.

Furthermore, even when deliberation does play a part, only God can know for sure what this part actually is. Suppose an employee loses his temper and nurses a grudge against a fellow worker. His uneasy conscience proves that to some extent, however minute, he sins knowingly and willingly. But what is this extent? How can he discover (*a*) whether he sins from disorder or (*b*) whether the deliberating reason turns from God as the final end of the soul? The answer is, he *cannot*; for his real motives are buried somewhere in the confusion of a totally ambiguous life. One never knows enough about his conduct to give a precise rational account of its causal connections. "I do not understand my own actions" (Romans 7:15).

Roman Catholicism does not appreciate the effects of original sin in the life of the Christian. And for this reason it does not appreciate the degree to which moral action is a rich blend of triumph and failure. There is "another law" at work in our members, a law that simultaneously attracts and repels our better faculties. The resulting ambivalence is so complex that one can never finally measure the quality of his own motives. This is what finally broke Martin Luther. Confronting the insecurity of a totally self-centered life, he knew he could never merit the favor of God—not even by works done in grace. A good man must love God with his whole heart and his neighbor as himself. But this was the one thing Martin Luther could not do; for the moment love must be conceived as law, one proves that he neither

The Finality of Jesus Christ

does nor can love. *Every* act of man is somewhat tainted by pride and self-sufficiency. Thus, the righteousness of Christ is our only hope. "For whoever keeps the whole law but fails in one point has become guilty of all of it" (James 2:10).

4. CHRISTIANITY AND OTHER WORLD RELIGIONS

Since we have deliberately restricted ourselves to a study of Christianity, an alert reader is bound to ask: "But what about the other major religions in the world? Does the Christian suppose he has a monopoly on truth?" Since the second question is the less important, we shall answer it first.

The Christian forthrightly denies that he enjoys exclusive access to the Logos of God, for God is revealed in nature as well as in Scripture. There are partial truths in every religious and philosophic tradition, truths that Christianity conserves rather than negates. But the Christian does not shrink from asserting that he, and he alone, can give a consistent answer to the question, "How can a sinner be just before God?" Only Jesus Christ can lead a sinner from moral ruin to judicial restoration without offending the major elements in man's fourfold environment—physical, rational, aesthetic, and moral and spiritual.*

Here is the heart of the Christian system: *"He saved us, not because of deeds done by us in righteousness, but in virtue of his own mercy, by the washing of regeneration and renewal in the Holy Spirit"* (Titus 3:5). God emptied man of virtue, in order that he might show the mystery of his justice through the consummate perfection of his love. Since man is defective in his will and in his affections, he cannot approach God on the merit of his own righteousness. "For by grace you have been saved

---

* It is not within our province to decide the destiny of those who may not interpret the Bible in quite the way we do. Pride would like to think that it has sole access to the mercies of God, but the sacred text seems to suggest otherwise. God looks for love, not uniformity. "And I have other sheep, that are not of this fold; I must bring them also, and they will heed my voice" (John 10:16). It is our duty to defend the truth as we see it; God will take care of judgment.

through faith; and this is not your own doing, it is the gift of God—not because of works, lest any man should boast" (Ephesians 2:8-9).

Here is the heart of all non-Christian systems: *Man can resolve the moral predicament by arousing dormant virtues within him.* Some systems distrust thought, some distrust passion, and some distrust spirit; but all agree that the real man—man in his inmost essence—is natively good. Machiavelli detects malice in those who are ruled, but not in the prince. Kant realizes that self-love preponderates over a pure reverence for law, but this does not make him pessimistic about Kant. Marx sees the threat of original sin in those who own the tools of production, but he sees no such threat in either Marx or the proletariat. With better opportunities and more effective resolution, man *can* overcome evil. Even Socrates believed that eternity could be mediated in time by a more perfect act of reminiscence.

Sin tempts a man to think of himself more highly than he ought. Pride will admit errors of prudence; it will confess faults and mistakes; it will resolve to do better in the light of unattained ideals. But pride will not admit that the will and the affections are defective. However pessimistic man may be about general evil, he remains optimistic about himself. Evil comes from adventitious sources; man is corrupted by outside influences. "For no man is voluntarily bad; but the bad become bad by reason of an ill disposition of the body and bad education, things which are hateful to every man and happen to him against his will."* Non-Christian positions are impressive for their antiquity, their wisdom literature, and their power to bind the conscience. But here is where their impressiveness ends.

When skeptics assert that there is no sure way to decide whether men are acceptable to God, they speak from ignorance; for the question is really not too difficult to decide. There are two families in the world: the family of sin and the family of righteousness. The first Adam is the federal head of the one family, while the last Adam is the federal head of the other. We can determine

---

* Plato, *Timaeus*, 86.

The Finality of Jesus Christ

our place in God by simply naming our federal head. All who strive to establish their own righteousness are of the family of the first Adam; they are rejected by God. All who repent are of the family of the last Adam; they are accepted by God. We have no final way of knowing who the members of each family are, for only God can read the heart. But we are reasonably certain of the principle on which the division is made. If a man clings to even a scrap of self-righteousness, he is guilty of not submitting to the righteousness of Christ; he renders the cross null and void.

God does not expect people to be experts in theology. But he does expect them to make a free and untaxed use of moral and rational self-transcendence. Love is the law of life—this we know from existence itself. And Christianity is the only world view built on it—this we know from even a cursory survey of comparative religions. Therefore, truth is quite within the reach of every normal man. A knowledge of the law of life leads to humility and repentance, while a knowledge of lesser laws leads to pride and self-sufficiency. If a man compares himself to a frog, he may think he has a fine voice; but if he compares himself to Caruso he soon discovers the true state of things. The difference in attitude is due to a difference in criteria. This is why it is easy to become self-righteous. One simply measures himself by a standard lower than the final norm of human nature, Jesus Christ. But this error will not make him righteous, for God judges by truth.

If one wants to know what God thinks of him, let him pose the right question. Is his life marked by repentance, or is it marked by self-sufficiency? To be received by God, one must despair of his own righteousness; but to be rejected by God one need only persist in personal pride.

5. THE HEIGHT AND DEPTH OF THE RELIGIOUS PERSPECTIVE

Calvin's opening sentences in the *Institutes* are very illuminating, for they sum up the paradox that man does not know God until he first knows himself; yet he does not know himself until he first knows God: "True and substantial wisdom principally consists of two parts, the knowledge of God, and the knowledge of ourselves. But, while these two branches of knowledge are so intimately connected, which of them precedes and produces the other, is not easy to discover. For, in the first place, no man can take a survey of himself but he must immediately turn to the contemplation of God, in whom he 'lives and moves;' since it is evident that the talents which we possess are not from ourselves, and that our very existence is nothing but a subsistence in God alone."

Christianity ends with a high view of man because it has the courage and the consistency to begin with a low view of man and a high view of God. As one despairs of his own righteousness, God robes him with the righteousness of Jesus Christ. Being nothing in his own sight, he becomes an adopted child in the sight of God. "See what love the Father has given us, that we should be called children of God; and so we are" (I John 3:1).

Other religions end with a low view of man because they begin with a high view of man and a low view of God. Trying to make man everything, they make him nothing. Since man's will and affections are defective, man incurs God's judicial displeasure with every new effort to be self-righteous. Man cannot please God until he humbles himself before God.

Let no one caricature this by saying that only those who contemplate the atonement can be saved. Abraham did not know of the cross, yet he was justified by God. *The Scriptures say that all who believe God will be saved.* Since conscience and the judicial sentiment announce God's displeasure with sin, men prove their respect for God by repenting. All who come to moral self-consciousness must humble themselves. They may die before they hear of Christ, but they do not die before they feel the accusing pricks of a guilty conscience.

Nor should one construe this as a disparagement of missions. Whenever theology relaxes the church's zeal to reach the lost, it is bad theology. There are at least two reasons why missionary activity is imperative. First, Christ has commanded us to take the gospel to every creature (Matthew 28:18-20). And since Christ is Lord as well as Savior, a consistent Christian must complete the ministry of the apostles by either going out as a missionary or by preparing the way for others to go. Second, God's love in nature is so obliterated by animism, magic, and witchcraft that the heathen are greatly confused about the nature of God. They know love as law, but not as love. Yet, men are not won to the law of God until they are subdued by the love of God. But how can they be subdued by the love of God unless they meet Jesus Christ? Christ is love incarnate. His life and death clarify distorted views of God, for God *is* love.

The perils and uncertainties of generic repentance prompted the Apostle Paul to limit repentance almost exclusively to the active preaching of the gospel. Not that men *cannot* repent without being confronted by Christ after the flesh, but that they *do* not repent without such confrontation. "But how are men to call upon him in whom they have not believed? And how are they to believe in him of whom they have never heard? And how are they to hear without a preacher? And how can men preach unless they are sent?" (Romans 10:14-15).

6. THE RIGHTEOUSNESS OF CORRECT THINKING

There are only three live alternatives to the righteousness of Christ, either purely or in combination: the righteousness of correct thinking, the righteousness of self-denial, and the righteousness of keeping the law. Let us show why each is self-defeating. In this way we shall expose the self-defeating elements in all non-Christian religions.

Some think they can answer to God's justice by entertaining correct thoughts, but their hope, quite sadly, is the daughter of either ignorance or sin. Thought may define virtue, but it is not virtue in itself. A morally wretched person can be quite skilled in theology and philosophy. " 'Knowledge' puffs up, but love builds up. If any one imagines that he knows something, he does not yet know as he ought to know" (I Corinthians 8:1-2).

If a person enters the circle of nearness and merely *thinks* about us, he arouses the judicial sentiment. He does not rightly know us, and thus cannot answer to our dignity, until he cordially accepts us. And since God and man are both persons, we would offend the truth if we were to suppose that God is consoled by the mere fact that men are orthodox in their theology. The essence of God is love, not thought.

This is why the Scriptures equate "doing the truth" with "doing righteousness," for righteousness is the third kind of truth—truth as personal rectitude. The third kind of truth has no existence until a person closes the gap between what he is and what he ought to be; and this can only be done by moral resolution. It was Christ's active obedience, not merely the consistent doctrine he taught, which gave merit to his passive obedience. Philosophers look to consistent thought, but Christ looked to consistent conduct; and he chose the better part, for God is love.

The error of confusing righteousness with correct thinking is by no means limited to those who have never repented. It is also characteristic of those who have repented in the past, but who sense no necessity to repent in the present. The Christian church is never entirely free from the error of supposing that a profession of right doctrine is the same thing as personal righteousness. The error is plausible because orthodox doctrine *is* an important element in a right view of God; for how can men come to God unless they are able to distinguish the will of God from the will of the devil? Doctrine tells us what God would have us believe and how he would have us live. Its indispensability is never called into question by a consistent Christian. "If any one refuses to obey what we say in this letter, note that man, and have nothing to do with him, that he may be ashamed" (II Thessalonians 3:14). Still, it is love, not thought, which answers to the nature of God. This is why Kierkegaard's attack on the established church is simply a modern counterpart to Paul's attack on the

The Finality of Jesus Christ

apostolic church; for a profession of orthodox doctrine *never* equals righteousness. "And if I have prophetic powers, and understand all mysteries and all knowledge, and if I have all faith, so as to remove mountains, but have not love, I am nothing" (I Corinthians 13:2).

Christians would like to believe that orthodox doctrine equals orthodox virtue, for it encourages pride to suppose that an absolute moral difference separates Christians from the world. Believers forget that, though the cross removes the judicial *sting* of sin, it does not remove the active *presence* of sin. When one stands on a busy city street and observes the milling throng about him, he cannot distinguish God's elect by the consistent way they love God with their whole heart and their neighbor as themselves. Quite to the contrary, Christians are never mistaken for Jesus Christ. With only rare exceptions, believers enter the competition of daily life with a shrewd eye on their own personal interests. Rather than enjoying exemption from pride and self-sufficiency, they simply vent these sins in more subtle ways. Christians may be relatively more virtuous than others, as indeed they ought to be; but their final ground of confidence is the righteousness of Christ in them. And there is no better proof of this than the refusal of Christians to admit it. Ministers preach against the sins of the laity, but seldom against the sins of ministers. Since they know more theology than the laity, they think they are less evil. This is ironic, however, for not only do the Scriptures teach that judgment must *begin* at the house of God, but one proves his love for God by a sincere confession that in himself he remains unrighteous. Professional holy men have one thing in common with the world: they do not seriously rest in the righteousness of Jesus Christ.

7. THE RIGHTEOUSNESS OF SELF-DENIAL

Ascetic rigors give every outward pretense of piety. Yet, the Apostle Paul does not hesitate to include them in his catalogue of spurious ways to please God. "If I give away all I have, and if I deliver my body to be burned, but have not love, I gain nothing" (I Corinthians 13:3). We may be brief here, for there is really not much to say. Right moral quality inheres in the will and the affections, not in the form of an act. If a person enters the circle of nearness, he can mortify himself until he wastes away; but he does not answer to our dignity unless he spiritually accepts us. Acceptance is affirmation; asceticism is negation.

Whenever one tries to love God by acts of ascetic devotion, he confronts the moral predicament. A man may ardently *desire* to love God, but he has insufficient moral resources to do it. We are not born with a natural love for God, and we are unable to arouse this love by works done in our own strength; for love is a fruit, not a work.

The rigors of self-denial may be good in themselves, even as thinking right thoughts is good; but in each case it is the love, not the work, which has moral value. Whenever God accepts our ascetic offerings, it is because the life of Christ is flowing through us. This is why repentance must precede fasting.

8. THE RIGHTEOUSNESS OF KEEPING THE LAW

It is not strange that Christ encountered his greatest opposition from those who meticulously observed the letter of the law. Since the Pharisees were engaged in professional religious duties, they not only felt no need of personal repentance, but they scurrilously attacked those who did.

But one must observe the kind of law which attracted the Pharisees. Rather than applying themselves to the heights of the law of love, they made righteousness easy by attending to ceremonial observances. Consumed in trifles, they exempted themselves from the things that really count. "Woe to you, scribes and Pharisees, hypocrites! for you tithe mint and dill and cummin, and have neglected the weightier matters of the law, justice and mercy and faith; these you ought to have done, without neglect-

The Finality of Jesus Christ

ing the others. You blind guides, straining out a gnat and swallowing a camel!" (Matthew 23:23-24). The Pharisees managed a high view of themselves by taking a low view of God; but Christ reminded them that truth is based on fact, not fiction. God is love, and those who seek to please him must love him. But they cannot do this of themselves; therefore, no man is righteous by keeping the law.

We pointed this out when examining Kant. The instant love must be conceived as law, we prove that we cannot meet its terms. The more we strive to love, the more affected our effort becomes. Love fulfills the law without any consciousness of law. That is why Pharisaism is self-defeating. Righteousness vanishes whenever men strive for legal righteousness. Although law codifies our duty, it has no power to make us good. "For if a law had been given which could make alive, then righteousness would indeed be by the law. But the scripture consigned all things to sin, that what was promised to faith in Jesus Christ might be given to those who believe" (Galatians 3:21-22). Christ met the terms of the law without legal effort, for his own will was perfectly united to the will of the Father. "My food is to do the will of him who sent me, and to accomplish his work" (John 4:34). Hungry men devour food out of vital, not lawful, necessity; and Christ was always hungry to do the will of God.

Some may chide us for dismissing other religions on the strength of such little evidence; but a charge of this sort overlooks the gravity of the evidence. If critics would come at the matter by way of moral self-acceptance, they would see that one *can* pass judgment on complex systems of religion without probing into fine details; and one not only can, but he must. A person may know everything and do everything, but we judge him delinquent if he fails to show a spiritual regard for our person. The same is true about systems of religion. When love is wanting, all else is inconsequential. A captious critic may call this scanty evidence; that is his privilege. But a more careful observer will know that, when testing for the presence or absence of the third kind of truth—

truth as personal rectitude—only one piece of evidence is needed. That evidence is love. The test is always swift and sure. When a religious system is not founded on this truth, it is defective in its very core.

If an individual will peruse the sacred books of the world, he will discover, as all candid observers before him have discovered, that non-Christian religions make the common mistake of supposing that man can please God by thinking something or doing something. They have lost what Christ calls the "key of knowledge" (Luke 11:52). Those who load men with thoughts to think, sacrifices to make, and laws to keep, but do not give men holy affections with which to perform these tasks, what are they doing but cutting off man's only escape from the judgment of God? Man cannot be righteous in God's sight until he repents of his expectation that he can be righteous in his own sight. God is not mighty toward man until man is weak toward God.

9. CONCLUSION

This is a book on Christian apologetics. Apologetics is that branch of systematic theology which shows why Christianity is true. "We destroy arguments and every proud obstacle to the knowledge of God, and take every thought captive to obey Christ" (II Corinthians 10:5). But apologetics *has* its limits. This must be pointed out, lest it be supposed that argumentation is a panacea for the loneliness and frustration of the human race. God is pleased to save men by the foolishness of preaching, not by the wisdom of apologetics (I Corinthians 1:21). Once apologetics has shown that the claims of Christ are continuous with truth, it is at the end of its tether. It cannot, even as it would not want to, encroach on the preaching ministry of the church. God is a living person, not a metaphysical principle. Evidences may point to God, but God himself must be encountered in the dynamic of personal fellowship. Only the Holy Spirit can illuminate the evidences.

The Finality of Jesus Christ

If a person refuses to heed the word of the gospel, he once again shows that man's trouble is not lack of knowledge, but lack of moral courage to act on the knowledge he already has. And more than this, he shows the degree to which sin dulls the moral faculties. Who can meditate on the life and death of Jesus without sensing his own distance from rectitude? Christ is the norm of righteousness; he is love incarnate. This, surely, is the final reason why all men ought to repent, for what standard *could* one meet that Christ has not already met? "So they sought to arrest him; but no one laid hands on him, because his hour had not yet come. Yet many of the people believed in him; they said, 'When the Christ appears, will he do more signs than this man has done?' " (John 7:30-31). If we deem a man foolish who scorns rare opportunities of advancement, what name is reserved for him who spurns the righteousness of God in Christ? "How shall we escape if we neglect such a great salvation?" (Hebrews 2:3).

Since Christ has satisfied God's justice through his active and passive obedience, God now invites all men to become reconciled to him. "Behold, I stand at the door and knock; if any one hears my voice and opens the door, I will come in to him and eat with him, and he with me" (Revelation 3:20). But God will not break down the door. He will not violate the sanctity of human personality. The door opens on the inside, and only man can turn the handle.

INDEX OF SCRIPTURE PASSAGES

Genesis 1:26, 189; 3:15, 251; 3:17-18, 147; 8:22, 43 n.; 9:6, 214; 12:1-3, 251
Exodus 4:11, 270; 20:5, 148
Leviticus 19:18, 97
Deuteronomy 7:7-8, 257; 8:17-18, 28; 13:1-3, 78; 29:29, 285
I Samuel 15:2-3, 270; 18:10-11, 12
Job 38:1-5, 280; 42:2-3, 280
Psalm 19:1, 135 n.; 28:3, 51; 103:13-14, 273; 119:99, 211; 139:1-3, 129; 139:8-10, 127; 139:23-24, 243
Proverbs 1:7, 4; 14:12, 236
Isaiah 6:5, 170; 40:13-15, 270; 53:4-6, 250; 55:9, 279; 57:20-21, 236; 59:1-2, 219
Jeremiah 2:19, 236; 13:23, 128; 17:9, 19
Ezekiel 45:9-10, 138
Micah 6:6-8, 151
Habakkuk 1:4, 274; 1:6, 274; 1:13, 144, 274; 2:1, 274; 2:3, 275; 2:4, 275; 2:8, 275; 2:20, 276; 3:17-18, 276
Matthew 5:8, 51; 5:16, 190; 5:44-45, 82; 5:48, 152; 7:1, 185; 7:1-2, 93, 287; 7:1-12, 194; 7:3-5, 185; 7:12, 82; 7:21, 268; 8:21-22, 225; 23:23-24, 301; 26:41, 222; 28:18-20, 297
Mark 10:17-18, 157; 15:34, 252
Luke 11:52, 302; 12:2-3, 184; 12:48, 239; 14:28-30, 26; 17:33, 231
John 1:17, 148; 3:6, 170; 3:20-21, 221; 4:34, 301; 5:24, 252; 7:17, 198; 7:30-31, 303; 9:3, 270; 9:40-41, 281; 10:16, 293; 12:27, 252; 14:6, 250; 15:22, 26; 15:25, 203; 16:2, 203

Acts 5:29, 229; 14:17, 282; 17:28, 218; 17:30-31, 255
Romans 1:4, 253; 1:18, 231; 1:19, 54; 1:19-20, 27; 1:20, 135 n.; 1:26-27, 236; 1:28, 236; 1:32, 53, 239; 2:1, 186; 2:14-16, 238; 3:10, 288; 3:20-26, 253; 3:23, 239; 4:11, 277; 4:20-21, 277; 5:1-2, 256; 5:15-19, 263; 5:20, 290; 7:15, 206, 292; 7:15-18, 197; 7:21-24, 202; 7:22-23, 228; 8:15-16, 261; 8:19-22, 146; 8:22-23, 258; 8:28, 277; 9:20-21, 148; 10:2, 77; 10:14-15, 297; 13:1, 131; 13:4, 192 n.; 13:8-10, 208
I Corinthians 1:21, 302; 1:25, 282; 1:28-29, 266; 2:14, 197; 4:4, 203; 4:7, 128, 8:1-2, 298; 10:32, 164; 13:1-3, 209; 13:2, 299; 13:3, 300; 13:4, 228; 13:4-7, 210; 13:7, 195, 257, 259; 13:12, 285; 15:45, 262
II Corinthians 5:13-14, 260; 5:21, 281; 8:12, 257; 10:5, 302; 10:12, 203; 11:16-18, 228; 12:8-10, 266
Galatians 2:20, 258; 3:10, 169; 3:11, 200; 3:13-14, 252; 3:16, 251; 3:21-22, 301; 5:14, 240; 5:17, 222; 5:19-22, 176; 5:22-23, 221
Ephesians 2:8-9, 294; 4:32, 254; 5:29, 92
Colossians 1:26, 284; 2:13-14, 255
II Thessalonians 3:14, 298
Titus 3:5, 293
Hebrews 2:3, 303; 4:12-13, 177; 9:27, 275; 11:6, 248; 11:19, 277; 12:5-11, 255
James 2:10, 293; 4:6, 151; 4:10, 152; 4:14, 154; 5:16, 182 n.

I Peter 1:16, 152; 2:22-23, 250; 3:15, 82
II Peter 3:8, 275
I John 1:8, 129; 2:2, 255; 3:1, 296; 3:2, 255; 3:3, 70; 3:6, 265; 3:9, 258; 3:21, 186; 4:1, 77; 4:9, 211; 4:10, 282; 4:16, 208

INDEX OF NAMES AND SUBJECTS

Abraham, 251-253, 262, 277-278, 283, 296
Absolute truth, 12
Absolutes, 30, 52-54, 64-66, 92, 107, 133, 234
Absurd, 76
Actions, 26, 35-36, 38, 40, 42-44, 47, 49, 51, 56, 98-99, 103, 114, 145, 188, 231, 261, 285
Active obedience, 250-251, 253, 264, 267, 273, 298, 303
Adam, 262-264, 294
Administer the law, 93, 95-96, 99, 106, 191, 192 n.
Administrator of justice, 102-105, 107, 109, 131
Administrator of the law, 106, 137
Adoption, 255, 257-258, 261, 264, 273-274, 296
Aeschylus, 223
Aesthetic experience, 33
Agamemnon, 223
Agape, 210
Age of reason, 107
Airliner, 173
American prosperity, 195
Analogy, 68, 137, 141, 149, 156, 247, 271
Anatomy of humility, 153
Angelic Doctor, 291. *See also* Aquinas
Anger, 124, 193
Animals, 54, 63-64, 81, 84, 113
Anselm, 130 n.
Anthill, 68
Antigone, 223
Anxiety, 147, 236
Apologetics, 3, 82, 96, 101-102, 152 n,. 197, 302
Apology, 105, 137, 162-167, 169, 233, 242, 259, 265, 271
Appreciation, 225, 228

Aquinas, Thomas, 75, 114, 130 n., 291
Archaeologist, 23
Archaeology, 286
Aristotle, 28, 38, 40-42, 70 n., 75, 88 n., 114-115, 120, 130, 210, 285
Arminians, 265
Art, 34
Artist, 213
Asceticism, 300
Athletic contest, 45
Atonement, 251, 255, 281, 284, 296
Augustine, 18, 41, 74, 88 n., 135 n., 201, 268
Aurelius Antoninus, Marcus, 53, 72 n., 119 n., 145 n.

Bach, J. S., 59
Beagle, 113
Beatific vision, 131
Being, 5, 14, 49-51, 54, 60, 64, 80, 188, 220, 279, 280
Bernard of Clairvaux, 283 n.
Bible, 82, 270, 273, 293 n.
Boasting, 228
Body, 8, 29, 294, 300
Boston, 232
Boswell, James, 195
Brinks robbery, 232
Brotherhood, 255
Burke, Edmund, 107
Butler, Samuel, 88

Calvin, 148, 265, 266 n., 278, 295
Capital punishment, 192 n.
Carlyle, Thomas, 61 n., 129, 231, 279 n.
Carroll, Lewis, 66
Caruso, Enrico, 295
Cat, 187
Categorical imperative, 20-21, 97-98

Index of Names and Subjects

Cervantes, 167, 261
Chain of being, 146
Channing, William Ellery, 134
Character, 55, 58, 65, 83, 88, 90-93, 95, 105, 116, 122-124, 131-135, 138 n., 139, 142-145, 148, 151, 153, 155, 158, 166, 179, 216-217, 220-222, 230, 248-249, 272
Christ, 82, 93, 96, 144, 148, 152 n., 185, 203, 211, 222, 225, 229, 250-260, 263-265, 267-268, 270, 281-282, 284-286, 288, 290, 293, 295-303
Church, 260, 268-269, 298-299, 302
Circle of nearness, 56, 66, 70, 81, 83, 85, 88, 92, 94, 100, 106, 124, 132, 149, 156, 160-162, 172-174, 187, 189, 192 n., 204, 208, 218-220, 240, 268, 298, 300
Claims to duty, 19-22, 33
Clytemnestra, 223
Coffeehouse, 57
Cogito, 37-38, 42
Coherence, 15
Comparative religions, 293, 295, 297, 301
Conditions of knowing, 29
Confrontation, 268-269, 297
Connotative definition, 210
Conscience, 21, 64-65, 83, 106, 110-111, 185, 232-239, 292, 294, 296
Consideration, 190, 194, 204-210, 218
Correspondence, 15
Council of Trent, 290 n.
Counsel of Christ, 93, 136-137, 185, 191, 287
Covenant of grace, 262
Covenant of works, 262
Covenants, 107, 128, 251, 262
Cratylus, 71
Creon, 223
Cross, 152 n., 249 n., 250-251, 254-255, 258-259, 281-282, 295-296, 299
Custodians of the law, 94, 103, 172, 183, 192
Cycle of fellowship, 59, 60, 122-123, 125
Cycle of guilt, 105
Cycle of pardon, 255

Darwin, Charles, 63, 111-113, 233-235
David, 12
Death, 33, 232
Declaration of Independence, 107 n.
Delphic epigram, 6
Demonic, 179, 203, 236
Denotative definition, 210
Dependence, 13, 16, 51, 102-104, 128, 154, 280
Depravity, 196, 198, 202, 235-236. *See also* Total depravity
De Quincey, Thomas, 17
Descartes, René, 37-38
Descriptive essence, 16, 171, 208
Descriptive mood, 19-20, 33, 72, 85
Devil, 77, 132, 298
Dickens, Charles, 231
Dignity, 22, 24, 48, 55-56, 58, 61, 78, 83, 85-88, 91-94, 96-99, 102, 104-106, 108, 112, 119, 120, 122-124, 127, 131-134, 136, 143, 147-148, 150, 156, 160-161, 164, 173-174, 183, 187, 189, 214-216, 218, 234, 240, 248, 298, 300
Direct fulfillment, 158-159, 200, 207, 213, 222, 233, 257, 259, 216, 264
Doctor, 224, 299
Doctrine, 298
Dog, 27, 64, 175
"Doing righteousness," 298
"Doing the truth," 298
Dominant instincts, 111, 113
Don Quixote, 105
Duty, 17, 19-23, 30, 33-34, 69, 71-75, 81-83, 85, 97-100, 102, 113, 126, 132, 142, 153, 159, 161-162, 164, 182-183, 186, 197, 206, 213, 223, 230, 234, 262, 265, 301

Education, 192
Edwards, Jonathan, 238
Empiricism, 4, 5, 36, 52-53, 65, 71-72, 84, 98-99, 106, 113, 116, 140
Encounter, 268-269, 302
Enlightened self-interest, 81, 99
Epictetus, 87
Eros, 210
Ethics, 74-75, 97-99, 232
Euthanasia, 221

Euthyphro, 6, 100
Evidences, 4, 61, 65, 77-78, 83, 99, 101, 105, 112, 119, 122, 133, 141-142, 148, 152, 155, 164-165, 174-175, 178-185, 189, 190-191, 193, 195, 198, 214-216, 218, 220, 231, 232 n., 238, 242, 259, 267-269, 282, 285-287, 294, 301-302
Evil, 143-144, 146, 166, 169, 175, 188, 197, 255, 269, 294
Existentialism, 74-75, 77, 78
Experience, 3, 4, 15-17, 24, 28-29, 32-33, 71-72, 74, 83, 86, 101-102, 108, 112, 122, 126, 131, 154, 158, 181, 218, 240-241

Faith, 75-77, 100-101, 114, 142, 198, 248-249, 267-269, 275-276, 280, 300
Fall, 251
False prophets, 78, 228
Family of righteousness, 294
Family of sin, 294
Father, 159, 201, 225
Father (God), 82, 190, 251, 253, 255, 261, 268, 273
Favor, 122, 163, 186-189, 219, 230
Federal headship, 262-264, 294-295
Fellowship, 55-60, 65-66, 69-70, 83, 85, 93, 101, 106, 118-121, 124-125, 127-133, 144-145, 149-154, 156-158, 160, 162-164, 166-167, 169, 172, 184, 230, 247-248, 252, 254, 260, 267, 275-276, 283, 302
Feuerbach, 138
Fichte, 114
Filial bond, 222, 255, 257, 259, 261, 266, 273-274, 276-277, 279
Final judgment, 137, 192-194, 242-243
Finitude, 11, 13, 131, 142-144
First condition of knowing, 25
Fishing, 50
Fission, 154
Flattery, 224, 226, 227
Flaubert, Gustave, 33
Foolishness, 25, 52, 56, 57, 64, 112, 197-198
Football, 45
Forced options, 99, 100, 103
Forgiveness, 248, 254

Formalistic ethics, 20, 74, 97
Fourfold environment, 46, 71, 126, 286, 293
Franklin, Benjamin, 192 n., 199 n.
Freedom, 11, 13, 16, 24, 26, 68, 72, 86, 88, 106, 108-109, 114-116, 120, 131, 180, 247
Friendship, 58-59, 69-70
Fruit, 176, 202, 206, 212-213, 216-217, 220-221, 227, 240, 261, 265, 289, 300

Generic faith, 76, 78, 267, 269
Gibbon, Edward, 227
God, 12, 27, 41-42, 48, 50, 52, 54, 56, 58, 60, 64, 66, 69, 70, 77, 83, 92, 93, 97-99, 101, 107-111, 114, 116, 118-121, 124, 126-129, 131-154, 156-158, 162, 164, 166, 169, 172, 173, 176-177, 182, 184-185, 191-193, 197, 206, 208, 212-215, 218-219, 221, 223, 231, 234-235, 237-239, 241, 243, 246-249, 252, 262, 265-266, 269-272, 274, 276-280, 286-289, 293, 295-296, 298-299, 301-302
Golden rule, 82
Goldsmith, Oliver, 3 n., 198, 240 n.
Good, the, 143, 149
Good will, 70, 175
Gorgias, 72
Gospel, 82, 253, 265, 297, 303
Grace, 147-148, 212, 253, 260-262, 265-266, 290-292
Gratitude, 122, 124, 128-129, 134-135, 154, 163, 166, 170, 195, 282
Grocery store, 178-179
Guilt, 13, 44, 59, 85, 91, 94-95, 99, 102-103, 105-106, 112, 119, 124, 126-127, 130, 150, 160, 164-165, 168, 170, 172, 174-175, 177-187, 190-191, 193, 201, 215-221, 231, 234-235, 237-239, 241-242, 281-282

Habakkuk, 274-278, 280
Hamilton, Alexander, 200 n.
Happiness, 57-58, 61-62, 86, 98, 115, 123, 142
Harvard, 108
Heathen, 237, 297

Index of Names and Subjects

Hegel, 72, 74-76
Hell, 261
Herder, 114
Highway, 178, 190
Hippocratic Oath, 62, 223
Hitler, 22, 232
Hobbes, 21, 63
Holy Spirit, 176, 179, 182, 186, 188, 215-217, 221-222, 235-236, 293, 302
Homo sapiens, 7
Honest self, 52
Humanism, 195
Hume, David, 140
Humility, 2, 69, 93, 109, 126-127, 147, 149-151, 153-154, 156-160, 162, 169, 187, 193, 198, 200, 228, 237-238, 242-243, 247-248, 295
Hypocrisy, 69, 184-185

Idealism, 4, 36
Idiots, 144-145, 147
Ignorantia facti excusat, 48, 237 n.
Ignorantia juris neminem excusat, 48
Image of God, 15, 37, 56, 64, 68-69, 86, 92, 97, 112, 114, 127, 133, 135-136, 142-143, 152, 173, 189, 190, 198, 214, 218, 222, 232, 237, 239, 246, 271, 284
Immortality, 114-115, 121
Imperative essence, 17, 19, 21-23, 36, 54, 56, 60, 80-81, 113, 119, 141, 153, 161, 171, 173, 179, 188, 194, 204, 206-208, 212-213, 217, 251, 253
Imperative mood, 19, 33, 56, 81
Imputation, 251, 257-258, 290
Inconsideration, 97, 103, 185, 190, 201, 209, 231, 287
Indian Thug, 111, 235, 237-238
Indirect fulfillment, 158-159, 200-201, 207, 213, 222, 228-229, 233, 256-257, 259, 261, 264
Ingratitude, 108, 123-124, 166, 272
Injustice, 90-91, 95-96, 103, 131, 145, 169, 173-175, 196, 209, 229, 264
Innocence, 27, 58, 182-184, 190-191, 218
Insomnia, 10
Intellectual love for God, 118

Irony, 74
"It-truth," 268-269

Jacobi, 114
James, William, 77 n., 97, 99, 100, 130
Jealousy, 148
Jesuits, 227
Jesus, 25
Job, 280
Johnson, Samuel, 18, 25, 79, 145-146, 194, 226, 263
Judging, 42, 93, 95-96, 102-104, 119, 132-133, 136, 147, 167, 172-173, 175, 177-178, 180, 184-186, 189, 191, 193-195, 199, 208-209, 216, 218, 235, 287, 289, 301
Judgment, 97, 181, 185, 189
Judicial predicament, 94-96, 99, 102, 105
Judicial sentiment, 69, 92, 97, 101-102, 104, 106, 108, 110, 112, 120-124, 127, 131, 133, 135-136, 139, 142-144, 147, 151, 153, 160-161, 163 n., 164-169, 172-175, 177-178, 180, 180 n., 184-185, 187-189, 191, 204-206, 208-209, 214, 216, 218-219, 226, 230-232, 233 n., 234, 237, 242, 247-251, 254, 267-268, 271-273, 281, 286-287, 296, 298
Justice, 54, 90-91, 93, 95, 105, 131-132, 138-139, 143-146, 148, 151, 167, 172-178, 180, 194, 201, 203-210, 237, 239, 253, 264, 266, 271, 274-276, 278, 281-283, 293, 297, 300
Justification, 248-249, 253, 255-256, 258, 261, 263, 273, 276, 282, 290, 293, 296

Kant, Immanuel, 20, 41, 44, 67-68, 70-72, 80-82, 97-98, 100, 110, 112, 115, 123, 130 n., 158-159, 161-162, 212, 235 n., 294, 301
Kierkegaard, Sören, 15-16, 73-78, 109, 130 n., 141, 277, 298
Know thyself! 5
Knowledge, 8, 24, 26-29, 61, 71, 90, 101, 114, 118, 125-126, 185, 267, 280, 296-297, 303

Knowledge by acquaintance, 17, 18, 20, 23, 29, 33, 36, 59, 72, 75, 101, 118, 120, 125-126, 128, 148, 150, 162, 210, 267
Knowledge by inference, 17, 18, 23, 29, 36, 59, 72, 75, 86, 118, 125, 210, 269

Law, 48, 56, 67-68, 93-98, 102-103, 105-106, 115, 123, 158, 161-162, 165, 167, 169, 170, 172, 175, 177, 180, 186, 189, 190-191, 200, 202, 207, 209, 213, 220, 223, 227, 231, 233, 237-238, 240-241, 249, 251, 253, 255-261, 264, 273, 288-289, 292, 294, 297, 300, 301
Law of consideration, 190-192, 194, 199, 201, 203, 205-206
Law of contradiction, 28, 38, 40-43, 56, 58, 66, 70, 85, 103, 109, 115, 135, 197, 246, 256
Law of legal necessity, 161, 176, 184, 197, 201
Law of life, 135, 192-193, 204, 208, 213, 220-221, 233, 235, 242, 250, 270, 284, 290, 295
Law of love, 207, 215, 221-222, 224, 226, 228, 230-231, 234, 237, 240-241, 288-289, 300
Law of sin and death, 256-257
Law of the spirit of life, 161-162, 176, 184, 194, 196, 206, 207, 213, 256
Law of uniformity, 42-43, 47, 49, 56, 85, 103
Law, William, 199
Lawyers, 177, 188
Leibnitz, 114, 270
Les Miserables, 33
Liability to law, 95
Liberty and equality, 107
Library, 180-181, 190, 204
Lie detector, 44
Limiting concept, 44
Lisbon earthquake, 27
Locke, John, 141
Logic, 4, 13, 18, 21, 41, 70 n., 71, 73-76, 102, 126, 241, 246-247
Logical positivists, 28, 50
Logos, 145, 269, 278, 293

Love, 17, 56, 70, 83, 92, 96, 119, 159, 202, 207-210, 212, 220-222, 224-225, 231, 233, 240-241, 250, 255-261, 265-266, 270, 273, 276-277, 282, 284, 288-290, 292-293, 293 n., 295, 297-298, 300-303
Luther, Martin, 292
Lying, 98

Machiavelli, 68, 226, 294
Madison, James, 200 n.
Man, 2, 7, 16, 45, 63, 84, 87-88, 119, 138, 141, 171, 181, 183, 185, 189, 194, 204-207, 223, 294-296, 302-303
Marx, 88, 146, 285, 294
Materialism, 36
Mercy, 169, 248, 290, 293, 300
Merit, 260, 275, 291-293
Methods, 3, 5, 6, 10, 14, 17, 23-24, 29, 36, 44, 52, 55, 109, 125, 141, 249 n.
Methods of knowing, 29
Methuselah, 84
Mill, John Stuart, 77 n., 98, 139, 148-149, 215 n.
Miracles, 43 n., 279
Missions, 296
Monastery, 260
Moral and spiritual environment, 2-4, 6-7, 17, 19, 22, 33, 39, 41, 50, 52, 54-58, 60-64, 66-70, 72-73, 75, 81-84, 86, 89, 91-97, 100-109, 112-113, 120-124, 126-127, 130-133, 135, 138-139, 141-142, 145, 148-153, 155-156, 158, 160-161, 163-165, 168-169, 172, 176, 179, 182-183, 185-188, 190-191, 198, 200-201, 203, 208-209, 212, 215, 217, 219, 220-221, 223, 227-228, 230, 233-240, 242, 246, 249-250, 253, 257, 265, 275, 284, 287, 289
Moral cycle, 94, 96, 101-102, 104, 108, 119-121, 127, 130-132, 135, 137, 142-143, 151, 166, 185, 218, 231-232, 254, 286-287
Moral holidays, 145
Moral limits, 195-196

Index of Names and Subjects

Moral predicament, 129-130, 134-135, 143, 154, 157, 166, 170, 199, 204, 216, 247-248, 256, 281, 286, 288, 290, 294, 300
Moral relativity, 52, 53, 65
Moral self-acceptance, 22-24, 29, 32, 34, 36-39, 42, 44-45, 48, 52, 55, 62-64, 68, 73, 81-82, 84, 88, 92, 95, 99, 102, 106, 110, 112-113, 125-126, 143-145, 149, 153, 157-158, 160, 167-168, 197, 217, 219, 248, 249 n., 271, 280, 284, 301
Moral sense, 23, 56, 67, 71, 73-74, 81-83, 100, 102, 111, 115, 125-126, 167-168, 204, 233-234, 275
Moral skepticism, 141-142, 152
Morals, 20, 36, 66-68, 75, 97, 100, 112, 116, 123, 159, 227
Mores, 52-53, 64, 113, 233, 237
Mortal sins, 222, 291
Motion, 4
"Mud, hair, and filth," 272
Muddy river, 122, 163, 220
Mysteries and particularities, 183-187, 189-190, 195, 205
Mystery, 279
Mystical union, 256, 258, 268, 281

Naturalism, 4
Nazis, 232
Nemesis, 62
Neo-orthodoxy, 268
Nervous breakdown, 12-13
Nobler faculties, 90, 95, 105, 179, 201, 216-217, 221, 258, 288-289
Noetic effects of sin, 198
Nursery, 89, 90, 172

"O sacred Head," 283
Oath, 61-62, 107-108, 224, 257
O'Keefe, Specs, 232
Ontological argument, 130 n.
Ontological truth, 14, 15, 17, 29
Orestes, 223
Original sin, 196-197, 199, 201-202, 292, 294

Pain, 24
Pantheism, 51 n., 138

Paradox, 77-78, 142, 157, 213, 237, 269, 295
Paradox of humility, 153, 157
Paradox of moral striving, 213
Paradox of morals, 69
Pardon, 254-255
Park, 34-35, 41, 55
Pascal, 15, 73, 99, 215, 227, 285
Passion, 75, 77-78, 95, 185, 254
Passive obedience, 250-251, 253, 264, 267, 273, 298, 303
Paul, 27, 60, 186, 197, 201-202, 210, 228, 233, 238, 260, 262, 264, 266, 297-299
Peccadilloes, 291
Pelagianism, 158, 260
Person, 3, 8, 41, 50, 51 n., 55, 86, 88, 108-109, 113, 118-120, 127-128, 130, 139, 145, 161, 173, 181, 183, 185-187, 189, 195, 204-208, 220, 247, 262, 269-271, 282, 291, 298, 302-303
Peter, 259
Pharaoh, 236
Pharisees, 300
Philosophers, 2, 4, 14, 28, 36, 45, 72, 76, 87, 125, 132, 135, 147, 202, 223, 239, 271, 298
Philosophy, 4-6, 15-17, 34, 37, 39, 41, 44, 73, 76, 87, 121, 182 n., 216, 247, 269, 271, 285-286, 297
Philosophy of history, 263
Physical cycle, 120
Pilate, 229
Pity, 169, 248
Plato, 53, 71, 74, 87-89, 133, 135 n., 143, 149, 221, 279, 285, 294
Plotinus, 72
Point of contact, 135-137, 139, 140, 142, 156, 190, 209, 234
Point of identity, 137
Politician, 176
Polynices, 223
Positional righteousness, 282
Practical imperative, 80-84
Pragmatism, 15, 100
Praxiteles, 59
Prayer, 182 n.
Predestination, 265
Pre-soteric synergism, 265

Pride, 4, 13, 68, 95, 105, 126, 145, 147, 150-151, 154, 158, 165-166, 176-177, 187, 191-192, 194, 196, 198-199, 218, 224, 228, 231-232, 236, 242-243, 256, 258-260, 264, 266, 272, 276, 281, 288-290, 292, 293 n., 294-295, 299
Principle of double fulfillment, 202
Private property, 88
Prize Essay, 67
Problem of evil, 143-148, 269-270, 272-273, 276, 278, 281-282
Proletariat, 294
Promise, 61
Prophets, 53, 78, 82
Propitiation, 136, 249, 251, 254, 260, 272-273
Propositional correspondence to reality, 29
Propositional truth, 15, 17
Prosperity, 196
Protestantism, 290
Providence, 215, 275, 277-278, 280
Psychiatry, 150 n.
Psychotherapy, 150 n.
Purity of heart, 277
Pyrrho, 44
Pythagoreans, 135 n.

Quicksand, 129

Race, 7, 8, 38, 65, 189, 195, 204-206, 250, 253, 255, 262, 281, 286
Radical evil, 68
Rahab, 229
Rapport, 165-166
Rational environment, 39, 41, 71
Rationalism, 4, 36, 71-72, 75
Reason, 72, 76, 82, 88, 97, 114, 197, 246-247, 284, 292
Rectitude, 4, 6, 16-17, 29, 33, 37-38, 48-50, 53, 60, 75, 93-94, 119, 124, 126, 129, 131-133, 148, 150-152, 157-159, 161, 171-172, 174-179, 190-191, 200-201, 206, 208-209, 212-213, 223, 227, 237, 242-243, 250, 254, 257, 272, 277, 289, 298, 302-303
Reformers, 258, 262, 268
Regeneration, 217, 258, 265, 293
Regret, 25

Regulative ideas, 114-116
Relativism, 5, 43, 65-66, 113
Remorse, 111
Repentance, 60, 167-170, 172, 203, 206, 212, 214, 221, 240-241, 243, 248, 254-255, 265, 272-273, 284, 295, 297, 300, 302
Republic, Plato's, 87, 89
Resentment, 195
Responsibility, 25-28, 34-35, 47-48, 52, 105, 152, 237-239
Responsibility of admission, 47
Responsibility of consequence, 47-48
Resurrection, 250, 253, 288
Revelation, 38, 51, 145, 150, 183, 187-188, 206-207, 262, 270, 284-285, 303
Revenge, 93, 96, 179, 191-192, 233, 254
Righteous indignation, 124
Righteousness, 203, 249-251, 253-254, 256-258, 260, 262-263, 265, 281-282, 284-286, 290, 293, 296, 298-303
Righteousness of Christ, 295, 297, 299
Righteousness of correct thinking, 297
Righteousness of keeping the law, 300
Righteousness of self-denial, 299
Rights, 86-87, 89, 91, 93, 99, 113, 173, 180, 204
Roman Catholic Church, 222, 258, 260, 268, 290-292
Romanticism, 4
Rousseau, 68, 107
Rowboat, 122, 163, 220
Royce, Josiah, 100

Sacred heart, 268
Sanctification, 258, 273
Saul, 12
Saving faith, 78 n., 267, 269
Savonarola, 198
Science, 4, 5, 8, 22, 30, 34, 43, 50, 52, 65, 76, 84, 112-113, 137, 171, 182 n., 216, 247, 269, 277, 279
Second condition of knowing, 25
Second justification, 222, 260-262, 290

Index of Names and Subjects

Self, 6-7, 11, 32, 34, 52, 54, 201, 207, 230
Self-love, 45, 97-100, 110, 123, 166, 193, 214-215, 225, 241, 258, 266, 288, 294
Self-transcendence, 13, 26-27, 29, 37, 48, 69, 111, 139, 186, 198, 207, 295
Selfishness, 58, 82, 91, 100, 107, 123, 204, 214, 216-217, 223, 230
Sense perception, 4
Shakespeare, 210, 243 n.
Sin, 26, 129, 137, 146-147, 184, 219, 224, 228, 236-237, 248, 250-252, 254-256, 258-259, 265-266, 271-272, 296, 288, 292, 297, 299, 303
Skeptics, 38, 40, 42-43, 58, 66, 108, 294
Slavery, 87, 221
Social self, 52
Sociologists, 65, 234
Socrates, 5, 6, 15-16, 18, 53, 55, 73-74, 80, 88, 100, 229, 294
Son of Man, 230
Sophocles, 223
Soteric synergism, 265
Sovereignty, 131-132, 137, 270, 282
Spinoza, 72, 116, 119-121, 146 n.
Spiritual nearness, 57
Spiritual preparation, 125-126
Starting point, 4, 36-38
Stoics, 115
Strangers, 57-59
Subjectivity, 5, 75, 78, 291
Suicide, 11
"Suppress the truth," 231
Swift, Jonathan, 202 n.
Syllogism, 18, 70 n.
Systematic consistency, 15
Systems, 284-286, 301

Tastes, 86, 90-91, 103, 108, 120, 139
Teleology, 114, 270-271
Telephone, 178
Telos, 279-280
Temptation, 292
Ten Commandments, 194, 221, 223, 235
Theaetetus, 71
Theodicy, 271

Theologians, 132, 135, 139, 198, 225-226, 265, 268, 285
Theology, 286, 295-297, 299, 302
Third condition of knowing, 25-28, 34-37, 43, 47-48, 52, 55, 67, 101, 128, 150, 152, 186, 218, 235, 237-239
Third kind of truth, 16-17, 50, 60, 298
Third method of knowing, 10, 12-14, 22-23, 32-33, 36, 38, 42, 44-45, 49-50, 52, 60-61, 65, 70, 79, 80, 84, 90-91, 93, 100-102, 109-110, 112, 115, 123, 126, 129, 134-135, 139, 141, 144, 152 n., 160-161, 171-172, 174, 208, 210, 214, 217, 219-220, 241, 249 n., 257, 268, 284, 286
Thomas à Kempis, 193
Thorn in the flesh, 266
"Thou-truth," 268-269
Thucydides, 173 n.
Timaeus, 279
Time and eternity, 134-136, 141-142, 146, 209, 275, 278
Toplady, Augustus M., 253
Total depravity, 128, 199-200, 236, 262, 264-266, 294, 296. *See also* depravity
Tourist, 24
Tragedians, 223, 229
Tragic moral choices, 202, 223-224, 227-230
Travelogue, 191
Tribes, 52-53
Trollope, Anthony, 225 n., 227
Truth, 5, 11, 13-15, 24, 29, 60, 72, 75, 86, 100, 132, 224-226, 246, 250, 269, 293, 295, 301
Tyrant, 68, 88, 106

University, 7, 10-12, 48
Univocal point, 51 n., 135, 137, 150, 152, 208
Unmoved mover, 120, 130
Unspiritual, 198
Utilitarian, 81

Values, 45, 49-50, 54, 59, 121, 166, 188, 217, 247, 271
Vengeance, 185

Venial sins, 222, 291
Verification, 15, 100-101, 109, 133-134, 138, 152, 197, 284-286, 294
Vindictiveness, 184
Voltaire, 271

Wager, Pascal's, 99, 285
Walton, Izaak, 94 n., 122 n., 210 n., 238 n.
Weltschmerz, 12

Wheat threshers, 32
Wholly other, 139
Wisdom, 25, 41, 52, 246, 262, 269, 282, 296
Wishful thinking, 116
Work, 176, 212-213, 240, 294, 300
World of Ideas, 143
World view, 2, 12, 27, 42, 71, 73-74, 83, 246, 270, 295